TESTING AMERICAN SEA PO

Joseph G. Dawson III, General Editor

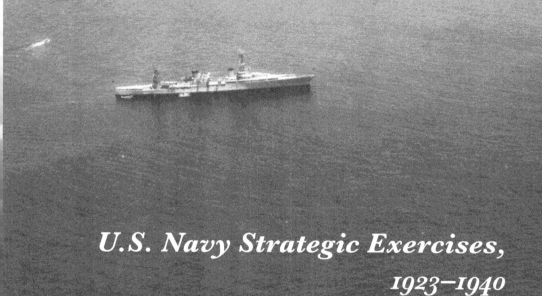

U.S. Navy Strategic Exercises,
1923–1940

CRAIG C. FELKER

Texas A&M University Press
College Station

TESTING AMERICAN SEA POWER

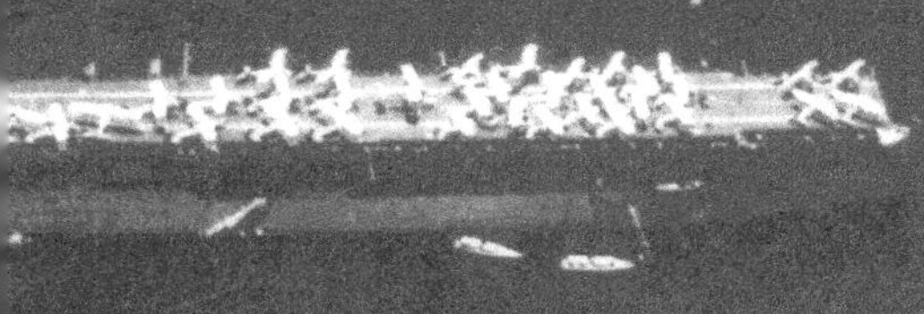

Second Printing, 2013

The paper used in this book
meets the minimum requirements
 of the American National Standard for Permanence
of Paper for Printed Library Materials, Z39.48-1984.
 Binding materials have been chosen for durability.

Library of Congress Cataloging-in-Publication Data

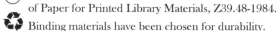

Felker, Craig C., 1959-
Testing American sea power : U.S. Navy strategic exercises, 1923-1940 /
Craig C. Felker. — 1st ed.
p. cm.— (Texas A&M University military history series)
Includes bibliographical references and index.
ISBN-13: 978-1-58544-560-8 (cloth)
ISBN-13: 978-1-60344-989-2 (paper)
ISBN-13: 978-1-60344-509-2 (ebook)
1. United States. Navy—Maneuvers—History—20th century.
I. Title. II. Series.
V245.F45 2007
359.4'80973—dc22 2006011427

CONTENTS

ILLUSTRATIONS

ACKNOWLEDGMENTS

The maxim, "Success has a thousand fathers, but failure is an orphan," seems to me an appropriate way to describe how this book came to be. As a naval officer, you learn early on that your success is determined by those whom you work for and with, but your shortcomings are yours alone. Despite the academic's tendency to spend hours surrounded by lifeless archival material, the same relationship applies.

I could not have reached this point without the support and mentorship of colleagues, friends, and family. Prof. Robert Artigiani and Dean Mary DeCredico set me on the path to graduate study at Duke. My time in Durham was made all the richer by the graduate students and professors in the military history community at Duke and University of North Carolina–Chapel Hill. Prof. Dick Kohn's guidance and mentorship not only shaped me into a historian but enhanced my understanding of the obligations of service to the nation. Prof. Alex Roland guided me through the big questions in military history and taught me the beauty of the short, declarative sentence. In the end he became both advisor and friend, and I am a better student because of him.

The faculty in the History Department of the U.S. Naval Academy truly embodies the definition of collegiality. Their support has proven instrumental to my success in the classroom. My thanks also go out to the staff of Nimitz Library, particularly its director, Dr. Richard Werking, and Research Librarian Barbara Manvel, who always made themselves available during my research trips to Annapolis.

My thanks also go out to those outside the academic community who shaped my career and life. Squadron mates kept me safe in the air, while their camaraderie made the navy more an adventure than a career. Friends, many of whom I spend hours with on trout streams, enriched those times away from the navy. Finally are my parents who inspired without pressure, brothers and sisters who shouldered family burdens when I could not, children who have been both a challenge and a blessing, and my bride, Mary, who as a mother and navy wife has made my life complete. I would not be sitting here typing if it were not for you.

There were many hands involved in the creation of this book. But as the maxim also goes, I am accountable for the content of this work. My intention was to explain the interwar U.S. Navy from the perspective of its annual exercises. I focused principally on documents created by those officers who planned and participated in those exercises. What errors are found reflect my own shortcomings as a "young" historian, who will only grow with criticism.

TESTING AMERICAN SEA POWER

CHAPTER 1

Introduction

From 1923 to 1940 the U.S. Navy held twenty-one major exercises, known as "Fleet Problems." While only a part of annual fleet training, these exercises differed from routine maneuvers and gunnery exercises. All available ships of the U.S. fleet would be assigned to one or more opposing naval forces, which were designated by a color (black, orange, blue, etc). The chief of naval operations would provide general guidance on the objectives of the exercise to the commander-in-chief, U.S. fleet. "CINCUS," as he was called, would then blend the CNO's training objectives with his own desires and provide the exercise fleet commanders specific strategic problems to be solved.[1] Fleet staffs would develop appropriate plans to address the requirements of the exercise and articulate their commanders' intentions in a strategic plan known as the "Estimate of the Situation." Subsequent operations orders would be developed for subordinate units participating in the exercise. At the conclusion of the operational portion of the exercise, representatives from all participating units and staffs would gather for a postexercise critique.

Normally held in a large auditorium to accommodate as many officers as possible, the critique provided the opportunity for all to see events in their entirety, as well as offering a forum for senior commanders to discuss their perspectives and lessons learned.

Seven of the fleet problems dealt with Caribbean security and the defense of the Panama Canal. Aspects of War Plan Orange, the navy's vision of war in the Pacific against Japan, were tested in ten of the problems. Exercises additionally tested the capabilities of submarines, the use of carrier aircrafts, and combined operations with the Marine Expeditionary Force (later changed to Fleet Marine Force) and U.S. Army in the seizure and defense of advanced bases.[2] In essence the fleet problems were simulated wars. They provided the only opportunity during the fleet's annual training cycle for flag and general officers to apply strategic thinking in an operational setting.[3] The aggregation of ships, submarines, aircraft, and marines provided an excellent opportunity for staffs and unit commanders to work through the problems of coordination and interoperability. Operational units experienced firsthand the perspectives of the navy's senior leaders.

The magnitude and scope of the exercises suggest that the interwar years were a dynamic period in the history of the U.S. Navy. Historical interpretations, however, have cast the period as little more than a proving ground for Mahanian notions of sea power.[4] The navy was tradition-bound and overly conservative. Its reluctance to break from a doctrine centered on decisive engagements between battleship-centered fleets squandered two decades of peace. Naval officers as a consequence spent their time doing little more than re-fighting the great World War I naval battle of Jutland, when they could have been determining how Jutland might be fought with submarines and aircraft carriers, or not fought at all for that matter.[5] This is not to say that the literature is fundamentally flawed. Elting Morison concluded that the navy's reluctance to adopt steam propulsion in the 1860s and continuous-aim gunnery at the turn of the century demonstrated a strain of unhealthy conservatism within its organizational ethos.[6] The dominant literature, however, has represented the interwar navy as little more than backward-looking or fanatically Mahanian, a military organization preparing for warfare in the twentieth century with eighteenth-century thinking.

What were naval officers trying to accomplish in their fleet problems? Were they, like Barbara Tuchman's generals in World War I, simply fighting the last war? The answer that the navy used the interwar exercises to resist reform is too simplistic. There is no question that much of the navy's thinking on doctrine and strategy was informed by lectures and books written by

Alfred Thayer Mahan in the late nineteenth century. The fleet problems were developed, and lessons were learned, within the broad contours of Mahan's principles of naval warfare. But unlike Mahan, whose ideas were deduced from the age of sail, twentieth-century naval officers could not completely ignore the implications of modern weapons. Limited experience during World War I only accentuated the gap between doctrine and technology. They had to reconcile principles drawn from battles between sailing ships to naval warfare fought with battleships, airplanes, submarines, and even marines.

It was during these fleet problems that the navy experienced the implications of modern technology on its doctrine. The exercises additionally proved to be an important medium through which naval officers used operational experiences to modify aspects of their conceptions of naval warfare. One of the reasons they learned so much is that the exercises took the form of sophisticated warfare simulation. The documents from the fleet problems reveal that naval officers attempted to create the conditions that they thought would arise in a future war. First, the exercise scenarios all had strategic relevance. In other words, the entire chain of command actively participated in the exercise. A second related condition was that the scenarios were written so as to inhibit a fleet commander from relying on "canned" solutions to a problem. The final condition of modern simulation is that participating units were employed in the environmental conditions that approximated actual operations.[7]

Given the navy's limited operational experiences, the fleet problem scenarios represented an amalgam of assumptions on geopolitics, technology, national defense, and naval warfare. As a consequence the exercises were inexact representations of reality. They were given the look and feel of what naval officers perceived to be real. But there was no guarantee that simulation would completely validate Mahan, even though many officers believed that would be the case.

Despite its limitations, warfare simulation exposed naval officers to what a modern war at sea might look like. The fleet problems helped to shape the navy's strategic vision of a future war. Naval officers learned how to integrate new technology. The exercises placed humans and machines as close to actual combat conditions as possible. Naval officers experienced the problems of coordinating three dimensions of naval warfare in an operational setting. Concepts such as dive bombing, independent submarine operations, antisubmarine warfare, and amphibious operations were explored in a medium that stressed not only machines and people but also the thinking of naval officers as to how best to employ them.

Perhaps an apt metaphor, and one that will resonate throughout the book, is that the interwar navy existed as if it had been placed inside a bottle. The bottle itself was molded by factors outside the navy's control. Diplomats used disarmament conferences during the period to contain the offensive capabilities of navies. The Harding, Coolidge, and Hoover administrations additionally envisioned naval disarmament as a way to relieve a strained U.S. economy and more conducive to a foreign policy of conditional engagement.[8] To the diplomats and politicians were added officers of the U.S. Army. Some of them sought to restrain the navy for fear of their own service's future. Others believed that the airpower revolution had made navies obsolete. Within the bottle, however, naval officers were left to validate their own sense of reality. Much of their effort was spent reinforcing a belief that the navy's purpose in war was to achieve *sea control*. The concept, which emphasized fleet action by capital ships to prevent an enemy's use of the sea, was first articulated in the lectures and narratives of Alfred Thayer Mahan. The problem facing naval officers, however, was validating that concept in peacetime with new tools of naval warfare, and few operational experiences. Consequently, not every issue raised through simulation was resolved. As Carl von Clausewitz noted, the only "lubricant" to the "abrasion" of friction was combat experience.[9] But the exercises served an important purpose to the interwar navy. Naval officers learned how to fight with modern technology.

An examination of the fleet problems serves to intervene in the established literature by revealing a different perspective on the interwar naval officer corps. Historians have crafted a particular image of the naval "culture" as committed to the most stringent interpretation of Mahanian sea-control doctrine. Airplanes, submarines, marines, and destroyers were not excluded from the naval hierarchy but were deemed of secondary importance to the battleship. To challenge the battleship's preeminence was heresy. To suggest alternatives to the decisive engagement was "defensive-minded." This interpretation represents the navy as a monolithic and hidebound culture, which seems an oversimplification. Mahan's vision of sea control was the wellspring from which the navy drew its strategic thinking. The canon resonated well after Mahan's death in December 1914. But American naval officers were not all catechismal throwbacks. Through simulation they developed a good, though incomplete, understanding of the new tools of naval warfare and a reasonable strategic scheme for applying them. The exercises also suggest that "the fleet" was somewhere between a monolith and a group of rival constituencies, each bargaining to enhance its position, and in some cases, its survival.[10]

This study will also add to the discussion on how military organizations transform. I. B. Holley and John Morrow, for example, both examined the development of aviation during World War I. Holley argued that the U.S. Army's failure to think through the employment of the new weapon prior to its construction was a principal reason for the problems that plagued U.S. military aviation. Morrow took the opposite tack. Innovations arising from battlefield experience, he contended, outpaced attempts at an inductive process.[11] Other commentaries focus on catalysts of change. Barry Posen, for example, offers a neorealist argument that links organizational reform to international behavior. He contends that international competition drives military organizations to change, with cooperation with civilian authority as the key to effective innovation. Stephen Rosen, on the other hand, argues that reform is brought about by "dominant social structures" within the organization's country. Finally, some historians focus on the impediments to reform. Tami Biddle's comparative analysis of interwar strategic bombing doctrine in Britain and the United States illustrates that assumptions and expectations attached to unescorted, high-altitude, precision bombers stifled development of other critical dimensions of air power, most notably escort fighters. David Johnson makes a similar argument to explain the army's lackluster efforts to develop the tank. The service was culturally constrained to viewing ground war as the province of the infantryman. The crews that had to fight with lightly-armed-and-armored tanks discovered, much to their dismay, that Germans in Panther and Tiger tanks had not been hindered by such bias.[12]

The fleet problems are extremely useful to this discussion, not only because they offer a naval example to the debate, but more importantly because the exercises illustrate the problems of explaining historical events within strict theoretical frameworks. The fleet problems are not a perfect fit. The exercises were the principal operational media from which naval officers began to understand the proper employment of new technology. Simulation emphasized a doctrine that accentuated offensive operations against enemy warships but did not altogether reject defensive measures, such as convoy defense against submarines. It also crafted a geopolitical reality that conflicted with foreign policy. Diplomats used arms limitation to reduce the offensive capabilities of navies. U.S. Naval officers used their imaginations to circumvent the diplomats. Simulated ships, which navy planners termed "constructive," were added to their exercises to validate their belief that future war would surely include the proscribed vessels. The political-military divide did not entirely inhibit innovation. The fleet problems suggest that a military organization can transform itself, even with untested principles or an unproven technology.

This study will also contribute to discussion on the medium that lies between a military organization's assumptions and expectations and the doctrine it develops. Organizational learning is viewed by sociologists Barbara Levitt and James March as "routine-based, history-dependant, and target-oriented." Direct experience, they argue, can be a productive means for organizations, particularly craft-based groups, to learn how to adapt to changing circumstances, develop "organizational memory," and transfer tradition to new members, or members who did not participate in the experience.[13]

In the late nineteenth century the navy incorporated much of the Prussian model in its strategy-oriented training programs. According to Ronald Spector and Michael Vlahos, war games played at the Naval War College not only nurtured the intellectual facet of strategy making but also reinforced the cultural ethos of the officer corps. The Royal Navy, for example, became a consistent opponent in many games but not because civilian policy makers perceived the British as a credible threat to national defense. Rather, U.S. naval officers used the Royal Navy as a means of reinforcing the two officer corps as equals.[14] But the difference between playing war *games* at Newport and solving fleet *problems* at sea was more than semantic. At-sea exercises provided a means of organizational learning through experience, or what historians of science refer to as tacit knowledge. The incorporation of technological "anomalies" such as aircraft and submarines and geographical features such as Pacific atolls tempered the temptation of commanders to resort to "canned solutions." Unlike Newport, failure in a fleet problem had to be explained to a much broader, and junior, audience.

The fleet problems were a collection of shared experiences that facilitated organizational learning. Navy and Marine Corps units, which normally trained alone or together in small groups, were assimilated into the larger fleet organization. At the conclusion of the exercise participants would gather to share their perceptions and learn from their seniors. Meaningful learning therefore relied on several important conditions of simulation. One was verisimilitude. Naval officers had to believe that the scenarios they were presented with, and the operating conditions they experienced, reasonably approached their expectations of what would happen in a future war. Secondly, the exercises had to convince participants that valid lessons could be gleaned from simulation. Finally, the fleet problems had to provide a medium that facilitated the transmission of lessons learned, nurtured organizational memory, and reinforced the navy's organizational ethos.

The interwar navy provides an excellent venue for a historically based inquiry on the behavior of a military organization, the doctrine it develops, the organization's capacity for learning, and how it innovates. But if there is a central theme that ties the history and the theory together, it is the enduring legacy of Alfred Thayer Mahan. Phillips Payson O'Brien observes in his introduction to *Technology and Naval Combat in the Twentieth Century and Beyond* that the naval balance of power changed very little in the twentieth century.[15] In 1907 Britannia ruled the waves, with the U.S. Navy in a respectable second place. Ninety-six years later the only change has been the elevation of the American navy. Both navies, O'Brien observed, successfully held off a slew of potential rivals. The Royal Navy dashed the hopes of the Spanish, Dutch, French, and Germans. The U.S. Navy foiled the aspirations of Karl Dönitz, Yamamoto Isoroku, and Sergei Gorshkov. Strong national economies, robust industries, and technological expertise were critical factors in the success of both organizations. But perhaps just as important was the consistent application of economic, industrial, and technological power to a coherent doctrine. Whether one views Mahan as a prophet or a popularizer, the interwar U.S. Navy cannot be properly understood outside the context of his ideas.

Since the fleet problems collectively have not been the subject of a scholarly study, primary source material has been used to the fullest extent possible. After declassification in 1975, documents specifically relating to the fleet problems were gathered from five series of records in three records groups and transferred onto microfilm. The document sources include: Office of the Secretary of the Navy Secret and Confidential Correspondence, 1919–26, and Confidential Correspondence, 1927–39; General Records of the Department of the Navy, Record Group 80, Division of Fleet Training Confidential Correspondence, 1927–41, and Confidential Reports, 1917–41; Records of the Office of the Chief of Naval Operations, Record Group 38, and Confidential Correspondence, 1939–40; and Records of Naval Operating Forces, Record Group 313.

Four additional sets of documentary sources provide important contextual information on the interwar navy. The *Annual Report of the Secretary of the Navy* and *Annual Report of the Chief of Naval Operations* are excellent resources on general operations and naval construction activity. The *Annual Reports of Fleets and Task Forces of the U.S. Navy, 1920–1941,* include the yearly status reports from the commander-in-chief, U.S. fleet, as well as his subordinate fleet commanders. These reports offer a variety of detailed information not found in the reports of the CNO and secretary of the navy, such as recommendations on fleet requirements, personnel status, and detailed discussions on technical issues. Finally, *Proceedings and Hearings of the General Board of the U.S. Navy, 1900–1950* offers testimony from naval officers and marines on a variety of policy and technical issues.

The final areas of primary source material are the professional journals of the navy and Marine Corps and unofficial commentaries on naval policy. The Naval Institute's *Proceedings* and Marine Corps Association's *Marine Corps Gazette* have long been considered as the principal media for officers to discuss and debate policies affecting the sea services. Professional commentary outside of these journals includes authors such as airpower theorist Giulio Douhet, navy advocates such as Bradley Fiske, Hector C. Bywater, and Dudley W. Knox, USMC Commandant John A. Lejeune, Alfred Thayer Mahan, and American air-power advocate William "Billy" Mitchell.

If history is, as Edward Hallett Carr contends, an "unending dialogue between the present and the past," then the duty of the historian is to offer the past as a way of understanding the present.[16] In January 2001 former Assistant Secretary of Defense Lawrence Korb criticized the Bush administration's plan to follow through on construction of DD-21, the navy's next-generation destroyer. The navy's intention to use stealth technology in its construction, Korb argued, would make these futuristic-looking ships twice as expensive as the existing *Spruance*-class destroyers and *Perry*-class frigates, which, like the proposed DD-21, "operate primarily on the high seas against another navy."[17]

Korb's remarks illustrate in one sense that the ghost of Mahan still walks among us. His observation that the purpose of a navy is an enemy's navy was Mahan's view over a century before. Just as important, Korb's comments demonstrate that the debate surrounding the weapons we ought to build, and how they should be used, is no less complicated now than in 1923. Whether to rely on the lessons of history, uncertain future enemies, technological innovations, or a combination of all to settle the debate requires a medium capable of testing the tools and the thinking of the people who operate them. In today's "net centric" navy, the computer offers an alluring temptation to use the microchip, rather than the sea, as the medium for simulation. Between 1923 and 1940 modern warfare simulation began with a more modest form: the U.S. Navy Fleet Problems.

Those far distant, storm-beaten ships, upon which the Grand Army never looked, stood between it and the dominion of the world.

Alfred Thayer Mahan

CHAPTER 2

The Origins and Persistence of Mahanian Doctrine

Henry L. Stimson, recalling his tenure as secretary of war during World War II, remarked on the "peculiar psychology of the Navy Department, which frequently seemed to retire from the realm of logic into a dim religious world in which Neptune was God, Mahan his prophet, and the United States Navy the only true church."[1]

Stimson's comments were correct in one sense. Much of the strategic thinking of interwar naval officers was informed by lectures and books written by Capt. Alfred Thayer Mahan in the late nineteenth century. But to consign his ideas to the realm of the metaphysical suggests an incomplete understanding of his work. Mahan was not a prophet. His conception of the navy's role in national policy was not spiritually divined but rather the product of experience and intellectual pursuit. At sea he experienced firsthand the navy's transition from sail to steam. Through books he came to a disturbing revelation on the prospects of successful modernization. Without a firm doctrinal foundation, the future of the navy was uncertain. He discovered that foundation in history. In a late nineteenth-century navy of practical sailors, Mahan became the service's first intellectual and America's first naval strategist. He looked to the past to serve both the popular and professional dimensions of military transformation. From history came a theory that Mahan believed justified America's need for a modern navy. And to his less theoretically inclined colleagues, history was the tool from which theory could serve the practical purposes of naval warfare.

History and Sea Power

One would be hard-pressed to find the makings of a prophet in Mahan's biography. His parents were Mary Helena and Dennis Hart Mahan, and his father was a professor of civil and military engineering at West Point. At an early age Alfred was sent off to boarding school in Hagerstown, Maryland, and in 1854 enrolled in Columbia College in New York City. Against the advice of his father, Mahan left Columbia and entered the U.S. Naval Academy, graduating in 1859. Though Mahan graduated second in his Naval Academy class, he gained the reputation as something of a misfit and loner. His early naval career provided no clear indication of future greatness. His sea duty service was particularly uneventful. He began his career on the sailing frigate *Congress.* During the Civil War he served in several steam sloops on blockade duty off the Gulf coast and on the staff of Rear Adm. James Dahlgren, the commander of the South Atlantic Blockading Squadron.[2]

Mahan survived the postwar contraction of the navy, and his life settled into the peacetime routine of alternating duty at sea and ashore. Were it not for the intervention of Rear Adm. Stephen Luce, the founder and first president of the Naval War College, Mahan's naval career probably would have ended as inconspicuously as it began. Luce, who had served with Mahan at sea and at the Naval Academy, invited him to join the faculty at the new Naval War College as a lecturer in history and strategy. Mahan arrived at Newport, Rhode Island, in 1885. He relieved the sea-duty-bound Luce the following year and served two tours as president of the war college.[3]

Mahan's lectures on naval history and strategy found their way to broad audiences as a series of historical narratives. In 1890 Mahan published his first work, *The Influence of Sea Power upon History, 1660–1783*. Two years later a two-volume history, *The Influence of Sea Power upon the French Revolution and Empire, 1793–1812,* was released. Command of the armored cruiser *Chicago* delayed Mahan's next effort, a biography of Horatio Nelson, until his return from sea duty. *The Life of Nelson, the Embodiment of the Sea Power of Great*

Britain, was finally completed in 1897. Mahan's last work in his sea power series, *Sea Power in Its Relations to the War of 1812,* was written in retirement and published in 1905.[4]

Mahan's writing career was relatively short but prolific. Over a twenty-three-year period he published twenty monographs, as well as numerous essays and articles for periodicals and professional journals. But Mahan's *Influence of Sea Power* series is of singular importance. In these volumes he synthesized disparate notions on the use of the sea and the purpose of navies into a coherent, historically based argument that formally linked "sea power" to national greatness.

Perhaps his most recognized work, *The Influence of Sea Power upon History* laid the foundation for his subsequent efforts by establishing the theory of sea power. To Mahan the term was multidimensional. States that possessed certain geographical, political, and societal characteristics were more likely to become sea powers than nations deficient in one or more qualities. Britain, for example, was an island nation populated by a sea-going, industrious people and lying athwart the access points to the Mediterranean and North Seas. It embodied Mahan's image of a sea power. Most of the other maritime states in the North Atlantic were considered sea powers as well. But in nearly all cases save Britain, Mahan was quick to point out significant deficiencies, such as Holland's political divisiveness, France's continental aspirations, or the United States' lack of a seafaring population.[5]

Sea powers to Mahan, however, were not just born. They were also made. To Mahan the world was a global system of producers and consumers. He conceived the oceans as great highways of international commerce. But for a state to enjoy the benefits of overseas commerce required an investment in what Mahan also called sea power. As a policy, sea power consisted of three components. The first was access to overseas markets. In the late nineteenth century the most dependable market to Mahan was a colonial possession. The colony provided raw materials to the mother country. In return, it was the principal purchaser of finished products. Second, nations that sought to become sea powers needed a sufficient merchant marine to move articles of trade. Third, since Mahan believed that increased competition for overseas markets might lead to war, a sea power needed some form of armed naval force to protect its shipping.[6]

Mahan envisioned prosperity as the key to national greatness, international commerce as the means to achieve prosperity, and sea power as the policy best suited to harness the world's commercial resources. Such a theory might in itself inspire popular and political support for a large navy. But Mahan understood that his colleagues would receive such intellectually based notions with skepticism. So Mahan made the theoretical appear practical. As a nation's prosperity was dependant upon overseas commerce, it seemed logical that whoever controlled the "well-worn paths" across the "wide commons" of the sea controlled their own destiny. Diplomacy and resourcefulness ensured a nation access to the sea in peacetime. In war, though, a nation required a navy to protect its commerce. "Sea control," the policy in which the navy guaranteed access to the great highways for its own nation's shipping, while denying it to an enemy, made the theoretical practical.[7]

Mahan was convinced that history revealed the relationship between sea power and national greatness. He also believed that studying the past provided practical principles of naval warfare, from which naval strategy could be derived. But exactly how was a navy to achieve sea control? And when sea control was attained, how was it to be exercised? The conflicts within the newly established European state system offered answers that Mahan believed were relevant to modern times. In 1660 there was relative equality amongst the maritime states of Britain, France, the Netherlands, and Spain. Yet by 1763 Britain stood alone as Europe's preeminent power. To Mahan, the predominant reason lay in the island nation's concerted national policy to use and control the seas. The years between 1660 and 1763 represented a blueprint for the application of sea power. In the course of a century, Britain eliminated its European maritime competitors through a variety of policies, all of which were related to Mahan's trilogy of sea power.

Spain was already in a deteriorating state at the outset of the narrative. In Mahan's opinion, the Spanish Navy made no substantive contribution to the course of events. Dutch maritime strength, on the other hand, did pose a challenge to Britain. Dutch sea power was reduced both diplomatically and militarily by Great Britain. In 1651 Parliament enacted a series of Navigation Acts that restricted the trade between Britain and its colonies to ships manned predominantly by English crews. The policy was an act of economic warfare. A series of Anglo-Dutch naval wars ensued, which finished Holland as a competitor on the high seas. Mahan observed that the difference lay in the Royal Navy's overpowering strength in ships of the line. They were used against the Dutch fleet in two significant naval engagements, and thereafter "shut the Dutch merchantmen in their ports and caused grass to grow in the streets of Amsterdam."[8]

The removal of the Spanish and Dutch from the ranks of sea powers left Mahan to concentrate on the rivalry that he believed best exemplified his ideas. Among the European states, France enjoyed almost as many of

Mahan's elements of sea power as did Britain. It had a stable government under the ambitious Louis XIV, good ports, and a navy growing in efficiency under the capable administration of Colbert. Conditions on the other side of the English Channel appeared to tip the balance of power further in France's favor. The ascension of William of Orange to the English throne in 1688 formally ended Anglo-Dutch rivalry. But the years of war left the Royal Navy in a declining condition. And the union with Holland only drew the island nation more deeply into affairs on the continent.[9]

The stage appeared set for an apocalyptic struggle between rival sea powers. What ensued was a series of wars that in Mahan's mind demonstrated how sea power shaped events on land. During the War of the League of Augsburg (1688–97), a single naval victory over the French at the Battle of Beachy Head in July 1690 forced the French navy back into port. Britain and Holland, having gained control of the sea, imposed a naval blockade on French ports. The blockade, Mahan concluded, checked Louis' advance into Spain. France ceded the sea altogether in its second war with England five years later. Of the four wars fought between 1688 and 1763, however, the Seven Years War was the crowning demonstration of British sea power in the eighteenth century. The French, Mahan noted, used their navy principally to support land operations. Britain, by contrast, used its navy independently to shape events ashore. Gibraltar was reinforced, blocking any chance for French fleets in the Mediterranean and Atlantic to unite. The Royal Navy took advantage of a divided French Navy and defeated the French Brest fleet at the Battle of Quiberon Bay in November 1759.[10]

Mahan characterized Quiberon Bay as the "Trafalgar" of the war, because the aftermath so clearly illustrated the advantages offered by controlling the sea. French ports were blockaded. British warships eliminated French privateering in the West Indies. Mahan pointed out that much of what the British gained during the war was used to dictate the conditions of peace during the conference in Paris in 1763. While much of the territory acquired through arms was returned, Britain nevertheless emerged as the world's preeminent sea power. And "at the end of seven years," Mahan concluded, "the Kingdom of Great Britain had become the British Empire."[11]

Mahan could point with some confidence to events between 1660 and 1763 as clearly demonstrating the ability of sea power to affect events ashore. The period was less clear, though, when it came to fully explaining the concept of sea control. The principal reason, he contended, was due to the flawed policies of the French. Rather than using their navy to directly challenge Britain, the Bourbon kings instead emphasized military operations on the continent.[12] Such asymmetry complicated Mahan's argument. From the British perspective, the evidence pointed to a general notion that the objective in a contest for sea control was the enemy's navy. Ships of the line appeared the most effective platform to be used. Decisive battle seemed to be the most efficient means of using the great ships. Yet in many cases, diplomatic initiatives had also contributed to the attainment of sea control. In others, sea control was achieved by default. Finally, there was the problem of explaining the American War for Independence. Britain was the world's preeminent sea power in 1776. Yet one could hardly point to naval operations as the determining factor in the war.[13]

Though the early history of the age of sail only intimated what sea control was, Mahan was convinced that it firmly established what sea control was not. After he had lost control of the sea during the War of the League of Augsburg, Louis XIV shifted naval operations away from attacking warships to British and Dutch merchant shipping. The Sun King embarked on *guerre de course,* a naval policy in which an enemy's merchant ships became the principal objective.[14]

Mahan was not blind to the notion that an enemy's merchant fleet was an appropriate objective in war. What concerned him was efficiency. Using warships to roam the seas for enemy merchant ships would undoubtedly be painful for the victimized nation's economy. And for a nation with little or no naval capacity, such a strategy was the only option available. But for true sea powers, *guerre de course* was an inefficient form of naval warfare. It was a piecemeal strategy that would spread a navy thin and could not guarantee complete success against a nation with global trade links. Better first to free the seas of an enemy's warships, Mahan argued. With the naval threat removed, blockades could be established off the enemy's ports, while those merchants who found themselves stranded at sea could be hunted down leisurely.[15]

Mahan's vehement criticism of *guerre de course* had contemporary relevance. In the 1880s a group of French naval officers, known as Jeune Ecole, or "New School," argued that modern technology had made commerce warfare a viable naval policy. Led by a progressive minister of marine named Hyacinthe-Laurent-Théophile Aube, the policy they crafted applied new weapons to close the gap between France and her principal naval rivals. The technological innovation upon which their confidence rested was the torpedo, mounted on a small, fast, and highly maneuverable boat. Swarms of these boats, they believed, would drive off a blockading British fleet, freeing cruisers to attack merchant ships at will. The ensuing effects of a weakened economy and plummeting civilian morale, the Jeune Ecole predicted, would force the British to sue for peace. Aube's policy was no less applicable to France's rival in the Mediterranean. Italy's economic centers lay beyond the reach of Aube's torpedoes. But her civilians, living in weakly defended coastal towns, were well within range of bombardment from gunboats.[16]

The Jeune Ecole posed a significant challenge to Mahan's argument. For centuries the prospects of sinking a capital ship had been the principal motivation of early efforts to develop underwater weapons.[17] Aube and his colleagues took the strategy of the weak to a dimension unforeseen by the early pioneers of underwater warfare. The merging of new weapons and strategy in French naval policy appeared to dramatically alter the complexion of war at sea. With the advent of a torpedo-carrying commerce raider, *jus ad bellum* ("justice in war") was subordinated to military practicality. The torpedo boat would not conform to Prize Law, the internationally recognized agreement that prohibited sinking unarmed merchants before an inspection of the cargo and the safe removal of the crew. The great tactical advantage of the torpedo boat was its ability to attack from a great distance at night. Proceeding to its target virtually unseen, the new weapon enhanced the psychological effects of the Jeune Ecole's policy.[18]

Mahan addressed the challenge of the Jeune Ecole by attacking the torpedo boat from operational and historical perspectives. He questioned its seaworthiness, contending that in heavy seas the small boats would impede the speed of a fleet that they were accompanying. The boats might have some utility closer to shore. But as the fire ships of the seventeenth century had been rendered obsolete by the invention of incendiary projectiles, Mahan was confident that simply adding torpedoes to larger ships would obviate the need for the smaller vessels.[19]

To Mahan, *guerre de course* and the torpedo boat constituted the antithesis of a prudent naval policy. The Jeune Ecole had adopted the torpedo and developed a naval policy from it. They had in effect replaced history with technology as the determinant of naval strategy. Mahan was not averse to technology. What did concern him, though, were the implications of technological change. He assumed that the appearance of new weapons would require a navy to adopt necessary tactical countermeasures. But Mahan believed that effective naval strategy should not be deduced from such an erratic and unpredictable environment. The proper foundation for conceptualizing strategy, he believed, lay in timeless principles, which could be deduced only through the study of history.[20] Mahan was convinced that history had shown that sea control was accomplished not by chasing individual merchant ships but by "the possession of that overbearing power on the sea which drives the enemy's flag from it." It was a power that could only be satisfied by "great navies," whose primary objective was the enemy's navy. Once the seas were cleared of hostile warships, the victorious fleet would be free to act as it pleased to destroy the opponent's merchant shipping.[21]

Sea Control

While Mahan's first book offered the historical justification for a national investment in sea power, *The Influence of Sea Power upon the French Revolution and Empire* was the apotheosis of Mahan's sea-control model. The period was marked by great naval battles, fought between concentrated fleets of the most powerful ships of the day. On Valentines Day in 1797 Adm. Sir John Jervis crushed a Spanish fleet off Cape St. Vincent. To Mahan the victory demonstrated the "worthlessness of the Spanish navy." It won for Jervis advancement to the peerage as the Earl St. Vincent. And to a rising young captain named Horatio Nelson, who had distinguished himself in the battle, came promotion to rear admiral. The following year Nelson, in command of his own fleet in the Mediterranean, attacked a French fleet anchored in Aboukir Bay. Mahan hailed the ensuing Battle of the Nile as "the most complete" and "most decisive" of naval battles. In his mind Nelson's victory secured control of the Mediterranean, left the French army trapped in Egypt, and thwarted Napoleon's grand strategic vision of loosening Britain's hold on India.[22]

With control of the Mediterranean attained, Britain next moved to secure its northern European reaches. Prime Minister William Pitt decided on a naval expedition to deter an alliance between the Baltic naval powers and France. The subsequent attack on Copenhagen in April 1801 did not exactly fit the Mahanian paradigm. The Danish fleet did not sail. Nelson, in command of the attacking naval force, directed his efforts against the city's fixed defenses, ignoring a signal from his apprehensive commander-in-chief to withdraw. Mahan nevertheless proclaimed the victory as "second in importance to none that Nelson ever gained" and "the most critical of all in which he was engaged."[23]

His tendencies towards insubordination aside, if there was one officer in the Royal Navy who Mahan thought embodied British sea power, it was Horatio Nelson. And if Mahan could point to one event during Britain's naval history to embody his vision of sea control, it was Trafalgar. The battle was Nelson's crowning achievement. It was also in Mahan's mind an incontrovertible demonstration of sea control. Having chased the French Toulon fleet across the Atlantic for most of the summer of 1805, Nelson eventually cornered the French in Cadiz. On September 29, his birthday, Nelson met with his commanders and issued his famous plan of attack. "The business of an English Commander-in-Chief," the order began, being "to bring an Enemy's Fleet to Battle," his objective was "a close and decisive Battle." Nelson's intention was clear to his captains. The objective of the battle was the annihilation of the French and Spanish fleets.[24]

On October 21, 1805, two great fleets totaling sixty ships of the line converged for battle. Nelson cut a combined French-Spanish line in two and concentrated his efforts on the center and rear of the enemy's line. When the battle was over, Pierre de Villeneuve, commanding the combined fleet, had lost twenty-two of his thirty-three ships of the line. Nelson was killed in the battle, which in Mahan's mind was a fitting end for England's greatest naval hero. "Finis coronat opus," Mahan wrote at the conclusion of *The Life of Nelson*, "has of no man been more true than of Nelson. He needed, and left, no successor."[25]

As Nelson was "the embodiment of the sea power of Great Britain," Trafalgar embodied the professional dimension of Mahanian sea-power theory. A concentrated force of Britain's most powerful warships had annihilated a similar force in a decisive engagement. Mahan was convinced that the battle completely altered the strategic environment. Napoleon's designs for an invasion of England evaporated in a single day. The general did not immediately abandon the sea. But his attempt to wrest sea control from Britain by resurrecting *guerre de course* proved futile. The Royal Navy countered by blockading French ports, convoying merchants, and patrolling the approaches to England. French merchant ships were trapped in port. British merchants roamed the sea with relative freedom. And Parliament, recognizing the diplomatic advantages of sea control, dictated more forcefully to neutrals that wished to trade with France.[26]

Britain's control of the sea remained unchallenged for the remainder of the war. But to Mahan the victory at Trafalgar had far-reaching implications. In his first book he had posited the critical relationship between sea power and commerce. Commerce fueled a nation's economy in peacetime. But Mahan also believed that international commerce was the principal means of sustaining war. A nation that controlled the sea in wartime was ensured an external source of revenue. A nation denied the sea would be forced to pay for war from within. The increasing demands of war on a national economy, Mahan believed, would act like a cancer. Without an external source of nourishment, war would eventually exhaust a nation.

During the dynastic wars the Bourbon kings consistently found themselves on the wrong side of the sea-control paradigm. Yet they were never completely isolated from their colonial possessions. In 1805, however, Napoleon was virtually cut off from the sea. British sea control, Mahan maintained, turned Napoleon inward. The general was forced to pay for war by extending French control over the continent. While crushing military victories consolidated most of Europe's resources under French control, Napoleon attempted to counter British sea control with his famous Milan and Berlin Decrees, which imposed a continent-wide trade embargo with England. England responded in kind with Orders in Council, which essentially prohibited all neutral merchant ships from landing in French-controlled ports.[27]

Between 1805 and 1812 the struggle between England and France resembled an encounter between a tiger and a shark. Each was dominant in its own environment yet unable to directly attack the other. The deciding factor, Mahan argued, was sea power. British merchants might be cut off from Europe, but they continued to trade with the rest of the world. As for France, the Royal Navy's ability to restrict its commerce exceeded Napoleon's ability to eke sustenance from his continental tributaries. The cancer of war, Mahan concluded, consumed the French treasury, drove Napoleon into a misguided invasion of Russia, and fomented revolution in Spain. Mahan acknowledged that Napoleon's genius had carried the war far beyond what the French Directorate could have imagined. But Napoleon was no match for British sea power, which "shut him off from the world, and by the same token prolonged her own powers of endurance beyond his powers of aggression."[28]

To Mahan the past was prologue. He viewed his country and navy as possessing potential but lacking clear direction. America enjoyed many of the geographic, political, and social conditions necessary to become a sea power. Even before Mahan published his first book, the United States had embarked on a modest naval construction program that included battleships. It was not necessarily the present, though, that worried Mahan. America's future concerned him. Would the United States adopt a maritime policy that ensured national greatness, as the British model so clearly illustrated? Or was the country to become another France?

Mahan was no less concerned with members of his own profession. The U.S. Navy had a rich tradition of capable mariners. Practical seamanship and gunnery had served a navy of frigates well. But unlike its wooden predecessors, steel battleships were national assets. They were too few and expensive to be used for purposes other than contesting the sea. If the United States was going to become a true sea power, Mahan argued, then its naval officers had to broaden their professional development to include strategic study. The stakes for a nation in a contest for control of the sea, he believed, were too high to delay strategic preparation until a war broke out.[29]

Mahan turned to history to accommodate both constituencies. The past provided the intellectual justification for a national policy of naval expansion. History also provided the means from which timeless principles of naval warfare could be deduced. Britain had prospered because of her colonial markets, her merchant fleet, and the Royal Navy. The navy was comprised of the most powerful ships of the day. Royal Navy squadrons might be dispersed at the outset of war but only to the extent that they could concentrate against an enemy fleet in a decisive battle. During the Napoleonic Wars decisive battles revealed the weakness of Spain, left Napoleon stranded in Egypt, and eventually shut France off from the outside world. In Nelson, Mahan had not only the embodiment of British sea power but also the model for the modern U.S. commander-in-chief. "Nelsonian boldness" was not impulse but courage and action tempered by intellectual insight. His "genius for war" was recognizing the importance of study prior to battle, which in Mahan's mind demonstrated the advantages of intellectually based risk taking.[30]

The Persistence of Mahanian Sea-Control Doctrine

Alfred Thayer Mahan was not the father of the modern U.S. Navy. Nor was he the sole instigator of the new navalism emerging in the late nineteenth century. As Peter Karsten observed, it was the generation preceding Mahan that initiated institutional reforms such as the Naval War College, the Naval Institute, and the Office of Naval Intelligence. Robert Seager II noted that political and business leaders were fashioning the ideological, commercial, and geographical arguments for a new navy well before *The Influence of Sea Power upon History* was published. The first ships of all-steel construction were authorized in 1882. By 1886 the navy had its first two battleships, *Texas* and *Maine*. By the end of the decade U.S. ship builders were producing warships of more modern design, prompting Secretary of the Navy Benjamin Tracy to call for the construction of twenty battleships, eight for the Pacific and twelve for the Atlantic.[31]

The naval officer corps understood that their future demanded broader professional horizons. Congress was authorizing a navy of capital ships. Americans were coming to understand that geography was no longer an impediment to expansion nor a guarantee of security. The only missing piece was a coherent message that brought all these forces together. Mahan provided that message, and the navy enthusiastically adopted it. In an address in Boston on April 15, 1894, Assistant Secretary of the Navy William McAdoo carried the message of sea power to the general public. McAdoo downplayed the navy's meager early accomplishments as the consequence of early U.S. history. The nation was too focused on filling its territorial borders, he explained, and had yet to fully exploit its vast resources. More importantly, McAdoo pointed out that "the great lesson that sea-power goes hand in hand with the right to rule on land was then little understood in the world." Even the greatest nations on earth had not recognized the connection between sea power and national greatness until Mahan wrote "his now universally accepted doctrine of the influence of sea-power on history." But now that the secret was out, McAdoo wanted his audience to understand that America's late entry into the world did not necessarily mean greatness was out of reach. "Our vast resources, our tremendous power, our advancing civilization," he exhorted, "make us a factor in the affairs of our neighbors." McAdoo's message was clear, and it was Mahanian. America was on the precipice of an explosion in commercial power. If Americans wanted to nurture this "doctrine of ascendancy," they needed more than presidential messages or congressional resolutions. America needed a strong navy.[32]

Responding to the Naval Institute's request to publish his Boston speech, McAdoo apologized in advance for the reception it might receive from professional officers. He reminded the secretary of the Naval Institute that his message was intended for the general public. Discussion of specific aspects of naval operations was never intended.[33] McAdoo clearly understood the multidimensional nature of Mahan's message. Sea-power theory was meant to reach out to the public. It was a grand vision intended to convince Americans of the connection between national greatness, prosperity, and a large fleet of battleships. Yet McAdoo also recognized that Mahan intended operational issues to be sorted out by naval professionals. Sea control, the professional dimension of sea-power theory, was vested to naval officers. And Mahan's colleagues in uniform proved as capable of sustaining his operational doctrine as McAdoo was of spreading the gospel of sea power.

The Mahanian canon was more than a balm to soothe professional anxiety. Naval officers perceived sea control as the means to redefine national defense in predominantly naval terms. Lt. Cdr. Richard Wainwright argued on the eve of the Spanish-American War that the navy's traditional role in coastal defense had become obsolete. Coastal fortifications, he contended, were not only expensive but also inefficient. Additionally, fixed coastal defenses failed to address America's increasing international responsibilities in the Western Hemisphere and Asia. Wainwright envisioned national defense in terms of a battle fleet, employed against an enemy's fleet near its own coast. Once the enemy fleet had been defeated, and "command of the sea" attained, then the navy would be free to operate in any way it saw fit to bring the war to a conclusion. Wainwright did not completely dismiss the relevance of fixed defenses. Forts might still be useful to defend important ports. But he viewed them as the last line of defense. The United States' "main coast defense" was a mobile battle fleet.[34]

Wainwright viewed sea control as the perfect fit for a modern navy of battleships. Critics of his position, he pointed out, had only to look at France. While Wainwright acknowledged that "Admiral Aube has a large following," he also noted the schizophrenic nature of French naval construction policy. The "ruling idea that appears to permeate those from the new school is that there is one type suitable for the strong naval power and another for the weak." But Wainwright also observed that Aube's ideas had not constrained France from continuing to build battleships. France's dilemma was its "misconception of the uses of sea power and the history of sea-fights." The Jeune Ecole offered an example of a naval policy the United States should avoid. Sea control, Wainwright concluded, would put the United States on the right side of history.[35]

Wainwright received an "honorable mention" award for his article, an indication that his recitation of Mahan was well received by his colleagues. One month after Wainwright's article was published, the navy found itself with an opportunity to put ideas to action. The war with Spain had not been completely unanticipated. Students and faculty at the Naval War College had provided the Navy Department with a plan in 1896 that proposed a joint army-navy assault on Havana in the event of war.[36] But the war college scheme was rejected in favor of a competing plan from the Office of Naval Intelligence, which wound up also being ignored. Strategy for the war with Spain regressed to the realm of ad hoc decision making. Admiral Dewey's orders for action against the Spanish in Manila came from assistant navy secretary Theodore Roosevelt. Public pressure to protect the east coast was the driving force behind the decision to divide warships between the Atlantic and Caribbean, which in Mahan's view resulted in a missed opportunity to catch the Spanish fleet before it entered Santiago.[37] Army and navy cooperation in Cuba deteriorated into a battle of personalities between Adm. William T. Sampson and his counterpart, Maj. Gen. William Shafter. American naval victories at Manila Bay and Santiago were due more to the Spanish navy's obsolete ships and incompetent leadership than to any strategic acumen within the Navy Department.

The war with Spain demonstrated that the practical application of Mahan's ideas was more complicated than his narratives had suggested. Yet the vitality of his sea-control doctrine was not diminished. Cdr. Bradley Fiske, in a March 1905 prize-winning article for *Proceedings*, showed how resolute the sea-control camp was. The navy's destiny, he argued, still lay in the battle fleet. The destructive power of the battleship outweighed arguments for any type of doctrine other than one that focused on the destruction of the enemy's battle fleet. The only technological advance that concerned Fiske was the torpedo. But as long as all ships in the fleet were outfitted with them, he did not envision technology significantly changing doctrine.[38]

Fiske's acknowledgement of a technological development unrelated to the battleship is noteworthy. Still, from the perspective of Fiske and most of his colleagues, the gun dominated naval warfare. Expectations were naturally muted, therefore, when weapons appeared that seemed to challenge the status quo. John Holland's submarine was introduced to naval officers by 1900, yet their enthusiasm for the new weapon was initially lukewarm. In one of the first articles on submarines to the *Proceedings,* Cdr. W. W. Kimball observed that they would pose a credible threat to surface ships that attempted to blockade U.S. coastal cities. But he also argued that limitations in speed and range, as well as the difficulty involved with underwater navigation, would diminish a submarine's effectiveness beyond the coast. Naval architect Lawrence Spear echoed Kimball's assessment. While he acknowledged great technical strides had been made in submarine development, Spear saw "no immediate prospect of the development of the large *submersible* into an *offensive* weapon." And in a 1905 article to the *Proceedings,* Lt. A. B. Hoff characterized submarines as slow, heavy, and "sluggish in all movements." Like Kimball and Spear, Hoff tempered his skepticism by suggesting that ships conduct maneuvering exercises to determine the best ways to chase down the boats. But the tone of the article reflected the emerging attitude of cautious optimism when it came to submarines. They might be useful but would not replace capital ships.[39]

Another potential challenge to Mahan was an even newer technological innovation, the airplane. The navy did not completely dismiss the potential of aviation. But it approached aviation with a caution that reflected the tenuous nature of the new technology. While European militaries were rapidly incorporating aviation in the early twentieth century, the first naval aviators were taking their flight training at Glenn Curtiss's cottage aircraft factory in Hammondsport, New York. In 1912, while the British were establishing the Royal Flying Corps, the four aviators in America's naval air force were training on a small air station on a spit of land across from the U.S. Naval Academy.[40]

The first naval war of the twentieth century appeared to validate a cautious approach. Naval officers might have been surprised that the first modern sea fights would occur in the western Pacific, but they did not seem surprised that a European power had been decisively defeated by an upstart Asian nation. Mahan provided a thoughtful interpretation of the war, arguing that the Russian naval disasters at Port Arthur and in the Tsushima Straits were object lessons in the improper application of sea control. Port Arthur fell because the Russian fleet had been mismanaged. The fleet, Mahan argued, had become nothing more than an extension of the land defenses, which in effect surrendered sea control to the Japanese. The naval battle in the Tsushima Straits additionally demonstrated the consequences of misidentifying the true strategic objective in a naval war. To Mahan, the Russian objective of getting their fleet safely to Vladivostok was ill fated from the start. Admiral Togo's decisive victory was due to his understanding that the fundamental objective of his fleet was to attain sea control, from which he devised a coherent strategy that defeated the Russian fleet in a decisive battle. Agreement with Mahan's interpretation is noted by the lack of commentary to the contrary. Officers did not challenge Mahan's assertion that the war illustrated the relevance of sea control.[41]

Still, it would be mistaken to infer that naval officers were simply enamored by the allure of the glorious victories implied in Mahan's work. The comments of Commodore W. H. Beehler in June 1909 exemplified the thoughtful attention given to the canon. Beehler wrote that the mere possession of battleships, cruisers, destroyers, auxiliaries, and bases was not sufficient to deter a potential enemy. What the navy had to demonstrate with its ships, he argued, was "efficiency." "They must be handled efficiently," Beehler wrote, "and foreigners, who might become possible enemies, must be convinced that our navy is handled efficiently." Beehler went on to define efficiency in the form of a battle fleet, free to operate on the high seas against an enemy's fleet in order to gain control of the sea. He pointed out that the war between Russia and Japan demonstrated that "the coast of Japan needed no protection against the formidable Russian fleet, because the Japanese first sought complete command of the sea." The destruction of the Russian fleet, Beehler observed, "rendered Japanese coast defences unnecessary."[42]

Naval officers often conflated the phrases "sea control" and "command of the sea" in their professional correspondence. But though they might confuse the semantics, they clearly understood the concept. That is, they understood what Mahan wanted them to. Sea control, the employment of concentrated firepower from battleships in a decisive naval engagement against an enemy fleet, was not just the most prudent use of the navy. It was, as Commodore Beehler repeatedly emphasized, the most *efficient* use of naval power. Mahan looked back to naval warfare in the age of sail and from the success of the Royal Navy crafted a positivist doctrine for a modern navy of steel ships. Sea control brought order to naval warfare. A line of battleships, in close formation, would converge on its opposite line. The doctrine additionally demonstrated the advantages of using the most powerful weapons available. Britain's unyielding faith in the ship of the line more than compensated for unorthodox ships such as commerce raiders. Finally, sea control was economical. Decisive battle eliminated the threat in a single event.

Scholars benefiting from the lens of history have identified the many deficiencies of Mahan's theory of sea power and doctrine of sea control. To take offense to my rather one-sided view of Mahan, though, ignores the historian's principal duty to explain the past within the context of the people who saw it as their present. The evidence suggests that most naval officers unconditionally accepted Mahan's sea-control doctrine well after the architect left active service. And at least for the foreseeable future, sea control would reign supreme in the U.S. Navy. Unlike the age of sail, however, naval technology in the late nineteenth and early twentieth centuries did not remain static. By the turn of the century the diesel-electric submarine was rapidly assuming its modern form. The torpedo was evolving into a more effective weapon. And aviation, although in its infancy, was beginning to show signs of a military application. For officers trying to come to grips with the transformation from wood and sail to steel and steam, sea control offered efficiency, order, and control. New weapons, at least for the time being, could be conformed to fit existing expectations. U.S. naval officers could only assume that they were prepared to fight a modern naval war, if presented with the opportunity.

The Navy Plans for a Modern War

As the 1896 Naval War College plan for war with Spain showed, naval officers had begun to think about and articulate war plans before the turn of the century. A navy of capital ships, fueled by commercial optimism and newly acquired possessions in the Caribbean and western Pacific following the Spanish war, made the United States a maritime empire. New imperial responsibilities intensified the need for coherence and consistency when it came to naval policy. The years prior to the U.S. entry into World War I were spent creating an administrative infrastructure capable of shaping naval policies to support the country's new global responsibilities. The Navy General Board was formed in 1900. Comprised of senior naval officers, the board was the principal medium through which the secretary of the navy received policy advice on issues ranging from ship construction to strategy. Two years later, a Joint Army-Navy Board was organized to coordinate planning and enhance interservice cooperation. The war-planning process became more formal in 1911, when Secretary George Meyer directed the General Board to designate the countries for which naval war plans were to be prepared. The Office of Naval Intelligence was assigned to provide the necessary background information on the specified country. The war college contribution was demoted to providing assistance, "as requested."[43]

The resulting plans, or "portfolios," were assigned a color representing the country the navy planned to fight. Although the imaginations of naval officers would lead them to develop twenty-three color-coded plans, efforts were predominantly focused on wars with the world's major naval powers. And with few direct experiences from which to draw, and little familiarity with emerging new weapons, planners shaped future wars using the doctrine that made sense to them.

Justification for the development of a "Red" portfolio against the British, for example, was made along historical, geopolitical, and economic lines. England was viewed as a historical thorn in America's side. British warships had blockaded the U.S. coast during the War for Independence and again during the War of 1812. No less egregious was Britain's apparent sympathy with the Confederate cause during the Civil War, reflected by the apparent ease with which southern naval agents were able to purchase English-built ships and turn them into commerce raiders.[44] The empire's geographic proximity to the United States also posed a potential strategic problem. Canada loomed to the north, while Britain's Caribbean holdings posed a potential challenge for control of the Panama Canal. Finally, Britain was a global commercial competitor. To officers educated in Mahanian sea-power theory, competition for overseas markets, the lifeblood of a nation, could certainly lead to war.[45]

Not unexpectedly, early versions of War Plan Red reflected a vision more in line with the eighteenth century than the reality of the twentieth. The first plan anticipated a massive reinforcement of Canada by the British, followed by a blockade of New England ports as a prelude for an invasion of

New York. The U.S. fleet, outnumbered and outgunned by the Royal Navy, would be forced to abandon the east coast. Michael Vlahos has characterized the early versions of War Plan Red as nothing more than a "pernicious inheritance of arrested evolution." The logistic constraint of transporting thousands of British troops to Canada alone was an issue, which if seriously considered, would have diminished the gravity of the British threat. Nor did Mahan seem to believe that a war with Britain was likely, viewing instead transnational cooperation as the key to keeping the United States relevant in world affairs. Perceptions of an Anglo-American war seem to have been more useful to generating some sense of self and mission within the U.S. naval officer corps than anticipating the reality of modern war.[46]

Similarly, the navy's 1913 plan for a war against Germany ("Black") was a model of Mahan's sea-control thinking. Navy planners envisioned the Kaiser's imperial designs in the western hemisphere as the most probable cause of the war. Upon learning of the German fleet movement, the navy would assemble in the lower Chesapeake Bay, then head to the Caribbean, the predicted destination of the enemy. Once concentrated in the Caribbean, the U.S. fleet would intercept the German Navy and destroy it in a climactic naval battle that would end the war.[47] The plan certainly remained loyal to Mahan. But it failed to address the salient question of why the German fleet would steam en masse to the Caribbean, leaving Germany vulnerable to its more proximate British rival. Nor did U.S. naval officers seem to consider the problem the Germans would face by moving a fleet across an ocean and fighting a major naval engagement without some sort of forward base.

In spite of some obvious deficiencies, plans for a future war with either Britain or Germany were crafted to fit nicely within the Mahanian paradigm. Between the United States and its possible European adversaries lay nothing but water, an ideal setting to choreograph the climactic sea battle. Even if the Germans made it to the Caribbean, the presence of the U.S. fleet would necessitate a naval engagement before the Kaiser could attempt to acquire an advanced base. But Japan, third on the list of most probable adversaries, was different. U.S. interests in the western Pacific were supported by a thin line of possessions taken from Spain following the war in 1898. The line was made even more tenuous by a mutual assistance treaty signed by Britain and Japan in 1902. Finally, just getting the fleet to the western reaches of the Pacific was problematic. Although the path from the west coast to the most western Hawaiian Islands was clear, the presence of numerous atoll chains between Hawaii and the Philippines seemed to imply that geography mattered a great deal.

Although the idea of war with Japan began germinating in the late nineteenth century, formal planning did not begin until 1906. By 1911, naval officers had what they believed to be a coherent vision of an "Orange" war. They predicted that Japan's increasing desire for hegemony in the western Pacific would increase diplomatic tensions between the two nations and threaten U.S. economic interests in China. Emboldened by its previous success against the Russians, Japan would eventually shift its activities from economic encroachment to outright aggression. The Japanese would initially attempt to drive the United States ("Blue") out of the region by seizing the Philippines and Guam and possibly threatening the Hawaiian Islands. In response, a U.S. fleet would assemble either off west coast ports or Hawaii and proceed en masse to the western Pacific. The Philippines, viewed as essential for sustaining fleet operations in the region, would either be relieved or retaken. Once the Philippines were secured, the U.S. fleet would then seek out and destroy the Japanese navy in a decisive battle. Having lost control of the western Pacific, Japan would either immediately sue for peace or be subject to a naval blockade.[48]

The sticking point in early versions of the plan was what to do about the islands. Planners dismissed geography, but not necessarily because they suffered from strategic myopia. Most of the intervening island chains were in the possession of European powers. The fleet would simply outrun any attempts by the Japanese to secure advanced bases in Pacific atolls. Still, unlike war plans with England and Germany, War Plan Orange added the problem of having to relieve or possibly retake islands in the western Pacific. The answer pointed to the U.S. Marine Corps. By the end of the nineteenth century, many of the Corps' traditional missions had been overtaken by the advent of modern warships. Marines had performed overseas expeditionary missions on several occasions in the nineteenth century and seemed the logical means of supporting Pacific contingencies.

Some naval officers even used the pretext of future amphibious requirements to push an agenda for the removal of marines from warships. Lt. William Fullam argued that the efficiency of the navy demanded bold personnel policies, chief of which was the removal of marines from warships. There was no responsibility given to them, he believed, that naval officers could not perform with equal competency. "A simple drill-book and a simple guard manual," he observed, "are needed—that is all." Fullam also believed that the presence of marines on board ships was "humiliating" to sailors, implying that they were untrustworthy. A more efficient use for the marines, Fullam believed, would be for them to be organized into shore-based battalions stationed at navy yards on the east and west coasts. A transport ship should also be assigned to each coast to facilitate their expeditionary responsibilities.[49] But in 1900 the Corps numbered only 174 officers and 5,200 enlisted men. Worse yet, the organizational culture of the "Old Corps" was lurching from waning missions, stagnant promotions, rivalry with the navy, and alcoholism amongst its officers.[50]

Nevertheless, it was to the marines that the Navy General Board looked to address the problem of seizing and defending advanced bases. The marines accepted their new mission enthusiastically. By the outbreak of World War I, a battalion-sized component had been formed and a rudimentary training school established to develop amphibious warfare techniques. But just as naval officers were intent on conforming the geography of the Pacific to fit their vision of a future war, the contribution of the Marine Corps was made so as not to conflict with established assumptions. The few exercises conducted by the navy and marines were extremely modest in scope and predominantly defensive in nature. Implied was the confidence that in a war with Japan the fleet would get to the Philippines before they fell. The offensive dimension of the amphibious-warfare mission was not fully explored.[51]

Soon after the war in Europe began, Pres. Woodrow Wilson suspended the war-planning process. The president feared that over-exuberant officers might compromise U.S. neutrality.[52] When the United States did enter the war in April 1917, it turned out that all parties had been grossly in error. Wilson's own exuberance to transform the international order more than made up for any possible embarrassment that the navy's war plans might have created. The navy's expectations proved no less accurate. The United States allied itself with two of the navy's three envisioned adversaries. And while planners could at least point with some satisfaction to Germany, the naval war in the Atlantic hardly matched the assumptions in War Plan Black.

Sea Control in the Crucible of War

Mahan's death in December 1914 was not particularly extraordinary. He had lived to the ripe age of seventy-four. The Naval Institute proclaimed in a memoriam that he "had used history as a tool with which to forge a philosophy whose effects, stupendous, titanic, are visible to this day."[53] But Mahan's passing was ill-timed in one respect. Naval officers were left to interpret World War I, with all of its technological nuances, without the calming influence of his observations. To complicate matters further, the U.S. Navy would spend the majority of the war not fighting but watching. By the time the United States entered, sea control had been transformed from seeking decisive battle to the unglamorous mission of protecting merchant convoys and troop transports from German U-boats.

There was little about the war's early progress that upset the navy's comfort level with its doctrine. Six months prior to the great naval battle at Jutland, Cdr. Dudley Knox offered a recitation of the sea-control canon. In true Mahanian fashion, Knox emphasized the principal objective of the navy as "the floating forces of the enemy." He characterized missions such as coastal raids and commerce warfare as "eccentric" and not justified until the enemy fleet had been decisively defeated. Knox then choreographed his vision of the modern sea battle. It would begin with converted merchants acting as distant scouts for the fleet. Once the enemy was located, cruisers, destroyers, and submarines would provide the commander-in-chief refined intelligence to help him shape the upcoming battle. Knox admitted that during this stage it would be natural to expect minor skirmishes to break out between the outer forces of the two fleets. Knox was nonetheless convinced that victory would be determined by the annihilation of the enemy in a decisive engagement between battleships.[54]

Even the German adoption of restricted and then unrestricted submarine warfare against Allied commerce following Jutland did not immediately lead to a wholesale change of attitudes. Prior to the war Ens. Holloway Frost observed that the torpedo, though dangerous, was no more immune from error than any other naval weapon.[55] Capt. Lyman Cotton viewed German U-boats with equal skepticism. He criticized *guerre de course* as a shortcut, an attempt to achieve "success in war without fighting." Cotton went on to use much of Mahan's historical evidence to reinforce the point that commerce warfare had always been an unproductive naval policy. As to the present, Cotton viewed the German employment of U-boats as a desperate measure resulting from the failure of their battle fleet to achieve sea control. He was confident that the U-boats would make only a tactical difference in naval warfare. Whereas the commerce raider of the nineteenth century captured its prizes, the U-boat simply destroyed its prey. Cotton was certain that technology had not elevated the strategic importance of commerce warfare.[56]

U.S. operational experiences appeared to reinforce the notion that the submarine threat was somewhat exaggerated. The few U.S. submarines that made it into the war failed to sink one ship. And operations against German submarines proved a dangerous yet manageable affair. Technological countermeasures such as underwater listening devices seemed to give surface ships an advantage over submerged submarines. Aircraft were demonstrating themselves as a useful antisubmarine search platform, though their success in attacking U-boats was mixed. Naval officers accepted their role as convoy escorts and testified to the Navy General Board that convoy operations were both an expedient and effective way to deter German submarines.[57]

What evidence naval officers could muster, either through observation or experiences, seemed to show that new weapons of naval warfare either suffered inherent limitations or could be minimized by countermeasures. Mahan's dictum that technology did not drive strategy seemed sound. Some officers, however, were less sure that the war offered no new lessons. Cdr. Yates Stirling was not convinced that the submarine had no strategic value. He did not disagree that the object of sea control was to ensure the use of the sea while denying its use to an enemy. But Stirling took issue with the notion that submarines played no role in the doctrine. The submarine was the natural tool for a weaker belligerent to challenge a stronger naval power. And should a navy fail to implement sufficient antisubmarine countermeasures, Stirling argued that submarines could achieve at least half of the sea-control mission by making the sea dangerous to a stronger belligerent. Bradley Fiske, who attained flag rank during the war, made a similar argument for aviation. He cautioned that it might be prudent to expand the term "naval power" to what he termed "mechanical power" and include aircraft along with the naval gun. Though Fiske admitted he was unsure how far aviation technology would advance, he was confident that aircraft would develop into a "major weapon of warfare" and predicted that a book might someday be written and entitled, "The Influence of Air Power on History."[58]

Even Jutland did not escape scrutiny. A more senior and wiser Cdr. Holloway H. Frost showed considerable professional courage by questioning the strategic relevance of the battle, which indirectly challenged the relevance of sea control to modern naval warfare. Frost was not impressed by the fact that the Royal Navy had achieved control of the North Sea following the battle. The Germans, he pointed out, still retained unfettered access to the Baltic. And as the U-boat campaign demonstrated, Jutland had not denied the Germans access to the sea. Frost then compared the alleged British victory with the accomplishments of the U-boats. The initial success of the submarine campaign had boosted the morale of the Central Powers. U-boats at one point reduced the flow of fuel oil to Britain to an eight-week reserve. Mounting merchant losses compelled the Allies to divert resources for the war to the construction of merchant ships. Finally, Frost pointed out an achievement that Mahan was convinced technology could not do. The U-boats had altered naval policy. Though the Allies controlled the surface of

the sea, submarines compelled them to adopt a defensive strategy emphasizing convoys.[59]

Conclusion

Writing in the April 1921 edition of *The World's Work,* Navy Lt. Cdr. Lee P. Warren, who worked in Chief of Naval Operations Adm. Robert Coontz's office, reflected the resiliency of Mahan. In Warren's opinion nothing that occurred in the last war compromised the notion that the battleship was "the backbone of the fleet." He admitted that submarines had sunk great numbers of merchantmen. But they had not sunk one "modern" capital ship and had failed to keep British battleships from cruising the North Sea and keeping the German fleet in its bases. The airplane appeared no closer to replacing the battleship than the submarine, suffering from limitations of range, weather, and bomb load. The "control of the air," he pointed out, "depends on control of the sea." Warren concluded that the United States was still best served by battleships, which represented "the maximum concentrated power" that could be put into one vessel. No other vessels could adequately support a national defense, which he interpreted might extend to an enemy's coast.[60]

Henry Stimson's characterization of Mahan as "prophet" implied the existence of a following of true believers. Looking back to the turn of the century, it is not difficult to understand the appeal of Mahan's ideas to imperialists, naval officers, and civilian naval enthusiasts. He advocated an internationalist policy for the United States and made the navy central to supporting it. He additionally provided a clear message that the only proper navy was one comprised of battleships. The national investment required for these ships would ensure the navy's organizational survival. Finally, sea control was a tonic for the self-esteem of the naval officer corps. Running down unarmed merchants paled in comparison to the promise of great sea battles between massive fleets.

And yet, while they found Mahan's ideas sensible enough, officers of the new navy had to face an emerging reality that Mahan's narratives had dismissed. Mahan's gaze was fixed on a period of limited technological innovation. Many of the ships that fought during the Seven Years War had seen service in the Napoleonic Wars. The age of sail was a time that suited Mahan's intellectual needs. The period left him unprepared, though, to fully appreciate the role that technology was playing in the transformation of naval warfare to three dimensions. Twentieth-century naval officers were caught in a paradox. Their strategic conceptions were based upon principles deduced from the age of sail. Yet their limited experiences in World War I implied that they could not ignore the relationship between new weapons and doctrine. What appeared so clear to Mahan through the lens of history was murkier when it came to actually dealing with submarines and airplanes. Even Lieutenant Commander Warren proved incapable of completely ignoring submarines and airplanes, admitting that the new weapons inhibited the battleships' ability to achieve or exercise "command of the sea" without sufficient escort.[61] Somehow history and the present had to be reconciled. The medium naval officers turned to was warfare simulation.

Has the Airplane Made the Battleship Obsolete?

The Former Now an Offensive Weapon Against which the Latter Has no Adequate Defence. Some Facts about Their Relative Speed, Destructive Power, Cost, and Utility

Brig. Gen. William Mitchell, April 1921

CHAPTER 3

The Airpower Pragmatists

The Fleet Problems and Naval Aviation

A little more than eighteen months after Billy Mitchell tossed down the gauntlet in the title of his article in *The World's Work,* the U.S. fleet assembled off Panama to conduct its first strategic exercise.[1] At issue was the security of the Panama Canal. Vice Adm. Edward Eberle, commander of the Black fleet assigned the objective of destroying the canal, launched an air attack on the Gatun Dam spillway in the predawn hours on February 21, 1923. Eberle's plan appeared to succeed. The aircraft arrived unopposed, dropped ten miniature, simulated bombs, and departed before army aircraft launched in response.[2] Fleet Problem One appeared to support Mitchell's claim.

CINCUS Adm. Hilary P. Jones offered a more cautious appraisal. Both exercise fleet commanders, he observed, had reached the same conclusion that the strategic objective was best achieved through air attack. CINCUS concluded that the exercise was therefore nothing more than a problem of getting airplanes into position. "In other words," Jones observed, "for

BLUE it became largely a problem in scouting, and for BLACK a problem of screening."[3]

There is no knowing whether Billy Mitchell's provocative title had any influence on Jones's low-keyed assessment of naval aviation in the first fleet problem. It is possible that CINCUS's enthusiasm was restrained for more practical reasons. In the first place, Eberle's aircraft carriers, each carrying fifteen bombers with a range of over eight hundred miles, were imaginary. USS *Langley*, the navy's first aircraft carrier, was undergoing initial underway testing. It was not a participant in the exercise. The navy's first fleet carriers, *Lexington* and *Saratoga*, were empty hulls of battle cruisers abandoned after the 1922 Washington Naval Treaty.[4]

Adm. Edward Eberle, Black fleet commander in Fleet Problem One, employed an air attack against the Panama Canal rather than using his battleships, yet his "airplane carrier" was fictitious, and his "airwing" consisted of a single sea plane. Courtesy U.S. Naval Institute.

Jones also criticized Blue fleet commander Jonathan McDonald's failure to fully utilize his own force, which also included aircraft. Had McDonald given greater consideration to Eberle's most probable route, the Black fleet would have been detected and attacked before it could close to within range of an air attack. As it turned out, Blue aircraft did locate the Black battleship *Oklahoma,* albeit ten hours after the attack on the canal.[5]

Finally, even Eberle's air attack was open to interpretation. Jones could not recall from World War I whether a plane had ever successfully launched from an aircraft carrier with a full bomb load. In the exercise, a lone navy seaplane from the Coco Solo Naval Station simulated Eberle's air force. The plane was pre-positioned in a secluded cay the day prior to the scheduled attack. The army was not informed of Eberle's plan prior to the exercise and was not warned of the air attack until the navy plane had closed to within thirty miles of its target.[6]

Jones's conservative appraisal of the capabilities of aviation did not keep him from advising its continued development. CINCUS recommended to the CNO the "rapid completion of aircraft carriers" and that the battleships should all carry aircraft "in order to insure control of the air."[7] The admiral's reluctance to embrace Mitchell's extreme view has been attributed to the psyche of conservatism that existed within the officer corps of the interwar navy. It has been suggested that Jones was culturally incapable of going any further in his assessment of naval aviation. As a member of the battleship "thought collective," he could consider aviation only in the context of the taxonomy of the navy's fighting ships. Billy Mitchell intentionally entitled his article to extol aviation as a "presumptive anomaly" that would supplant the battleship. It was Jones's duty to ensure that aviation would remain as an auxiliary form of naval warfare.[8]

The idea of operating aircraft at sea was certainly an anomaly in naval theory. But could it become the presumptive replacement for the battleship? On twenty-one occasions the U.S. fleet came together to work out strategic problems. Fifteen exercises tested the capabilities of naval aviation. It was during the fleet problems that a middle ground was reached on the role of aviation in the navy's strategic vision. Early exercises revealed the practical problems of operating aircraft at sea. Aviators learned that they had to crawl before they could walk and walk before they could run. It would be the arrival of the navy's first fleet carriers in the late 1920s that propelled the development of aviation doctrine. Admirals could still point out enough limitations to argue that the battleship was the backbone of the fleet. But by the final fleet problems, aviation had established itself as an important weapon in the navy's sea-control strategy. The reality posed by the exercises was that fleet commanders ignored aviation to their peril. Battleship admirals validated aviation by unleashing airpower against their own ships.

Postwar Years: Naval Aviation and the Billy Mitchell Crusade

Despite a rather lackluster operational record during the war, U.S. naval aviation had grown to almost 7,000 pilots, 33,000 enlisted men, 1,800 seaplanes and flying boats, 242 land-based aircraft, 15 dirigibles, and air stations in both the United States and Europe.[9] And yet, such impressive growth was not matched by a comparative development in doctrine. America's naval aviators had been assimilated into the European war and spent little if any time thinking about the future of airpower. Learning to fight from the air, whether over the Western Front or the sea, was for the most part an ad hoc affair. Given that Wilbur Wright had demonstrated his flying machine only ten years earlier, it is not hard to understand how the pace of events outstripped the ability of experts to define the weapon before it could be employed.[10] It was only when the war ended, and the pace slowed, that the airpower prophets emerged to challenge the status quo.

Naval aviation enthusiasts could hardly point to the war for incontrovertible evidence that seaborne airpower was integral to the fleet. America's late entry into the war left the navy little to do other than the dull yet strategically critical mission of convoy escort. Aviators flew thousands of missions at sea, none of which were launched from or landed on the deck of a ship. The navy's surface and air forces fought together but as separate entities. Efforts following the war to integrate naval aviation faced challenges from within and without the navy. The navy's most serious internal challenge came from its own top officer. Adm. William Benson, the first chief of naval operations, did not share his aviators' enthusiasm, characterizing aviation as "just a lot of noise." Benson reorganized the small office of aeronautics, eliminated most of the staff, and reassigned the director to the CNO's plans division.[11]

Fortunately for aviators, the Navy General Board did not share the CNO's disdain for aviation. In hearings begun in January 1919, the senior advisory group agreed that aviation's future lay principally in scouting for the fleet. The board members further decided that the mission was best supported by placing aircraft on ships, rather than relying on seaplanes or land-based aircraft. After five months of deliberations, the board recommended that the collier *Jupiter* be converted into an experimental aircraft carrier and that the fleet's battleships be equipped with planes. Aircraft had become "an essential arm of the fleet." And for the navy to maintain its position relative to other naval powers "fleet aviation [had to] be developed to its fullest extent."[12]

Aviators courted a sympathetic General Board with practical demonstrations of their capabilities. In February 1919, an aircraft provided spotting support for the battleship *Texas* during gunnery exercises off Guantanamo. With a smoke screen thrown in front of the target to obscure the ship's spotters, aircraft spotting increased *Texas'* accuracy by two-fold. Several months later, naval aviators embarked on a more daring initiative. The attempt by four Navy-Curtiss flying boats led by John Towers to cross the Atlantic was both publicity stunt and operational demonstration. Only one of the four aircraft actually reached the European continent. But even with limited success, the flight provided important practice in the use of aircraft flight instruments such as the gyrocompass, celestial navigation procedures, and wireless radio operation. Towers and his group showed fellow officers that airplanes could extend the eyes of the fleet.[13]

Dealing with skeptics within the service was one thing. But as naval aviators worked to prove themselves to their shipmates, a more serious threat loomed from outside. The threat came in the form of the airpower zealots, officers who looked upon aviation as so revolutionary that history was no longer a relevant reference for understanding war.

David MacIsaac has characterized airpower theory as so confounding as to defy attempts at analysis. Terms such as "strategic bombardment," "command of the air," and "air supremacy" appear to have no firmly rooted definitions but are nevertheless useful tools for the various proponents (and critics) of the theory.[14] Holding dear to their core belief that the Wright brothers had signaled the end of history, the early prophets sought to validate airpower not from empiricism but rather from expectations. Since World War I offered no concrete lessons of the potential of aviation, aviation enthusiasts deftly leapt to the conclusion that the travesty of war was due to antiquarian means of fighting. It was the armies and navies of the world that were responsible for dragging out the conflict and causing untold numbers of casualties. Future stalemates, the prophets argued, could only be avoided by utilizing the third dimension to its fullest. Unrestricted by geography or national borders, airplanes could provide the "knockout blow" by over-flying navies and trench lines and taking the war directly to a nation's interior. The theory assumed the fragility of civilian morale and the vulnerability of national infrastructures from an unabated attack from the sky.[15]

America's foremost airpower advocate was Brig. Gen. William ("Billy") Mitchell. The son of a U.S. senator from Wisconsin and grandson of a railroad and banking tycoon, Mitchell began his army career as an enlistee in a Wisconsin militia regiment during the Spanish-American war. He served in Cuba as the war ended and thereafter in assignments in the Philippines, the Far East, and Alaska, joining the general staff as an intelligence officer in 1912. Duty in Washington exposed the young captain to reports from Europe on the growing use of aircraft for military purposes. Mitchell was so inspired by aviation that he obtained orders to the Aviation Section of the Signal Corps in August 1915. He began training at Glenn Curtiss's flight school at Newport News, Virginia. By the following January, Mitchell had accumulated enough flight time to obtain orders to Paris as an observer of French aviation development.[16]

Mitchell's wartime experiences propelled him to the forefront of U.S. airpower advocates. He was the first American to fly over enemy lines and the first American to be awarded the Croix de Guerre for bravery in combat. Mitchell commanded the largest aggregation of Allied air forces at St. Mihiel in September 1918. By the time he arrived back in the United States following the armistice, he was convinced that America's future lay in the exploitation of the sky.[17]

Yet after his return from the war Mitchell turned out to be more airpower activist than airpower prophet. He appropriated ideas from Europe's principal aviation enthusiasts to promote a radical change in the way the United States defended itself. From Hugh Trenchard's Royal Air Force and Independent Bombing Force, Mitchell found a useful model for the organization, procurement, education, and training of an autonomous air service. And in the theory of Italian aviator and airpower prophet Giulio Douhet, Mitchell drew the central idea that to be beaten in the air is to lose the war.[18]

In Mitchell's mind, the conservative pace of aircraft development by the army and navy was a "wasteful trial and error process" that inhibited aviation's full potential. Only through the establishment of a separate air service, controlled naturally by the "air-going fraternity," would warfare be revolutionized by aircraft capable of protecting the nation's coasts, as well as threatening the interior of an enemy's nation. Should the United States shift its reliance from the "obsolete theory" of battleships to an independent force of bombing and pursuit aircraft as its principal means of defense, war would be quick, decisive, and cost-effective.[19] While Mitchell's emphasis on both bombing and pursuit aircraft strayed somewhat from Douhet, he nevertheless remained true to the central tenet of Douhet's airpower theory.

Airplanes could wrest control of the responsibility for national defense from the grip of armies and navies. Future wars would be won by the nation that gained command of the air and denied its use to the enemy.[20]

Mitchell eclipsed Douhet in a respect that had important implications for the U.S. Navy. The returning war hero quickly embarked on a campaign to convince the public and Congress of the necessity for an independent air service. The navy became the primary target. Mitchell's piece in *The World's Work* was just one of many articles and public speeches aimed at stirring up the public. As for Congress, Mitchell cultivated relationships with influential members such as New York's Fiorello La Guardia and Wisconsin's Robert La Follette and Florian Lampert. They in turn held committee hearings to give Mitchell's ideas political voice, resulting in legislation sympathetic to his cause.[21]

At first, the navy appears not to have considered Mitchell much of a threat. In a General Board discussion on March 5, 1919, on the status of naval aviation, Director of Naval Aeronautics Capt. Noble Irwin identified Mitchell as one of several "subordinate officers" who "strongly advocated a united air service." But Irwin also pointed out that he had recently spoken with Gen. Charles Menoher, director of the Army Air Service, whose opinion on the separation of responsibilities for the two air services, Irwin reported, "was the same as mine." The discussion quickly shifted to other matters.[22]

The navy's confidence that Mitchell could be contained by his chain of command proved short-lived. In 1920, Mitchell convinced congressmen friendly to his cause to attach a rider to the House Army Appropriations Bill giving the army complete control over all military air operations conducted from land. Recognizing the consequences to navy shore-based aircraft, Navy Secretary Josephus Daniels used his own political connections to have the legislation amended to ensure that the navy could continue to fly from its own air stations.[23] Undeterred, Mitchell went back to Congress in January 1921. In testimony to the House Military Affairs Committee, he claimed that he could prove that ships were vulnerable to aircraft attack and asked Congress to press the navy to provide a target for the demonstration.[24]

The resulting bombing trials, held off the Virginia Capes in the summer of 1921, are well enough known to require only a brief overview. Over a period of several days army, navy, and marine aviators bombed captured German naval vessels, ranging in size from a submarine to a cruiser. The coup de grace, however, was the test on the German battleship *Ostfriesland,* veteran of the battle of Jutland. For two days, pilots dropped bombs ranging in size from two hundred to two thousand pounds and made nineteen direct hits before sinking the ship.[25]

Mitchell would later write that the *Ostfriesland* test "conclusively proved the ability of aircraft to destroy ships of all classes on the surface of the water." Adm. William Fullam, who was among the senior military and civilian dignitaries who witnessed the test, remarked that when the "Ostfriesland joined Mr. McGinty's Navy," the emotions of the admirals were "indescribable."[26] From a publicity standpoint, the tests certainly added fuel to the controversy swirling between Mitchell and the navy. Whether the tests proved that the age of airpower had arrived, however, was another matter. Mitchell had succeeded in validating the theory that bombs dropped from the sky could sink a ship. Beyond that narrow context, verisimilitude and validity fades. The *Ostfriesland* was neither manned nor even moving during the bombing trials. Its watertight compartments were not secure. The ship did not fight back. No damage control teams were onboard.

By attacking the navy, Mitchell hoped to convince Congress of the necessity for a united defense establishment, of which an independent air service would be a member. It appears, though, that the navy was on to Mitchell's convoluted strategy before the *Ostfriesland* test. Following hearings held in April 1921, National Advisory Committee on Aeronautics chairman Charles Walcott recommended that each service retain its aviation component and that the navy establish a bureau of aeronautics, with responsibilities consonant with the navy's other powerful bureaus. The navy responded by assisting sympathetic members of Congress in drafting the legislation. The Mitchell lobby attempted to stall the legislation by introducing a rider requiring the director be a qualified aviator. The navy won the battle over the legislation. The final bill, attached to the Naval Appropriations Bill and signed by Pres. Warren G. Harding in July 1921, provided a one-year grace period for the new director to qualify.[27]

Mitchell's campaign had succeeded in ways that he did not intend. Interservice rivalry trumped intraservice rivalry between naval aviators and battleship sailors. The navy reacted to Mitchell by circling the wagons. The Bureau of Naval Aeronautics effectively ended the external threat to naval aviation. Its first director was chosen to further ensure that the fleet and its air arm would remain united. Rear Adm. William A. Moffett was a battleship sailor and Medal of Honor recipient during the Mexican Crisis in 1914. His formal relationship with naval aviation began in 1917 as commander of the Great Lakes training station, where he successfully lobbied the navy to add aviation training facilities. As commanding officer of *Mississippi,* Moffett oversaw installation of its flight deck. And as the newly assigned director of the Bureau of Aeronautics (BUAER), he responded to Mitchell's tactics in

Congress by establishing a naval aviation observers school in Pensacola and completed the five-week course in May 1922.[28]

Moffett was the right person in the right place at the right time. While not a fully qualified aviator, his appreciation of aviation convinced junior aviators that they had a voice in senior navy circles. Moffett proved as capable as Billy Mitchell at cultivating relationships in Washington. To those officers skeptical of naval aviation, Moffett offered a policy that even the most salty battleship sailor could not fight. Naval aviators were naval officers first. The airplane was a naval weapon. And naval aviation would go to sea "on the back of the fleet."[29]

In contrast to Billy Mitchell's prophetic vision of airpower, Moffett recognized that naval aviation would succeed only if its utility to the fleet could be demonstrated. Diplomatic initiatives would prove of inestimable help to his cause. The treaties marking the end of the Washington Naval Conference in February 1922 not only reduced battleship tonnages for the major naval powers but prohibited new construction for ten years. Of even greater importance was the agreement signed by the United States, Britain, and Japan not to fortify their western Pacific holdings. As Japan already held key island chains athwart any U.S. advance across the Pacific, it became apparent to U.S. Navy planners that the fleet would have to bring its aircraft along with it.[30]

The answer seemed to lie in the aircraft carrier. During the Washington conference, diplomats applied to carriers the same 5:5:3 tonnage ratios set for battleships. This authorized 135,000 tons of construction to the United States. Additionally, the United States was permitted to convert two of its uncompleted battlecruiser hulls into aircraft carriers. Moffett chaired the aviation subcommittee of the conference and succeeded in convincing diplomats that restricting the development of military aviation would not only hinder its civilian counterpart but would also be impossible to verify.[31]

Moffett left the Washington Naval Conference confident that naval aviation would remain part of the fleet and that accommodations had been made for growth. Beyond that, however, naval aviators could not with any confidence make the claims of their army counterparts. *Langley* had yet to join the fleet. More importantly, there was yet no venue for aviators to validate airpower to the fleet's leadership. The opportunity would arrive in January 1924, when *Langley* made its first appearance in a fleet problem. Aviators by this time were no longer crawling. But as the first fleet problems would demonstrate, first steps prove to be the most difficult.

While Billy Mitchell's crusade made for good headlines, it failed in all its objectives. Unification initiatives in Congress failed. The navy circled the wagons around its air arm. Even the battleship admirals could breathe easy. The Joint Army-Navy Board, of which General Pershing was the senior army member, was not swayed by the *Ostfriesland* tests. The board asserted that the battleship remained central to the fleet.[32]

In September 1924, navy secretary Curtis Wilbur convened a Special Policy Board on aviation matters that supported the navy's conservative view. Many of the board's recommendations, such as expanding the aircraft production program, expediting completion of *Lexington* and *Saratoga,* and the construction of a new twenty-three-thousand-ton aircraft carrier, pointed to the navy's commitment to aviation. But the board also concluded from testimony by civilian and military experts that the trend of aviation technological improvement would not require radical changes in the navy's force structure. The battleship could be modified to retain its central position. All other types of combatants were deemed to be complementary.[33]

The navy's early strategic exercises appeared to confirm the board's opinions. Any conclusions drawn from the first fleet problem had to be tempered by the "constructive" employment of *Langley* and the shore-based airplane that represented her air wing. The fleet defending the Panama Canal did fly shore-based patrols during the exercise, but they failed to locate the opposing force before the successful attack was launched.

Langley's physical appearance in Fleet Problem Four in January 1924 solved at least one aspect of aviation's credibility issues. In fact, it is interesting just how quickly the aircraft carrier was integrated into the exercise. *Langley* was made part of a Blue fleet simulating the final phase of an envisioned Orange war. Under the command of Adm. Robert Coontz, the fleet's mission was to seize the Puerto Rican island of Culebra and "establish an advanced base within 500 miles of the vital sea and trade routes of the constructive enemy," which in this exercise meant Japan.[34]

For the first three days of the exercise, *Langley*'s aircraft flew daily reconnaissance patrols for the Blue fleet without coming into contact with the enemy. As the fleet closed Culebra, however, aviators were provided the opportunity to demonstrate some tactical acumen. On the afternoon of January 30, five *Langley* planes engaged an incoming force of nine navy and USMC bombing aircraft from Culebra. Other fighters were sent to prevent an air torpedo attack on the Blue transport *Henderson.* Capt. Stafford H.

Doyle, *Langley*'s commanding officer, remarked following the exercise that his aviators had held their own against the air raid. The carrier's fighters continuously harassed black bombers and torpedo aircraft. Doyle was also confident that the few aircraft that had succeeded in getting to the ships were at so low an altitude as to have been shot down by anti-aircraft fire. The Black fleet commander's assessment was less enthusiastic, but he did credit *Langley*'s aviators as having provided "prompt," "energetic," and "effective" opposition to the air attacks.[35]

Captain Doyle was confident enough in his assessment of *Langley*'s performance to conclude that "the one who first gets control of the air in a future naval battle is the one who will come out the winner." But he also distanced himself from any inference of sympathy with Mitchell. He was not to be considered "one of those fanatics who believes that all one needs is aircraft." Any claims that aircraft would put the battleship "on the fritz" was in his mind "bunk."[36]

Doyle's deference to the battleship might be construed as due to the powerful grip of the battleship admirals on the navy. It is also likely that his remarks were due to the limitations exposed by the practical problems of conducting flight operations at sea. Rough weather on the first day of the exercise pitched *Langley*'s flight deck beyond the limit for safe flight operations. Pilots had no experience in landing on the carrier at night. Aircraft were so prone to mechanical problems and navigation beyond the sight of land was so difficult that fleet commander Coontz restricted flying to within "easy reach" of the fleet.[37]

Fleet Problem Four also pointed out an operational limitation of aviation that could not be reconciled easily through simulation. To augment her actual complement of fourteen aircraft, *Langley* was given an additional forty-two "constructive" aircraft. Given the artificiality, the commander of the Black aircraft operating from Culebra did not completely share his fleet commander's assessment of the effectiveness of *Langley*'s efforts against his bombers. Capt. W. C. Gherardi cautioned that in actual war, air attacks would be "timed for daylight, dusk, or thick weather," requiring that the carrier have her aircraft in the air to meet the attack. "One well-placed bomb under the great deck," he observed, "will close the campaign for that carrier, perhaps leaving her squadrons no place to land except in the sea with a certainty of material casualty."[38]

Implied in Gherardi's comments were other practical problems that naval aviators would have to master before becoming credible fighting platforms. Night flying, for example, was an inherent part of the training regimen for

USS Langley, *the navy's first aircraft carrier, formerly the collier Jupiter, first appeared in Fleet Problem Four in 1924.* Langley*'s slow speed, limited carrying capacity, and the practical limitations of operating aircraft at sea prevented aviators from making bold predictions about the future of naval aviation. Courtesy U.S. Naval Institute.*

all naval aviators. But the training was not designed to make carrier pilots proficient in night combat operations. Emphasis was placed on ensuring that pilots could safely launch from the carrier prior to dawn, and recover after dusk. Concerted efforts in night combat proficiency were not made until the spring of 1943, with the first night-capable combat air squadrons deploying on *Independence* in July 1943.

Air navigation over the water and out of sight of land was another vexing problem. With no geographic references available, aviators would have to find their way from the ship to their target and back again using dead reckoning techniques. At issue was correcting for the error encountered from the winds aloft, known as "drift." Crews in larger, more stable aircraft, such as flying boats, could use celestial navigation to fix their position. In smaller, less stable aircraft, however, the rigors of flying monopolized the attention of the one- and two-man crews. The only reliable means for carrier pilots to determine drift (a procedure still in use) was to look at the wave action on the surface of the sea. Waves tend to break in the direction of the true wind. Knowing the general direction of drift, the pilot would then have to estimate the wind speed by the height of the waves and multiply the error by the time in the air to determine an estimated position from the ship. Air navigation for tactical aircraft remained an inexact science until the advent of data links and ground searching Doppler radars in the 1960s and in the 1990s with global positioning systems.

Lt. Frank "Spig" Wead wrote soon after Fleet Problem Four that aviation was too new to draw conclusions beyond the fact that "the airplane is a necessary aid and adjunct to the operation of the battle fleet, and is no way a substitute for it."[39] Given the performance of carrier aviation in its first strategic exercise, Wead's conservatism was prudent. *Langley*'s aviators demonstrated enough tactical proficiency to have justified their integration into Coontz's strategic plan. More importantly, they had appropriated a facet of Mitchell's airpower theory that was palatable to battleship sailors. But given the limitations of both *Langley* and her aircraft, to extend beyond a defensive strategy would have been unrealistic and counterproductive. Unlike Mitchell, both aviators and ship drivers agreed that the navy's airpower doctrine was not going to be determined by prophecy. Aviators would be employed based on a realistic assessment of the contributions aircraft could make to the fleet at the moment.

Progress was slow over the next several exercises. Fleet Problem Five, held in March 1925, was so flawed as to leave very few tangible lessons. CINCUS Adm. Robert Coontz devised an eastern Pacific scenario, in which a Black (Japanese) fleet of warships and auxiliaries was to establish itself in the area in anticipation of an engagement with a Blue (U.S.) fleet transiting the Panama Canal. While conceptually sound, too little time was allocated for the exercise. As a result, neither fleet made contact with the other. USS *Shenandoah*, the navy's first rigid-hulled airship, failed as a long-range scout for the Blue fleet. *Langley*, which was assigned to the simulated Japanese fleet, accomplished little more. The ship was limited to flying air defense patrols as part of Black fleet commander Samuel S. Robison's defensive screen. Capt. S. E. Moses, commander of the aircraft squadrons on *Langley*, voiced his frustration in his comments following the exercise. The carrier, he argued, was not capable of carrying out its responsibilities both as an experimental platform and as an operational asset in a fleet exercise.[40]

Moses criticized Fleet Problem Five not so much because of conflicting missions for his aviators but because he viewed the exercise as a missed opportunity. As part of Admiral Robison's task organization, *Langley*'s aircraft were assigned not only to defend the fleet from attack from the air but also to "attack enemy vessels when ordered."[41] Moses viewed Robison's decision to fix his aircraft within his defensive screen as overly cautious. He made his feelings apparent by noting that fleet umpire reports of aircraft being of little use during the exercise were inaccurate. Moses countered that aviation had been "little used" and hoped that in future exercises it would be "utilized in all types of prescribed employment."[42]

In contrast to Fleet Problem Five, the exercise held in 1926 included an air squadron commander intent on pushing aviation beyond a strictly defensive role. Owing to the failure of the previous exercise to bring forces to an engagement, opposing fleets in Fleet Problem Six were positioned at the outset of the exercise as to make contact certain. Robison's conservatism had not entirely faded from memory. In his "Estimate of the Situation," Black fleet commander Vice Adm. Josiah S. McKean was skeptical that aircraft assigned to either side would be effective. Though *Langley* was assigned to his opponent, McKean felt that her aircraft would be too closely tied to the Blue fleet to prevent it from being located and destroyed by his Black fleet.[43]

McKean anticipated his counterpart's intentions, with one important exception. Blue fleet commander Vice Adm. Charles F. Hughes did provide general guidance that his carrier aircraft were to be used "economically, conserving them for spotting and repelling bombing attack." What McKean did not anticipate was Hughes' decision to delegate all air operations to Capt. Joseph Mason Reeves, aircraft squadrons' commander onboard *Langley*.[44]

A former battleship officer who had taken the naval aviation observer's course in 1925, Reeves pushed his aviators. Aircraft assigned to the Blue fleet flew continuous daylight operations throughout the weeklong exercise. Flight deck operations on *Langley* were pressed particularly hard to meet Reeves's requirement that the carrier operate all fourteen planes.[45] By placing such demands on his pilots, Reeves was able to fully support his fleet commander's requirements for the exercise. Blue fleet aircraft logged 116 hours in the air during the exercise and made 174 contact reports on Black ships. Enemy ship location was passed promptly to the fleet commander, who used the information to prevent McKean's fleet from penetrating the Blue defensive screen.[46]

But Reeves also took advantage of his authority to employ his aircraft in an unprecedented way. On February 13, fighters launched to provide air defense for *Langley* spotted a light cruiser on the horizon. Reeves ordered the aircraft to investigate the contact and attack it if it was determined to be an enemy. Upon discovering the ship to be of the Black fleet, the aircraft simulated an attack with light bombs and machine guns.[47]

This attack by carrier aircraft on a ship (other than a carrier) was the first in a fleet problem. Yet it is possible that Reeves's motivation was not to emphasize the offensive potential of aircraft but rather to make a statement about the vulnerability of the carrier. Reeves made no mention of the attack in his postexercise report. What he did emphasize was that the carrier's mission of air control required that it be kept well away from hostile surface forces. "The primary objective of the plane carrier," he argued, "is the enemy air force. A plane carrier should never be employed with a vessel carrying guns."[48]

There are sound reasons for Reeves's conservative estimate of the role naval aviation should play in the fleet. The Billy Mitchell crusade had yet to abate. Comments by a naval officer promoting the air attack on the cruiser would be even more damaging than Mitchell's aerial demonstrations. To make too much out of the attack would also have been contrary to Moffett's strategy to make aviation appear as more a tonic than irritant to nonaviators. And Moffett's strategy was beginning to have an effect. Submarine officer Capt. Yates Stirling echoed the mantra of conservative officers in the *Proceedings* a few months after Fleet Problem Six. In his article he wrote that when "an air force goes to sea, it must be carried on the backs of the vessels of the fleet." But Stirling also predicted that "airplane superiority will have a decisive effect upon the battle."[49]

The early fleet problems provided unique opportunities for naval aviators to demonstrate the basics of at-sea operations in front of the navy's senior leadership. *Langley* tested improved arresting gear and catapults, crash barriers, and landing signal officers on the flight deck. Flight deck operations became efficient, expeditious, and relatively safe.[50] But the exercises also revealed important tactical limitations, which checked doctrinal development. *Langley* was not designed as a fleet carrier. Her maximum speed of fourteen knots limited both her ability to launch and recover heavier aircraft, as well her ability to outrun hostile warships.[51] Her complement of fourteen aircraft was another important tactical limitation. Without a carrier capable of carrying more aircraft, aviators could not reasonably expect to expand their operational capabilities beyond defending the fleet from an opposing air force. Unlike Mitchell, naval aviators bided their time. They eschewed prophecy, chose a pragmatic path, and awaited the arrival of the fleet carriers promised in 1922.

From shared experiences during the first fleet problems, aviators and their surface brethren achieved a consensus on the framework within which the navy's air arm would function. The navy would retain its aircraft and aviators. Naval aviation would indeed go to sea on the back of the fleet. The task at hand for aviators was first to protect the fleet from air attack and then to spot for the battleships to achieve sea control.

The prospects of aviators brightened significantly toward the end of the 1920s. The furor over the control of naval aviation was over. William Mitchell's provocative tactics proved instrumental to his demise. In 1925, he charged the War and Navy Departments with "criminal and treasonable negligence" following a spate of aviation mishaps, the most spectacular of which was the crash of the navy dirigible *Shenandoah*. The army responded by charging Mitchell with insubordination and conduct prejudicial to the service. The ensuing court martial ended Mitchell's career and with it any hopes for a united air service. Army aviators shifted their emphasis from bombing battleships to bombing enemy airfields and other "terrestrial objectives."[52]

Mitchell's fall from grace had an additional benefit for naval aviators. In the wake of the controversy surrounding the *Shenandoah* crash and Mitchell's trial, Pres. Calvin Coolidge convened a committee to examine the state of military and naval aviation. Headed by Dwight Morrow, a distinguished financier and personal friend of Coolidge, the board recommended that the services retain their respective air components. The Morrow Commission went on to propose that legislation be enacted to create a top civilian aviation position within the navy secretary's office and that commanding officer positions of the navy's aircraft carriers and naval air stations be reserved for aviators. BUAER chief Moffett personally guided the board's recommendations through the legislative process. By the time Coolidge signed the recommendations into the appropriations act in June 1926, a five-year aircraft production program had been added, which would give the navy one thousand operational aircraft by 1931.[53]

The Morrow Board was one of several initiatives that addressed the personnel, professional, and material needs of naval aviation.[54] Important technological developments and tactical initiatives pushed aviation further beyond the experimental realm. The fleet carriers *Lexington* and *Saratoga* became available for operational missions. Each ship carried over five times the number of aircraft and steamed at over twice the speed of *Langley*. Naval aviators also looked with great interest in the dive-bombing tactics used by

Marine aviators in Nicaragua in 1927. BUAER's desire to expand the mission of carrier aviation led to the purchase of the F8C-2 Helldiver, a two-seat fighter originally built for the army. Though the aircraft's deficiencies in speed and rate of climb in flight tests demonstrated its unsuitability in the attack role, by 1928 BUAER had submitted design proposals for an aircraft capable of delivering a one-thousand-pound bomb. The Martin BM-1, the first navy aircraft specifically designed for the dive-bombing mission, was accepted in September 1931.[55]

The notion that carrier aircraft would be employed against ships had been played out at the Naval War College as early as 1921.[56] But it was not until the end of the decade that the concept was given serious consideration. It appears that the imposing appearance of the new nine-hundred-foot-long ships was one catalyst to new thinking. CINCUS Adm. Charles F. Hughes remarked in his 1928 annual report that the fleet would have to reconsider the way it employed its air arm. "The advantages of suppressing an air offensive before it is launched," he observed, "may have a far reaching effect upon the engagement of main forces."[57]

In January 1929, the navy put Hughes's prediction to its first operational test. Fleet Problem Nine was the first strategic exercise in which both fleets had carriers. On January 26, Black fleet commander Adm. William V. Pratt detached the carrier *Saratoga* and cruiser *Omaha* from his main fleet and staged a dawn air attack on the Panama Canal. While thirty-two fighters provided overhead protection, thirty-four bombers initiated dives from nine thousand feet, released their simulated bombs on the Miraflores locks and spillways, and pulled out from their dives at five hundred feet. Coordination between army and navy defenders in the Canal Zone proved no more efficient in 1929 than during the first fleet problem. Army aviators acted independently during the exercise and were out of position when the attack was made.[58]

Fleet Problem Nine has often been considered as something of a watershed for naval aviation. Pratt's strategy to separate his carrier beyond the protection of his battleships was the first of many challenges to the Mahanian maxim of concentration. *Saratoga*'s dash from the main body of the fleet to her launch position, some 149 miles from the canal, was also a clear demonstration of the strategic value of the fast carrier. Pratt's strategic plan, however, came with a heavy price. The Blue cruiser *Detroit*, which had made contact with *Saratoga* on January 25, reported the carrier's position throughout the night. Soon after the carrier launched her aircraft, she was engaged by battleships from the Blue fleet and soon thereafter by planes from the Blue carrier *Lexington*.[59]

Perhaps Pratt had let his confidence obscure an important shortcoming of naval aviation. Only the day before, his own battleships had emerged out of rainsqualls within gun range of *Lexington* and attacked the carrier before an air attack could be launched.[60] At the critique following the exercise, Pratt acknowledged that his plan placed *Saratoga* in jeopardy but insisted that the strategic mission of destroying the canal justified the potential loss of the carrier. Joseph Mason Reeves, Pratt's air commander and now a rear admiral, agreed. Reeves went on to add that *Saratoga* was actually safer when acting independently. Being tied to a slower main body, he believed, made the carrier more vulnerable to attack. Reeves used as an example the cruiser *Omaha,* which had been assigned to escort the carrier. *Omaha*'s fouled bottom, Reeves believed, had hindered *Saratoga* from moving at top speed to elude *Detroit.*[61]

CINCUS Adm. Henry Wiley was unhappy with both of his fleet commanders. Blue commander Vice Adm. Montgomery Meigs Taylor was chastised for his decision to launch planes from *Lexington* during its unplanned encounter with the enemy on the twenty-fifth. Wiley felt that the carrier's "preferable" course of action would have been to turn away from the attacking ships and "utilize superior speed to avoid punishment." As for Pratt, Wiley observed that the decision to detach *Saratoga* and *Omaha* placed the carrier "in grave peril." The fact that it was Cdr. Kenneth Whiting, one of the navy's first aviators, who judged *Saratoga* sunk, only enhanced the credibility of Wiley's criticism.[62]

Wiley remarked that while naval aviation had "found a place in the fleet," the exercise pointed to the "battleship as the final arbiter of Naval destiny." The comment was a practical reminder to aviators of the limitations in their trade. In his concluding remarks, however, Wiley also noted that the exercise had accentuated that the "heavy capital ship is still the backbone of the fleet."[63] Wiley was no doubt referring to battleships in both comments. But his use of the term "capital ship" in the latter implies that some room was left for the aircraft carrier. Given that this was the first opportunity for naval officers to employ the fleet carriers strategically, Fleet Problem Nine pointed to the potential, as well as the limitations, of applying airpower at sea. Both fleet commanders in the exercise had used their carriers offensively. But the exercise was not a watershed event in naval aviation. It was rather the first practical demonstration to fleet commanders of a potentially powerful new weapon. The door was left ajar for investigating missions beyond achieving control of the air.

Fleet Problem Nine marked a significant turning point for the navy. For the first time, fleet carriers were pitted against each other. The 261 land- and sea-based planes assigned to the Black and Blue forces represented an unprecedented number of participating aircraft. *Saratoga* alone carried 20 percent of the navy's commissioned flyers and 60 percent of the navy's carrier-qualified aviators.[64]

Mahanian maxims were proving increasingly tenuous when tested against weapons operating in three dimensions. Mantras celebrating the battleship as the "backbone of the fleet" did not entirely disappear after Fleet Problem Nine. Enough limitations existed with the new technologies to permit at least the hope, if not the actual possibility, for a decisive engagement with great guns. But it also became increasingly evident to naval officers in the 1930s that the air weapon should neither be ignored nor restricted to a particular mission.

In the years following Fleet Problem Nine the navy refined its aviation doctrine. The torpedo-carrying aircraft was one of the earliest casualties. The popularity of airborne torpedo attacks had actually begun to wane late in the 1920s. Torpedo planes were large, which reduced the total number of aircraft that a carrier could hold. Furthermore, the requirement to maintain a straight and level attitude when attacking made the aircraft vulnerable to faster and more agile fighter aircraft, as well as the anti-aircraft defenses of the ships they were attacking. Most importantly, dive bombing offered a more promising alternative. More dive bombers meant more bombs. Planes at altitude were more difficult to spot. And the dive bomber in attack provided a more difficult targeting problem for ship's gunners. As a consequence, by 1929 only one of the navy's three torpedo squadrons had the primary mission of conducting torpedo attacks. The other two were assigned the primary mission of dive bombing, a tactic Henry Wiley characterized as the "most serious problem in anti-aircraft defense."[65]

Torpedo squadrons continued to remain part of the navy's air arm, but the fleet problems reflected the limited confidence naval officers had in their effectiveness. In Fleet Problem Ten, only one torpedo squadron was among the nineteen squadrons assigned to the exercise. Six years later, only 12 torpedo planes could be counted amongst the 253 carrier-based aircraft that participated in Fleet Problem Seventeen.[66]

While the navy held the door slightly open for torpedo aircraft, it closed it completely on the dirigible. BUAER chief William Moffett had envisioned the huge airships as meeting the navy's operational and publicity needs. Airships appeared a solution to the fleet's reconnaissance problem in a future Pacific war. Moffett was also convinced that the impressive appearance of the airship, with a huge "U.S. NAVY" painted on its sides, would serve a useful purpose when flown around the country.[67]

In a moment of tragic irony, both Moffett and his dream died when in April 1933 the airship *Akron* flew into storms off the coast of New Jersey and crashed into the sea. Admiral Moffett was among the seventy-three sailors killed in the accident. But the promise of the rigid airship was also defeated by its operational limitations. A year before its crash, *Akron* was damaged while being moved out of a hangar and missed its scheduled participation in Fleet Problem Thirteen. Airships also proved to be tactically unwieldy. In 1934, *Macon* made an appearance in Fleet Problem Fifteen. Although the airship carried fighters for protection, both were easily overwhelmed by carrier-based fighters. The rigid airship was killed soon thereafter by Rear Adm. Ernest King, Moffett's successor at BUAER.[68]

An important consequence of the elimination of the airship program was an increased emphasis on the flying boat for long-range patrol and scouting. While flying boats participated in the early fleet problems, the aircraft were—for the most part—of World War I vintage. In April 1930, however, the navy introduced a flying boat prototype during Fleet Problem Eleven. Built by the Consolidated Aircraft Company and designated XPY, the biwinged aircraft flew daily surveillance flights in the Caribbean for the Blue fleet, some lasting as long as nine hours. The aircraft located and attacked Black submarines and on April 17 located and reported the first contact with the Black main body.[69]

While the navy's fleet problems in the 1930s increasingly focused on the Pacific, it became apparent that a reliable long-range flying boat might be critical to the success of an Orange war. Naval officers began eyeing the numerous atolls that lay along the navy's proposed advance. Many of these small islands were too small to accommodate land-based aircraft. Flying boats, however, could operate from them. The first significant attempt was made in 1935. Forty-five flying boats operated from French Frigate Shoals and Midway Island during Fleet Problem Sixteen in April 1935. In this case they made only a limited contribution because air operations were terminated following the crash of one of the flying boats. Two years later, however, over ninety flying boats were employed by Black and White fleets during Fleet Problem Eighteen. The XPY (designated by the navy as P2Y) was augmented by a newer Consolidated patrol plane, the mono-winged PBY. Operating from island chains stretching from Hawaii to Midway, patrol planes on both sides flew long-range reconnaissance and attack missions. Rear Adm. Ernest King, air force commander for Adm. Arthur Hepburn's White fleet, concluded after the exercise that the patrol planes demonstrated the ability to extend the eyes of the fleet to a distance of one thousand miles. King was more reserved as to their offensive potential but did believe flying boats showed promise as attack platforms against lightly defended surface ships.[70]

The navy's de-emphasis on torpedo aircraft and increasing reliance on flying boats were threads being woven into a larger tapestry of the sea-control mission. Long-range patrol aircraft served not only as the eyes of the fleet but also provided the aircraft carrier some relief from the fleet's scouting requirements. Fewer torpedo aircraft left room on the flight deck for more aircraft to carry bombs. Naval aviators in the 1930s did go to sea on the back of the fleet. At the same time, fleet officers were becoming increasingly aware that the sea-control mission, or at least the initial engagement with the enemy fleet, would be carried on the backs of the dive bombers. In October 1928 Rear Adm. Frank Schofield, director of the War Plans Division, read into the proceedings of the General Board a memo he had written outlining his thoughts on the direction naval aviation should take. Schofield advocated that the navy keep to a minimum the number of different types of aircraft, "consistent with the accomplishment of the necessary missions afloat." Citing improvements in anti-aircraft procedures and the difficulties of high-altitude horizontal bombing against maneuvering warships, Schofield recommended that all future naval bombing aircraft be designed principally as dive bombers. As to construction priorities, he further recommended that if separate types of aircraft were to be designed for dive bombing and torpedo attack, then "the maximum effort be devoted to bombing planes." But, should the navy decide to build a single aircraft type capable of both dive bombing and torpedo attack missions, he proposed that "the requirement of bombing be given precedence." Schofield went on to express his lack of confidence in the capability of air-launched torpedoes against capital ships to further justify an emphasis on dive bombing.[71]

The perils of underemploying the new fleet carriers became evident not long after Fleet Problem Nine. In the spring of 1930, the navy held Fleet Problem Ten in the Caribbean. Ostensibly designed to simulate a sea-control campaign in a Red war, the scenario could as easily have been a template for the navy's arrival in the western Pacific. Blue fleet commander Adm. Louis Nulton envisioned his air force as the instrument necessary to gain command of the air over the battle area. In his "Estimate of the Situation," Nulton's air strategy included a variety of missions for his carrier- and land-based aircraft. The carriers *Saratoga* and *Langley* were to remain within three miles of the main body of the Blue fleet. Aircraft would spot for his battleships, defend the battle line from air attack, and participate in a coordinated attack on the enemy fleet, when Blue battleships had closed to within gun range of the enemy.[72]

Nulton's adversary opted for a more offensive and aggressive air strategy. Vice Adm. W. C. Cole directed his shore-based aircraft and *Lexington* air wing to "locate the Blue fleet and deliver surprise attacks on capital ships, preferably aircraft carriers. . . ." *Lexington* operated independently from Cole's battle line. Her air wing was specifically directed to begin attacking the Blue main body when it got to within one hundred miles of the carrier. Cole went so far as to have some of his battleship-based aircraft refitted with landing gear and reassigned them to *Lexington*'s air wing.[73]

The two contrasting air strategies were played out off the coast of Haiti on March 14. In the early morning, with visibility reduced by rainsqualls, aircraft from *Lexington* surprised Blue fleet air patrols and dive bombed both of Nulton's carriers and the destroyer *Litchfield*. With the carriers' flight decks having been judged destroyed, Black fighters next went after Nulton's battleships, dropping thirty-pound bombs on *West Virginia*, *California*, and *New Mexico*. Observers imposed conservative damage assessments following the air attack but still concluded that anti-aircraft guns had been destroyed, topside personnel injured, and *California*'s main battery fire reduced by 15 percent.[74]

While both lines of battleships did manage an engagement at the end of the exercise, it was clearly overshadowed in the postexercise critique by the work of the aviators during the March 14 engagement. Nulton tried to pin the blame for the loss of his carriers on his aviators. Had they only been able to find the Black fleet sooner, he argued, the tactical situation might have been reversed. But CINCUS William Pratt refused to accept Nulton's excuse. Instrumental to Nulton's failure, Pratt pointed out, was his conservative and defensive employment of airpower. He had kept his carriers *Saratoga* and *Langley* closely tied to his main body of battleships and used his air force too conservatively. Nulton's emphasis on air cover for the battleships made any offensive use impossible. Pratt's chief observer added his own criticism of Nulton for having failed to adequately scout ahead of the fleet. He noted that there was no reason, given the good weather, why Nulton had not extended his air patrols as "far out as wind and sea permitted." The commander of the Black fleet's air forces shrouded his criticism of Nulton in metaphor. He

As a vice admiral and Blue fleet commander in Fleet Problem Ten, Rear Adm. Louis Nulton rigidly adhered to the Mahanian canon and sought a decisive engagement with his battleships. Instead of the anticipated gun battle, Nulton experienced waves of dive bombers attacking his carriers and battleships. Naval aviation had a destabilizing effect on naval warfare that could no longer be ignored. Courtesy U.S. Naval Institute.

compared carriers to "blindfolded men armed with daggers in a ring. If the bandage over the eyes of one is removed the other is doomed, and a decisive advantage is obtained."[75]

Unlike the preceding exercise, Fleet Problem Ten had all the earmarks of a watershed event in the development of the navy's airpower doctrine. The attack on *Saratoga* and *Langley* demonstrated the futility of using an air force in a purely defensive role. Even when operating en masse, carrier aircraft proved difficult to spot in good weather and nearly impossible to detect in reduced visibility until they were diving onto their targets.[76] Air-control strategy shifted from the enemy's aircraft to the enemy's aircraft carrier. And as carriers were launching strikes at great distances from the fleet, it was only natural that the aircraft should be used not only against the enemy carrier but against other strategically significant targets as well.

By 1930 naval aviators were beginning to upset the notion that only battleships were capable of fighting other battleships. Exercises after 1930 validated much of what was learned in Fleet Problems Nine and Ten. In the 1932 exercise, Blue fleet commander Adm. Richard Leigh used *Saratoga* in an independent task force to screen his main body as it proceeded to seize a simulated Pacific atoll on the west coast of the United States. Blue carrier aircraft searched as far as 120 miles ahead of the main force. Leigh succeeded in getting his convoy to its exercise objective unscathed, but in the process *Saratoga* was damaged by Black aircraft from *Lexington* and sunk during a night torpedo attack by destroyers. The Blue battleship *Pennsylvania* was also attacked from the air and given a noteworthy 44 percent damage assessment from the dive-bombing attack.[77]

That the exercise ended before the Black fleet could exploit Leigh's tenuous position left room for debate following the exercise. Blue air force commander Harry Yarnell concluded from the loss of *Saratoga* that any trans-Pacific campaign would require no less than six aircraft carriers. Black fleet commander Adm. A. L. Willard drew the opposite conclusion. "The battleship is still the backbone of the fleet," he said, not because of any success achieved by battleships during the fleet problem, but because the mighty carrier had been sunk in a night destroyer attack. It was up to CINCUS Adm. Frank Schofield to point out the strategically important middle ground. "There is a too strong tendency in the Fleet to make operations pivot around Airplane Carriers—they should pivot around the essential focus of the great effort being undertaken in these operations." Though directed principally to his aviators, Schofield's remark was aimed at all of the assembled officers. He would not tolerate parochialism, be it from carrier pilots or battleship sailors.[78]

This 1930s photo illustrates not only the changing face of naval aviation (note USS Langley *in the foreground, compared with fleet carriers USS* Lexington *and* Saratoga*) but also symbolizes the increasing relevance of airpower to the navy's sea-control mission. Courtesy U.S. Naval Institute.*

Conclusion

In a January 1936 article for the *Proceedings,* Lieutenant J. C. Hubbard demonstrated just how much naval aviation doctrine had changed. Entitled "Aviation and Control of the Sea," Hubbard articulated what had been made evident in simulation. While he objected to the claims of "air-minded zealots that the airplane had no peer," he recognized the utility of aircraft to the fleet. "The truth is," Hubbard wrote, "that control of the sea must embrace control not only of the surface, but also of the air. The air force protects the battle fleet, which in turn guards the air force."[79]

Hubbard's ideas were put into an operational context the following spring. Fleet Problem Eighteen was one of the navy's most ambitious strategic ex-

USS Lexington *was one of the navy's first fleet carriers. The nine-hundred-foot-long ships, which carried more than seventy-two aircraft, made naval officers in the 1930s increasingly aware that the sea-control mission, or at least the initial engagement with an enemy fleet, would be carried on the back of naval aviators. Courtesy U.S. Naval Institute.*

ercises. Its geographic dimensions extended from the U.S. west coast north to the Aleutians and west to Hawaii and Midway Island. The navy deployed 152 ships and 496 aircraft to simulate a future Orange war. For the first time, *Lexington* and *Saratoga* were operated jointly in the exercise, opposed by the navy's newest fleet carrier, USS *Ranger.*

The exercise incorporated the full spectrum of naval aviation. Carrier task forces had become commonplace. A Black carrier striking force consisting of *Lexington* and *Saratoga* attacked navy and army installations in Hawaii. PBY flying boats assigned to the White fleet flew long-range patrol missions from the strings of atolls between Pearl Harbor and Midway and made attacks on the Black troop convoy heading to seize Midway. *Ranger* aircraft attacked *Saratoga*. *Saratoga* and *Lexington* aircraft attacked *Ranger.* Aircraft from all three carriers made dive-bombing attacks with five-hundred-pound and one-thousand-pound bombs on warships of all types. Commanding the air forces were future air navy architects Vice Adm. Ernest King, Vice Adm. Frederick Horne, Capt. Aubrey Fitch, and Capt. William Halsey.[80]

For naval aviators, Fleet Problem Eighteen was the coup de grace to an incremental process that had begun back in 1922. Under the guidance of pragmatic leaders, naval aviation was initially sold to the skeptics as the eyes and protectors of the fleet. As aviation technology improved and more capable platforms arrived, operational demonstrations extended the definition of "protection" into the navy's sea-control doctrine. The aircraft evolved from an observation platform, to a tool of fleet defense, and then to a weapons delivery platform. By the end of the 1930s, command of the air became integrated within control of the sea.

What Adm. William Moffett had "prophesied" in the 1920s materialized in the 1930s. Naval aviation did physically go to sea on the back of the fleet. Successful demonstrations of the new technology also proved instrumental to the development of a more sophisticated thinking on the part of fleet commanders. Aircraft carriers and battleships were becoming comparable means to accomplish the objectives in a naval war. "In every encounter with hostile forces," Black fleet commander and future CINCUS Claude C. Bloch commented, "it is expected that *all* our forces present will be employed, in greater or lesser degree, to accomplish the complete destruction of the enemy."[81]

A fitting postscript to this chapter can be found in one of the tactical exercises conducted during Fleet Problem Nineteen in April 1938. Billy Mitchell had passed away two years earlier. His disciples were presently concentrating on the ability to annihilate the industrial capacity of a nation with an airplane they called a "flying fortress." Two more fleet carriers, *Yorktown* and *Enterprise,* were entering operational service. The navy had an all metal, mono-wing dive bomber and its first mono-wing fighter was soon to join the fleet.

Fleet Exercise 74 committed three carrier air groups and a wing of flying boats in coordinated attacks on the fleet. Among other things, the exercise would test the fleet's anti-aircraft proficiency. On April 5, over two hundred aircraft from *Lexington, Saratoga,* and *Ranger* attacked the fleet's battleships, cruisers, and destroyers with simulated five-hundred-pound and one-thousand-pound bombs. Flying boats followed the dive bombers with their own attacks on the ships. No empirical assessments were made as to the number of ships damaged or the number of aircraft lost. None were possible, as the battle was simulated. But the commander of the fleet's battleships concluded that "the efficacy of this type of coordinated attack cannot be doubted."[82] Naval aviators had succeeded through practical demonstration where Mitchell's provocative strategy had failed. Unlike Icarus, the navy's flyers stretched air superiority both vertically and horizontally, without flying too close to the sun.

The fire-ship disappeared from fleets whose speed it delayed.

Alfred Thayer Mahan

CHAPTER 4

Employing the "Engines of Fulfillment"

The Fleet Problems and Submarine Warfare

Around one o'clock in the morning on May 10, 1934, submarine *SS-53* was patrolling the western Caribbean in the vicinity of the Panama Canal. Attached to the Gray fleet as part of Fleet Problem Fifteen, its assignment was to intercept and attack Blue fleet, bound for an amphibious landing on a Gray island base. Cruising on the surface, the submarine encountered an unknown ship off its starboard bow. Unable to discern whether the ship was friend or foe, the commanding officer of *SS-53* decided to attempt a ruse by passing his boat off as a yacht. The signalman was instructed to respond to any challenge in a slow and improper manner. After allowing several challenges from the unknown warship to go unanswered, the signalman blinkered the message "Where are your running lights?" The answer received was, "You are in the midst of the U.S. Fleet, darkened." *SS-53* then identified itself as "Steam yacht Arrow," bound for San Juan, Puerto Rico. Just as the submarine was preparing to inquire if the Virgin Passage was clear, lookouts spotted another ship that was lying dead in the water. Realizing circumstances had become untenable, the *SS-53* fired four simulated torpedoes at the ship ahead, turned toward the stopped vessel, then altered course away from both ships. *SS-53* escaped to the south unscathed.[1]

SS-53's participation in the 1934 exercise illustrates that the airplane was not the only technological anomaly to see service in the fleet problems. But of what value were submarines to the exercises? The generally accepted view is that the interwar years were a period of stagnant development for submarines. Diplomats used Germany's unrestricted warfare campaign in World War I as the pretext for postwar initiatives to eliminate submarines entirely. Battleship-oriented admirals tried to eliminate them entirely and when that failed simply relegated them to auxiliary status.[2] Submarines were to be confined to service as scouts and "ambushers." They were placed under restrictive operating conditions when exercising with surface ships. Years of neglect led to the erosion of tactical expertise and the "calculated recklessness" needed in a successful submarine commander. In its place emerged a pandemic of excessive cautiousness, which spread from the operational realm into the psychology of the submarine community.[3]

The actions of *SS-53* suggest another interpretation. The commanding officer demonstrated initiative with his successful ruse. His attack prior to departing the scene appears not the behavior of a person consumed by caution or confined to fighting chivalrously.

The navy did not conspire to inhibit the submarine. Naval officers struggled to shape a technological anomaly to exist within a tightly bounded strategic framework. Interwar development was conditioned predominantly by diplomatic pressure to prohibit unrestricted submarine warfare and the navy's own vision of Mahanian sea control. Submarines were consequently fitted to conform to the navy's vision of a trans-Pacific war. They would be the eyes of the fleet as it proceeded across the Pacific. In the climactic battle for sea control they would play only a supporting role but would be the principal means of exercising sea control as a participant in the ensuing naval blockade of Japan. But practical limitations exposed during the early fleet problems forced navy leaders to reconsider the utility of the fleet submarine concept. They subsequently divorced the submarine from the sea-control mission, in favor of independent submarine operations. Submariners aided their cause by exercising both initiative and aggressiveness during the exercises. The submarine never became predominant in the naval hierarchy. But as the fleet problems stretched the geographic and strategic dimensions of naval warfare, the submarine became a useful instrument to the navy. And while the navy was validating the operational utility of its submarines, opinions expressed in other venues kept alive the employment policy abhorred by diplomats and rejected by Mahanians.

Postwar Attempts to Abolish Submarines

Perhaps the greatest contribution made by submarines during World War I was fueling the enthusiasm of diplomats afterward to abolish them. While naval armaments in general were viewed as a cause of the war, the heinous policy of unrestricted submarine warfare provided an even more compelling reason to reduce the offensive capabilities of the world's navies.[4] When Secretary of State Charles Evans Hughes declared at the first plenary session of the Washington Naval Conference on November 12, 1921, that "preparation for offensive naval war will stop now," his aspirations were not limited to the battleship. Consensus on battleship tonnage restrictions was reached, and a ten-year construction "holiday" was approved.[5] Comparable efforts to eliminate the submarine, though, proved futile. The French, who had grudgingly acquiesced to Hughes's conditions on battleships, refused to budge on commensurate restrictions on submarines. Albert Sarraut, representing the French delegation on the submarine committee, declared that the submarine was an "essential means of preserving her independence," which France would not surrender.[6] Italian representative Sen. Carlo Schanzer agreed that the submarine was essential to securing Italy's "vital lines of communication." He even questioned the applicability of any agreement signed by the five powers to nations not invited to the conference.[7]

As a consequence, the attempt to restrict submarine tonnage failed. In its place arose a compromise proposal by Sen. Elihu Root, the senior U.S. delegate on the submarine committee. Root avoided the construction issue completely. He offered instead to remove the temptation of unrestricted submarine warfare by providing legal protection to unarmed merchant ships. Submarine attacks on merchants were to be restricted in accordance with "Prize Law," requiring them first to surface, board, and inspect the merchant for contraband cargo. Ships found carrying contraband could be sunk but not until the crew was disembarked and placed in a position of safety. Violations would be considered a violation of international law, in effect an act of piracy.[8]

While Root's compromise was incorporated in the Washington Naval treaties, the French refused to ratify the article.[9] Subsequent diplomatic efforts to restrict submarine warfare met with similar mixed results. At a naval disarmament conference in Geneva in 1927, the British attempted to extend the Washington Naval Treaty restrictions on battleships to cruisers, destroyers, and submarines. On the submarine question, the British desired that the 5:5:3 ratio to battleship tonnages be applied to the number of submarines a nation could possess. The U.S. delegation, which was dominated by naval officers, countered with a proposal that agreed to restrictions in overall tonnages for submarines but not the numbers that could be possessed. The French and Italians refused to participate in the conference but sent observers to report on the proceedings.[10] A third attempt was made in London in 1930. The United States, Great Britain, and Japan sought to resuscitate the idea of submarine tonnage restrictions and reaffirm the Root resolution from 1922. Once again France and Italy demurred.[11] By 1935, diplomacy had run its course. The strengthening "fleet faction" in Japan was by this time eager to embark upon a naval construction program that would guarantee both supremacy in the western Pacific and parity with the United States and Great Britain.[12] When the United States and Britain refused to accommodate their demands at the London Conference, the Japanese walked out.

The postwar period initially offered little hope that submarine warfare doctrine would continue in the way Aube and his followers had envisioned for the torpedo boat. In their fury over the catastrophe of world war, diplomats pointed to navies as one of its principal culprits. Neutralizing the battleship was deemed necessary to curb the offensive tendencies of the great powers. The ban on unrestricted submarine warfare was used to reaffirm international law at sea. But as the actions of the French and Italians demonstrated, diplomats were not entirely successful in closing the book on submarine warfare. The burning question remained: Could a weaker naval power use whatever means were available for its defense?

For the time being, U.S. naval officers did not have to address the underlying reality of submarine warfare. Their country had embraced the battle fleet. Like the airplane, the submarine was considered an auxiliary to the battleship. The Root resolution, though rejected by the French and Italians, framed the employment policy for the submarines operated by U.S. Navy crews. Submariners were caught in a reality bracketed by both diplomatic antipathy and the legacy of Mahan. Any movement of submarine doctrine beyond commerce raiding under Root's strict constraints would require a demonstration of the submarine's usefulness to the fleet. That the crew of *SS-53* demonstrated characteristics outside the bottle shaped by diplomats and line officers is an indication that the navy's strategic exercises provided that venue.

Construction of the so-called "fleet submarine" did not begin until just prior to U.S. entry into World War I. Authorized as part of Woodrow Wilson's 1916 Navy Act, the first boat of this new class of submarines, the *S-1,* was launched on October 26, 1918. Displacing 854 tons surfaced and 1062 tons submerged, she was rated at 14.5 knots on the surface.[13] The lack of wartime experience, however, left further development of the fleet submarine to the realm of simulation. The early fleet problems suggested that the concept of the "fleet submarine" was fundamentally flawed. The culprit was mechanical. The S-boats could not make the sustained 14-knot speed envisioned as necessary for the trans-Pacific movement of the fleet in an Orange war.[14] The S-boats launched in 1923 and 1924, for example, averaged a maximum surfaced speed of 13.5 knots.[15] Material problems also plagued the new submarines. During Fleet Problem One, Black fleet commander Edward Eberle experienced the deficiencies first hand. His advance to the Panama Canal was slowed due to the submarines, half of which suffered material casualties that required their withdrawal from the formation.[16]

USS S-1 *was the first of the so-called "fleet submarines." Early fleet problems suggested that the concept was fundamentally flawed when it became apparent that the boats would not be able to keep up with surface ships on long transits. Instead, naval officers used the fleet problems to explore the possibility of using submarines as independent attack platforms. Courtesy U.S. Naval Institute.*

CINCUS Hilary P. Jones remarked at the conclusion of the exercise that the submarines "did not have sufficient speed to warrant using them as scouts" for the fleet.[17] Lt. Cdr. F. C. Sherman, the submarine division commander, agreed. He pointed out that the submarines were capable of a sustained maximum speed of only 11.5 knots. Furthermore, extensive maneuvering required the submarine to run on two engines, increasing fuel consumption. This violated the fleet's commitment to fuel economy. The evidence argued for removing the submarine from the battle line. In Sherman's opinion, submarines needed to run on both engines to have any chance of keeping up with the fleet and should be positioned well in advance of the fleet to allow single-engine operations, as well as maintenance, when necessary.[18] Vice Adm. William Shoemaker, who acted as the commander of Eberle's battle line in the exercise, brought the discussion into strategic clarity. The navy's submarines lacked the "necessary speed to accompany the Fleet in war—especially in a war in the Pacific."[19]

Subsequent exercises confirmed the deficiency of submarine speed. During Fleet Problem Two, which simulated a wartime transit of the fleet to the Philippines, submarine performance left senior naval officers skeptical of their strategic utility. Since they could not risk the sea-control mission to a vessel that might not be able to make the trip, they decided to cut submarines from the battle line.[20] By 1925 naval officers were convinced that their original conception of a fleet submarine was unfeasible. Commenting at the postexercise critique for Fleet Problem Five, CINCUS Adm. Robert Coontz concluded that the "submarines, even the newest (S-type) are not fleet submarines, nor are they capable of being made to perform the duties of fleet submarines." He implied that alternative tactics had to be considered.[21] Even the submariners faced reality, arguing that the demands of keeping up with the fleet severely limited the submarine's operational capability. Better to sacrifice speed, argued Cdr. Tom Withers of Submarine Division Four, for endurance, range, and habitability.[22]

While naval officers showed no inclination to remove submarines from the naval inventory, the nagging problem revealed by their exercises was how best to employ them. The navy had two options. Submarines could be used for coastal defense, or naval officers could find a way to keep them relevant to the Mahanian paradigm. Exercise fleet commanders adjusted by exploring the possibility of the submarine as an independent attack platform. Fleet Problem Four was the first of thirteen exercises to demonstrate the advantages of independent submarine operations. Grouped with Fleet Problems Two and Three, the fourth exercise represented the last phase of a Pacific campaign. The problem posed to Blue fleet commander Robert Coontz was to take the war to the enemy's home waters by establishing an advanced based within five hundred miles of Japan. From there, Orange trade routes could be threatened.[23] Both fleets were provided with substantial numbers of submarines, and both fleet commanders by this time accepted the reality of independent submarine operations. Vice Adm. Nulton McCulley, commander of Coontz's scouting force, was directed to employ his submarines in a reconnaissance role at least 240 miles ahead of the battle fleet. McCully came to the conclusion following the exercise that submarines were the only vessels "capable of operating unsupported at great distances."[24] Coontz's opponent in the exercise viewed the submarines assigned to him as his "principle offensive force," whose duty "should be the destruction of enemy capital ships and transports."[25] Under the direction of Lt. Cdr. R. H. English, the seven submarines that constituted the Black fleet attacked elements of Coontz's Blue fleet, including one battleship, as it approached the island of Culebra.[26] While no damage assessments were levied by observers of the exercise, the activity of the Black submarines did not escape CINCUS Coontz's attention. In his report to the CNO, Coontz called for additional submarines as one of his top ten recommendations, ahead of all other fleet assets, save cruisers and destroyers.[27]

Throughout the Coolidge and Hoover administrations, the prospects of adding significant numbers of submarines to the fleet suffered along with the rest of the navy's needs. The navy's emphasis on testing the concept of independent submarine operations, however, persisted. An independent submarine striking force was introduced during Fleet Problem Five. For the first time, a submarine flag officer was given command of the group and authorized to develop an employment strategy for his submarines.[28] Control Force commander Montgomery Meigs Taylor planned to disperse his force across the most probable line of the enemy advance. When contact was made, submarines would converge on the opposing fleet, submerge to evade the outer rings of escorts, and attack.[29] Taylor's submarines did not disappoint. The striking group successfully intercepted the opposing fleet and attacked the battleships *Maryland* and *Wyoming*, as well as the carrier *Langley*.[30]

Independent operations had an important implication. Detaching submarines from the battle line entailed a de facto removal from the central tenets of the sea-control mission. Submariners adapted by fitting in and making the most out of the assignments given to them. Even the introduction of an improved submarine, capable of maintaining higher speeds than the S-boats, did not alter the perceptions created by the exercises.[31] By the 1930s, the fleet submarine was transformed completely to fit the navy's vision of its utility. The submarine would not participate in the great battle for sea control. But neither was it to be completely freed from the control of the fleet commander. Adm. Luke McNamee, commander of a Blue force in Fleet Problem Fourteen in 1933, exemplified the changed perspective. Assigned the problem of defending Puget Sound, San Francisco, and Los Angeles–San Diego, McNamee delegated the defense of Puget Sound to his submarines.[32] McNamee was comfortable enough to assign them sole responsibility for one third of his strategic objective. But then again, McNamee's decision was also informed by the assumption that Puget Sound was not his adversary's principal objective. The fleet submarine was a useful tool. But it was not a weapon of strategic decision.

The Submarine as an Offensive Threat

Limitations experienced during the early exercises transformed the notion of the fleet submarine from an extension of the battle line to an independent part of the fleet. But while naval officers proved willing to detach the submarine from the sea-control mission, they rejected any further doctrinal development in the direction of the Jeune Ecole's emphasis on commerce raiding. The submarine, like the aircraft carrier, would be shaped into an offensive weapon commensurate with Mahanian doctrine.

Simulation made it difficult to validate the submarine as an effective offensive weapon. A submarine could reasonably be expected to approach warships unseen in a training environment. But the climax of a submarine's work would be difficult to assess. During the fleet problems a variety of measures were used to register attacks on ships. Submarines would use their blinker lights or fire flares to signal warships that they had been shot at. Umpires and observers also provided some means of objectively measuring effectiveness. But validation also required acknowledgment from the fleet. Gaining an admission from a commanding officer that his ship had been successfully attacked would not come easily. Such was the case on February 21, 1923, during Fleet Problem One, when the Blue submarine *O-4* crossed Black USS *California* on the port bow at approximately 250 yards. Running submerged, the boat's periscope was sighted by lookouts on the battleship and fired upon at once.[33] Black fleet commander Edward Eberle corroborated *California*'s story by a report from a destroyer, which also acknowledged sighting the sub. The admiral concluded that the submarine had been put out of action prior to its attack on the battleship.[34] The report of Eberle's adversary offered a contrasting account. While acknowledging that *O-4* had been detected as it passed through the outer screen of ships, the Blue commander found no evidence that any Black vessels had attacked the submarine. The attack on *California* was judged successful by the Blue force commander.[35]

Four years later *California* was assigned to the Blue fleet in Fleet Problem Seven. *S-19*, assigned to intercept and attack a heavily escorted Blue convoy, sighted the Blue screen in the early afternoon. Submerging, the submarine conducted attacks on three battleships, firing torpedoes on USS *Colorado* at a range of twelve hundred yards, attacking *West Virginia* seven minutes later with four more torpedoes, and finishing up her run by hitting *California* with four torpedoes at a range of eight hundred yards. Surfacing two minutes later on *California*'s port beam, the crew of the *S-19* received a distinct two-word message from the commanding officer of the offended battleship: "Well Done."[36]

Two explanations suggest themselves for the difference between the attacks on *California* in 1923 and 1927. First, observers were added to the fleet exercises after 1923. While not empowered to assess damage, these naval officers, who reported directly to CINCUS, could conceivably have discredited any protest from *California* during Fleet Problem Seven. But the different outcomes also suggest the emergence of an attitudinal change. Were the actions of *S-19* an anomaly, it would be easy to agree that the submarine crews lacked the aggressive nature to be an effective fighting force. But the fleet problems provide evidence that *S-19* was not an anomaly. Submariners were no less immune from Mahan's influence than their colleagues on the surface or in the air. Their aggressiveness in attacking the main battle fleet appealed to their colleagues. The submarine might not be the arbiter of sea control, but it nevertheless became accepted as a useful weapon.

The emergence of an offensive mindset began to take root as early as 1924 during Fleet Problem Two. While Coontz was bemoaning his submarines' speed limitations, his adversary in the exercise envisioned his submarine force as acting independently and offensively to prevent the Blue fleet from thrusting to its destination. "While a concentrated submarine attack would be undoubtedly the most desirable," Rear Adm. J. H. Dayton wrote in his "Estimate of the Situation," "attacks by submarines operating in small groups or singly would prove very effective against so large and unwieldy a force as BLUE."[37] The following year, the employment of submarines in offensive attacks was acted out as one of four primary assignments for the Blue fleet during Fleet Problem Five. Organized as a separate striking group, the force of eleven submarines was directed to locate and attack Black force units prior to a general engagement with the remaining Blue fleet units.[38] The concept of the submarine striking group continued to develop in later exercises. Submarine attack groups, the precursor of the U-boat wolf pack, were part of Vice Adm. A. L. Willard's operational plan for Fleet Problem Thirteen in 1932. Willard divided his submarine force into three attack groups to defend simulated atolls from a Blue amphibious invasion force.[39]

The increasing inclination of battleship admirals to send submarines into dicey tactical situations demonstrated a growing confidence that submarine crews would aggressively carry out their assignments. Accounts from the fleet problems also suggested that fleet commanders were not restricting submarine operations just to protect the cherished battleships. It is true that submarines were restricted during night operations in some of the exercises. The intent of commanders, however, was not to inhibit submarines or to protect the reputation of the battle line. The safety of the submarine personnel was the driving force behind exercise restrictions. And concerns of fleet commanders were not without merit. On the night of September 25, 1925, *S-51*, conducting engineering trials off Block Island, collided with the merchant steamer *City of Rome*. The submarine sank instantly, taking commanding officer Lt Rodney Dawson, five other officers, and thirty-one sailors to their deaths.[40]

Two years later the submarine *S-4*, while submerged, was accidentally rammed and sunk by the Coast Guard destroyer *Paulding*, with the loss of all hands. Even when running navigation lights, a submarine was difficult, if not impossible, to spot on the surface at night. Add the elements of weather and sea state and the submarine was nearly as invisible on the surface as submerged.[41] Such safety restrictions were not lost on operational commanders. Adm. Joseph Mason Reeves commented following Fleet Problem Sixteen that the "WHITE submarines, because of restrictions imposed on their operations for reasons of safety, were not able to demonstrate their capabilities. There appears to be no doubt that their presence in a comparable war situation would have strongly affected BLACK's operations."[42]

Artificialities imposed for safety reasons in peacetime did not lessen navy expectations of the submarine's tactical value. To the contrary, the fleet problems demonstrated an inclination on the part of fleet commanders to employ them fully. Submarine crews responded with a commensurate aggressiveness. The exploits of *S-19* and *S-53* have already been recounted. The after-action report of Lt. A. E. King, commanding officer of *S-11* during Fleet Problem Five, provides an additional example that challenges the characterization of submarine crews as overly cautious. The young officer deftly maneuvered his submarine around a heavy screen of destroyers to accomplish his mission of attacking the Black battleships. Attacking at night, and in a darkened condition ("the best way to get at it"), he successfully maneuvered to within fifteen hundred yards and fired. *S-11* signaled the ship that she was sunk and received the reply that it was the battleship *Wyoming*.[43]

Additional evidence suggests that the actions of *S-53* and *S-19* were not anomalies. The four submarines assigned to the Black fleet commander during Fleet Problem Three conducted thirteen attacks on submarines and three on battleships.[44] In Fleet Problem Seven, exercise observers and umpires formally acknowledged submarine tactical successes. Two separate submarine groups totaling five submarines were awarded attacks on battleships, one attack on the aircraft carrier *Langley*, and an attack on an oil tanker.[45] Later exercises show that submariners continued to press attacks when opportunities arose. In the pre-dawn hours of April 20, 1934, Brown submarines located a Blue fleet steaming to the Panama Canal as part of Fleet Problem Fifteen. The chief umpire acknowledged afterward that by noontime nine attacks had been recorded on battleships, two on carriers, and two on cruisers.[46] By Fleet Problem Nineteen submarines were not only firing actual (but unarmed) torpedoes at ships but also were successfully penetrating SONAR-equipped destroyer screens. Ten of the thirteen submarines participating in the exercise penetrated the screen—three undetected—and conducted eleven attacks. Six of their torpedoes found their targets.[47] CINCUS Adm. Arthur J. Hepburn commented that the opportunity to attack was not lost on the submariners but was "seized upon avidly" and provided "excellent training" to the crews.[48] Contrary to characterizations of the submarine community as constrained and cautious, the fleet problems demonstrated a level of aggressiveness and tactical initiative that fit in nicely with an offensive-minded navy.

Perhaps the most telling recognition comes from the defensive tone of the report prepared by Adm. Harris Laning, commander of the White fleet during Fleet Problem Sixteen in September 1935. Black submarines made numerous attacks on Laning's fleet as it sortied from Pearl Harbor. The chief umpire assigned hits on the battleships *New Mexico*, *California*, and *Idaho*, which together constituted 30 percent of Laning's battle line.[49] Laning's observations following the exercise are particularly instructive. The Black submarines had it easy, the admiral rationalized, as they had a good idea when the fleet would sortie. Actual conditions during war would be completely different. Submarines would be required to maintain station for extended periods of time and would be subjected to constant surveillance and attack from air and surface patrols. Moreover, not every attack from a submarine would be successful, as they themselves were vulnerable to attack. Finally, Laning's fleet had been restrained from aggressive maneuvers to reduce the chance of collision. Laning raised these issues to reassure his officers that "in actual war we can nullify the effectiveness of enemy submarines, and *second,* to bring home to submarines that they cannot in war operate as they do in our fleet problems." It is interesting though, that Laning neglected to comment on the damage sustained by his force from the submarines.[50]

In 1924 U.S. submarines had so disappointed their navy masters that they were excommunicated from the battle fleet. But by 1935 the submarine community had claim to a significant victory. They had gotten into Harris Laning's head. The following year the submarine was formally incorporated into the navy's Pacific strategy. A CINCUS staff report entitled "Employment of Blue Submarines, Orange War" posited a Mahanian role for its submarines in the war. The primary employment of submarines, the staff concluded, would be in offensive operations directed against "enemy larger combatant vessels." Additionally, submarines would be used to survey various islands in the Marianas and Carolines prior to the arrival of the fleet. The issue of *guerre de course* was moot. The report specifically stated that no submarines would "be assigned in the early stages of the war to operate against enemy trade routes."[51]

The Fleet Problems and Unrestricted Submarine Warfare

To the Jeune Ecole the submarine could be viewed as the theoretical successor to the torpedo boat as a blockade breaker and commerce raider. Yet despite its pioneering efforts in submarine development, French enthusiasm for the submersible waned as its relationship with Great Britain warmed in the twentieth century.[52] It would be Germans who would demonstrate its practical utility against unarmed merchant ships. U.S. naval officers nevertheless shaped submarines to conform to their own strategic vision. Warfare simulation validated the tactical utility of submarines. Fleet commanders learned how to employ the weapon effectively and without compromising the predominance of the sea-control mission.

The fleet problems provided the only venue through which submarines could be tested against the Mahanian canon. Submarines were consequently fashioned into independent actors, though they did not escape Mahan's grip entirely. Exercise fleet commanders, with submarine crews as willing accomplices, used the fleet problems to reinforce the submarine as an offensive weapon. But the increasingly aggressive employment of submarines also had consequences that went either unnoticed or perhaps unsaid. The more Mahanian the submarine became, the closer it actually moved to the Jeune Ecole.

At no point during the exercises were submarines specifically assigned to practice tactics related to unrestricted commerce warfare. Such activity would have certainly raised the suspicions of civilian policy makers. But that is not to say that the concept was beyond the strategic horizon of exercise planners or the tactical expertise of submarine crews. One hint can be found in the general plan for Fleet Problem Nineteen, conducted in late April 1938. One particular aspect of the problem posited the employment of Purple fleet units, including submarines, against Green "vital centers and coastal shipping."[53] The assignment implied that once sea control had been achieved, the navy anticipated turning its submarines on enemy merchant ships. The fleet problems also provided training that could be easily applied to hunting and attacking unarmed merchant shipping. Submarines in virtually every exercise scouted for enemy fleets, tracked warships, penetrated defensive screens, and conducted attacks. Given the level of rigor experienced during the exercises, it was but a small operational leap from *guerre de escadre* to *guerre de course.*

Unlike other facets of naval warfare, the conceptual framework and tactics of unrestricted submarine warfare existed in separate venues. The fleet problems prepared submarine crews for the tactical aspects of the mission. The conceptual framework was sustained in official testimony and published opinions. Skepticism from naval officers that the prohibition on unrestricted submarine warfare could be enforced ran along several themes. Big-navy advocates like Dudley Knox believed that British initiatives to abolish submarines were nothing more than a ruse to ensure her supremacy on the seas. If the great powers were going to restrict the employment of submarines, Knox argued, then why had they not also restricted artillery and aircraft, which also had a reputation for indiscriminate use?[54]

Technical arguments against the prohibition on unrestricted warfare revived themes invoked by Aube and the Jeune Ecole. "The submarine," contended Yates Stirling, "has proved a most efficient weapon to that end," implying that unwarned attacks were not only operationally expedient but necessary.[55] The submarine was simply inadequately designed to comply with the requirements of the Prize Law. On the surface, a submarine, even with a gun, was vulnerable. Its instability in heavy seas made a surface engagement impractical, as well as dangerous, for the crew manning the deck gun. And as the collision between *S-51* and *City of Rome* demonstrated, submarines on the surface could be easily sunk by ramming.[56] The submarine was designed to be employed under the water. Any attempt to force it to operate on the surface would render it ineffective.

Finally, naval officers were skeptical that international law would prove an effective deterrent to unrestricted submarine warfare. Testifying before the Senate Committee on Naval Affairs about the 1930 London Naval Conference, Adm. George Day remarked that the restrictions imposed on submarines were so ambiguous that enforcing the law would be impossible.[57] Yates Stirling offered the perspective of the pragmatic warfare technician on the prospects of restraining any weapon. Despite the efforts of diplomats to contain the submarine, he cautioned his colleagues, "we must be prepared to discover that in war necessity acknowledges no law."[58] Junior officers shared his opinion. Lt. Hyman G. Rickover, who would one day oversee the nuclear navy's submarine program, observed that the continuing controversy over submarine warfare only served to ensure that diplomatic initiatives would fail. Since diplomats had yet to reach unanimity on the submarine issue, "it is almost certain that the submarine practices of the World War will be repeated in a future war."[59]

Arguments posed by naval officers outside the venue of the fleet problems present an interesting paradox. How could the navy remain true to the Mahanian canon in their fleet problems, and yet pose arguments that seemed to contradict that doctrine? The answer is that naval officers acknowledged anomalous shades of reality to address an anomalous technology. The fleet problems reinforced the Mahanian-inspired perception that a submarine was a naval weapon, to be used against other naval weapons. Outside the realm of operational exercises, however, the submarine was a tool of war to be unrestricted in its use. In the minds of naval officers, political leaders were responsible for the moral decision to go to war. War itself was an amoral activity. Naval officers expressing such views were careful in their choice of words. Not one of them advocated a policy of unrestricted submarine warfare. They were simply pointing out what they viewed would happen in a future modern war. In their minds the utility of the submarine would outweigh political objections to unrestricted warfare. The weapon would be used to its fullest capacity. In the words of Capt. Walter Anderson, by not ratifying the Root proposal at the Washington Naval Conference, France had "done a service to the United States."[60]

On November 27, 1941, CNO Adm. Harold Stark sent a memorandum to Adm. Thomas C. Hart, commander of the Asiatic fleet. Hart was notified that in the event of war with Japan he would be given authority to conduct unrestricted submarine warfare "south of a line from Shanghai to Guam."[61]

The seamless transition to unrestricted submarine warfare can be explained by events that preceded Stark's memo. In fact, the ease with which the order was given represents the failure of both diplomats and Mahanians during the interwar years to contain the submarine. Diplomats were confident that international law had made the bottle strong enough. Within the bottle, Mahanian sea control rejected the ideas of the Jeune Ecole. Diplomacy failed because the promise of submarine warfare to naval "Davids" such as France, Italy, and Germany proved stronger than the measures by "Goliaths" to restrain their employment. Naval officers proved to be only slightly more successful. They confined the submarine so as not to detract from the sea-control mission. But they also could not resist the inclination to use the submarine for what it did best—commerce raiding. While submarines were attacking warships in operational exercises, naval officers sustained the utilitarian argument that a weapon once invented could not be restrained. Expertise gained against fast and maneuverable warships in simulation could be married easily to the argument when expediency allowed.

Like the "fire-ships" in Mahan's historical narrative, the fleet submarine failed to fulfill the early expectations of naval officers, who envisioned it charging across the Pacific with the battle fleet. Unlike the fire-ship, however, the submarine did not disappear. Naval officers reconciled the technological anomaly of underwater warfare to fit their sea-control paradigm. But they also left open the possibility that the submarine would be used in a way that would have been rejected by Mahan. The submarine would become an engine of fulfillment in the Pacific, when on December 8, 1941, CNO Harold Stark ordered the U.S. Navy to ignore the international law sponsored two decades earlier by the American secretary of war.

Actually, the problem of combating the submarine was like that of lifting an immense jellyfish. Grasping it with two hands accomplished nothing, but with hands all around and heaving together, one could really do something to the so-and-so.

Samuel Eliot Morison

CHAPTER 5

Getting a Grip on the "Jellyfish"

The Fleet Problems and Antisubmarine Warfare

From late April to early May 1940 the U.S. Navy held its last fleet problem before World War II. Maroon fleet commander Adolphus Andrews was assigned the problem of defending Hawaii from invasion by Adm. Charles P. Snyder's Purple fleet.[1] At Andrews's disposal was an impressive fleet of battleships, aircraft carriers, and cruisers. He also commanded eighteen submarines. Submarines had been employed in earlier fleet problems with mixed success. They were no longer considered integral to the attainment of sea control. The future pointed to independent operations. Andrews was prepared to put his submarines to good use. He believed that they would contribute to the success of the exercise as an irritant to Snyder's fleet. "Submarines are especially suited for attrition tactics," he remarked in his "Estimate of the Situation." Andrews was so confident that he decided to advance them far to the west of Hawaii to locate and intercept Snyder's fleet. It seemed "unduly cautious" to hold them back in a defensive posture close to Hawaii.[2]

Andrews's strategy failed miserably. Snyder divided his fleet into task forces to mask the location of his transports. He stationed his carrier within range of both his main fleet and the convoy. Aircraft could protect the convoy and attack the Maroon fleet should the opportunity arise. Snyder additionally positioned destroyers well ahead and astern of the convoy to work in cooperation with patrolling aircraft. Andrews's submarine commanders consequently found themselves too widely dispersed to converge on Snyder's fleet. The Purple fleet arrived in Hawaiian waters virtually intact and successfully carried out air raids against the port facilities at Lahaina.[3]

Andrews took responsibility for his plan's failure but attempted to rationalize his shortcomings at the postexercise critique. Maroon submarines, he argued, had been successful in forcing the enemy to engage constantly in antisubmarine operations. A premature engagement against the main elements of his Maroon fleet had been avoided. But Andrews did not absolve his submarines completely. His disappointment apparent, Andrews cautioned against drawing any "false conclusions" as to the submarines' "actual value or lack of value."[4]

How ironic that, less than two years later, the weapon that failed Andrews would be a source of so much alarm to him. Six weeks after the Pearl Harbor attack, German Navy Lt. Reinhard Hardegan, commanding *U-123,* torpedoed four merchant ships off Cape Hatteras.[5] The opening blows of Operation "Drumbeat" had been struck. To Adolphus Andrews, now commanding the U.S. Eastern Sea Frontier, the situation was bleak. He commanded only twenty-eight ships to defend the eastern seaboard from New York City to Jacksonville, Florida. By March, U.S. merchant losses off the east coast mounted to over one million tons of shipping. Andrews had two options. He could institute coastal convoys and use his few ships as escorts. Or he could use his ships on offensive patrols. Andrews recommended to "COMINCH" Adm. Ernest King that "no attempt be made to protect coastwise shipping by a convoy system until adequate number of suitable vessels are available."[6] The few ships on hand would conduct patrols to seek out and engage enemy submarines. A poorly escorted convoy, Andrews concluded, was worse than none.[7]

The navy eventually established coastal convoys in April 1942, but the delay raises an important question. Why did the admirals so quickly dismiss the idea of coastal convoys in lieu of offensive patrols? Some scholars have looked to the interwar years for the answer. The literature characterizes the naval officer corps as culturally averse to considering the submarine as a threat. Its Mahanian vision prevented the trespass of ideas emphasizing the defensive measures implicit in convoy operations. As a consequence, line officers spent very little of their time doing anything about combating submarines. Naval exercises emphasized only Jutland-type engagements, main surface battle fleets in head-on confrontation of big guns. Unorthodox strategies, such as the defense of civilian merchant shipping, were neglected.[8]

Implied in the literature is Mahan's suffocating grip on the interwar navy. His canon offered no alternative to the sea-control mission. It further stipulated that sea control could only be achieved by battleships in a decisive fleet engagement. The fleet problems bear out some of this criticism. The navy used its strategic exercises to reinforce sea control as the fleet's raison d'être. Naval officers shaped new technologies to ensure the relevancy of the canon. Submarines were freed from the sea control fraternity. Aviators were accepted as provisional members. But while the fleet problems tightened Mahan's grip in some areas, they were loosening it in others. Independent submarine operations and carrier task forces challenged the relevance of his canon of concentration. Carriers were acknowledged as capital ships.

The fleet problems resolved the submarine menace in a similar mottled fashion. Naval officers did not neglect antisubmarine warfare (ASW). They simply coped with the submarine by treating it as a manageable threat. ASW technology and tactics were employed in ways that fit comfortably within the broad contours of sea control. The fleet problems sustained the navy's confidence that submarines posed no strategic threat to the sea-control mission. Officers believed that they had a sufficient hold on the "jellyfish." What they did not recognize were the limitations of warfare simulation that informed their conceit. Their confidence was actually born of complacency, nurtured by peacetime exercises.

The Early Fleet Problems: Reinforcing Tested Techniques

Of the twenty-one fleet problems held between 1923 and 1940, thirteen incorporated one or more aspects of antisubmarine warfare as a major objective.[9] Early exercises were devoted principally to practicing convoy tactics used during World War I. But unlike their wartime experiences, naval officers used warfare simulation to shape antisubmarine warfare to fit their strategic vision. The defensive flavor of the convoy was fashioned to suit the offensive ends of the sea-control mission.

Given that the U-boat had been defeated and the submarine conceived as merely a tactical problem, it is surprising that naval officers felt compelled to include convoys in their early fleet problems. Fleet Problems Two and Four, for example, were planned "primarily as a test of a Screening Formation and Plan of Action for the protection of the Train in an overseas advance."[10] In Fleet Problem Two a Blue U.S. fleet steamed from U.S. west coast ports to the Panama Canal. The route was intended to simulate an unopposed advance of the U.S. fleet to the Philippines. After passing through the canal, the fleet engaged in Fleet Problem Four, which addressed the final phase of the Pacific war. As CINCUS Robert Coontz orchestrated both exercises to be conducted with little enemy opposition, there was very little to be learned by the limited combat that occurred. But Coontz could not conceal deficiencies imperiling his strategy. One glaring problem was that the fleet was too slow. Submarines, transports, and other auxiliaries could not sustain the fourteen-knot speed anticipated for a Pacific transit. And the slower the speed of the fleet, the more vulnerable it was to attack from submarines. Coontz considered cutting loose the slowest ships on his transit. But abandoning vital supply ships to almost certain attack would in effect compromise the entire campaign.[11]

The problem of fleet speed was one easily revealed by simulation. A slow ship was a slow ship, whether in an exercise or in combat. But the emphasis of the exercise on an Orange war had strategic implications that went unnoticed. In Fleet Problem Two the logistics ships Coontz was escorting were naval vessels. These ships might slow the fleet, but the sailors who operated them were no different than those on the warships. The Blue fleet in an Orange war was essentially a homogenous entity. Navy logistics ships could conform to the requirements of the escorting battle fleet. The prospect that the fleet might have to conform to the needs of civilian merchants was understandably, but unfortunately, ignored.

Naval officers had to work out an important conceptual paradox in the early fleet problems. In 1924 War Plan Orange was the only viable war plan in the navy's dossier. But the plan was founded on a tenuous premise. The fleet had to reach the western Pacific intact and in fighting form. This flew in the face of the geopolitical reality. The Washington Naval Treaties had secured Japan as a regional naval power. The nonfortification clause further imperiled the navy's notion of an uninterrupted transit to the Philippines. Both the Philippines and Guam, the two navy outposts in the western Pacific upon which the strategy depended, were vulnerable. The emerging circumstances had to give even the most ardent naval officers pause. Could they guarantee that the fleet could outrun Japanese submarines operating from their central Pacific possessions?

The navy faced the mismatch between its offensive sea-control mission and its reliance on a defensive convoy strategy. The solution was found in simulation. Naval officers simply glossed over the inherent problems and vulnerabilities in convoy operations. In Fleet Problems Two and Four, Coontz's entire fleet, including his battleships, guarded his auxiliaries. Coontz satisfied the Mahanian canon. He kept sea control at the forefront. Escort was a necessary defensive measure to achieve the greater offensive end. The convoy was further institutionalized into the fleet's task organization in subsequent exercises. In his "Estimate of the Situation" for Fleet Problem Five in March 1925, Black fleet commander Samuel Robison noted that the sixteen submarines of the opposing fleet represented a "serious menace" to the slow convoy of tankers, repair ships, and tenders he was assigned to defend.[12] Robison crafted the first formal task organization for a convoy in a fleet problem, which included every warship at his disposal. Additionally, he planned on using a carefully developed set of zigzag plans to avoid contact with submarines. The frequent course changes would serve to frustrate any submarine attempting to track or intercept the force.[13]

Robison's organizational initiative was formally incorporated in the navy's tactical lexicon the following year. Fleet Problem Six was conducted to test the "defensive qualities of a screen around a convoy" as well as the problem of the opposed entry of a convoy into a port.[14] The "Fleet Screening Formation," consisting of three to four concentric circular rings of destroyers, was employed during the exercise and credited in postexercise remarks as "well adapted to keeping submarines down."[15] Convoy seemed the only reasonable means to prevent submarine attacks on the fleet's vulnerable troop and supply ships. But as its defensive nature clashed with the offensive-mindedness of U.S. naval officers, the convoy was shaped to fit the Mahanian paradigm. Simulation set the strategic precedent of absorbing convoys within the fleet organization. Throughout the remaining exercises, some form of the Fleet Screening Formation was employed. The physical machinations going on in simulation was no different than what went on during World War I. The important difference was that reality could be shaped in simulation. Sea control could still retain its predominance. The convoy was simply reconceived as a defensive means to a greater offensive end.

Naval officers successfully shaped the convoy in their exercises to suit the Mahanian canon. A submarine that could not stop the fleet was not a strategic threat. Antisubmarine warfare technology, much of which originated during World War I, was also used to keep the submarine problem at the tactical level. One of the first technological initiatives attempted was signals intelligence. Submarines operating in dispersed patrolling stations were prone to using their radios to pass along contact reports. Radio direction finding showed early promise in Fleet Problem Five, when a submarine contact report was intercepted and used to determine the sending submarine's location. Signals intelligence was used in later exercises, but its effectiveness as an antisubmarine tool proved spotty. Submarine crews obviously learned that radio silence was the most effective means of countering the direction-finding capability of the enemy.[16]

Acoustic technology showed similar promise and equally inconsistent results. The commanding officer of the destroyer *Melvyn* noted in his critique following Fleet Problem Five that a submarine had been located by "listening device" at an approximate range of between five and six thousand yards.[17] Later fleet problems, however, showed few references to the use of passive listening devices. Funding constraints appear to have been the principal reason for the limited use of acoustic technology. CINCUS Joseph Mason Reeves complained in his report on Fleet Problem Sixteen that none of the destroyers in the exercise had been equipped with listening gear, which he believed was second only to aircraft as an effective means of detecting submarines.[18] The navy was no less sluggish in its development of SONAR. In 1918, British scientists produced the first acoustic instrument capable of emitting an underwater sound pulse and detecting the returning echo from the hull of a submerged submarine. This device, code-named "ASDIC" (called SONAR by the U.S. Navy), was developed too late for use during World War I and remained a closely guarded secret for many years.[19] The first use of SONAR in a fleet problem appears to be during the 1938 exercise. Thirteen destroyers tested the effectiveness of "supersonic screening" against thirteen submarines assigned to penetrate the sound barrier. Results were mixed. Nine of the thirteen destroyers reported successful SONAR contacts. But destroyer commanders also noted numerous false echoes, acoustic interference, and deficiencies in operator proficiency. The submarines, conversely, were able to conduct twelve torpedo attacks, although only six were assessed to have hit their targets.[20]

CINCUS Claude C. Bloch offered a lukewarm assessment of the demonstration. He described the supersonic screen as "encouraging" but in need of increased testing.[21] Bloch's cautious approach was not without merit. Acoustic detection devices were major technological breakthroughs in antisubmarine warfare. The fleet problems demonstrated that underwater detection technology had potential. What the problems also pointed out, though, were limitations indicating that SONAR alone was not a panacea in antisubmarine warfare.

The technology that did show great promise was the airplane. Naval aviators were cautiously optimistic that their machines would be an integral part of a future war. Land-based aircraft were well suited to antisubmarine warfare and were employed extensively in antisubmarine operations throughout the fleet problems. What is surprising, however, was the increasing contribution of carrier aviation to antisubmarine warfare in the exercises. USS *Langley* became an inadvertent ASW platform during Fleet Problem Five in 1925. While on patrol on the afternoon of March 10, one of *Langley*'s planes was spotted by a submarine. The submarine dutifully reported the bearing of the plane by radio. The message was intercepted. The position of the plane being known, the reciprocal of the bearing was plotted, and the submarine was located.[22]

Langley's inauspicious introduction to antisubmarine warfare reflected her experimental nature and the novelty of carrier aviation. But the prospect of using submarines to further the aviation agenda was not lost on the aviators. Battleship admirals had limited carrier-based aircraft to defend the battle line from other aircraft. Antisubmarine warfare appeared an excellent means to broaden the mission. Carrier aviators became increasingly proficient in antisubmarine warfare. By the 1927 fleet problem, aircrews from *Langley* not only flew convoy escort missions but also sighted submarine periscopes and conducted attacks.[23] Carrier-based aircraft were thereafter routinely assigned with continuous daylight patrols as part of the antisubmarine screen, extending protection as far as thirty-five miles from the center of the fleet's formation.[24]

The role of carrier aviation in antisubmarine warfare increased as the warfare community matured in the 1930s.[25] The introduction of *Lexington* and *Saratoga* greatly increased the number of carrier aircraft available to fleet commanders. Sustaining continuous daylight antisubmarine patrols was now possible without compromising fleet defense against the air threat. The employment of carrier aviation in antisubmarine warfare also led to important developments in coordinated tactics. Combined operations between aircraft and surface ships had originated in World War I.[26] Interwar exercises refined the concept. Fleet Problem Thirteen in 1932 was something of a watershed demonstration of the capabilities of coordinated antisubmarine operations. During the initial phase of the problem, Black submarines were stationed east of the Hawaiian Islands, with orders to locate Blue forces as they departed their anchorage at Lahaina Roads. On March 9 and 10, Blue minesweepers, minelayers, and planes from Pearl Harbor made repeated attacks on submarines, with aircraft bombing and placing out of action the submarine *Narwhal.* Later in the exercise, two land-based antisubmarine patrol planes sighted the wake of a submarine. The submarine was completely submerged yet visible from the air. While one aircraft continued to track the submarine, the other flew to a destroyer ten miles away. The destroyer was directed to the submarine and attacked it with depth charges. Aircraft from *Saratoga* joined in the action and continued to track the submarine until it eventually surfaced, at which time it was attacked again.[27]

Fleet Problem Thirteen validated an important lesson in antisubmarine warfare. The combined efforts of aircraft and surface ships would make the submarine's work extremely difficult. The exercise also pointed to some important limitations of aircraft. Detection capability from the air was conditional. Most of the antisubmarine action occurred in Hawaiian waters, an area known for consistently excellent weather conditions and clear water. Aircraft operating in inclement weather would suffer from restricted visibility, if they could fly at all. And during the hours of darkness, the fleet's air arm was completely grounded. A second important limitation was the effect of antisubmarine missions on the readiness of aircraft and aircrews. The desire of fleet commanders to maintain continuous airborne patrol affected aircraft maintenance. The requirement for continuous patrols also took its toll on airmen, who became fatigued from continuous flying.[28] The lessons pointed to the realistic side of antisubmarine warfare. Under most conditions, the submarine had little chance against teams of destroyers and aircraft. But the fleet would not always operate in perfect conditions. Both machines and humans could be exhausted. The submarine still had some chance of avoiding detection or escaping from an attack.

The fleet problems of the 1930s revealed the complications of holding too tightly on the Mahanian canon. The geographic and strategic dimensions of a Pacific war pointed to the utility of dividing the fleet into task forces. Fleet carriers and dive bombers intruded upon the battleship's dominion as the arbiter of sea control. Mahan was being stretched in many ways. In spite of this, doubts about the strategic importance of the submarine persisted. The submarine remained, in the minds of many, a tactical problem. CINCUS Joseph Mason Reeves illustrated the navy's conflation of strategy and tactics in May 1935. Reeves commanded the White fleet during the initial phases of a simulated Orange war during Fleet Problem Sixteen. Facing significant submarine opposition to his movement from the U.S. west coast to Hawaii, Reeves drew on many lessons gleaned from earlier fleet problems. He integrated carrier aircraft into his defensive screen, which extended its protection out to twenty-four miles beyond his surface escorts. A false screen of destroyers was positioned twenty-five miles ahead of Reeves's main body in the hope of misleading submarines. And as the White fleet neared Hawaiian waters, Reeves deliberately took the longer course to the north and west of Oahu to avoid contact with Black submarines.[29]

Reeves's plan was successful. The formation and air patrol successfully prevented submarines from attacking the fleet on its transit to Hawaii. Two Black submarines did detect Reeves's ships as they circled Oahu. But the submarines were located and attacked by the White fleet's air patrol before they could attack. Submarines lying off Pearl Harbor were kept down by an advance patrol of eleven destroyers and army aircraft, which permitted Reeves's main body to enter the harbor unmolested.[30]

It certainly appeared from Reeves's performance that the navy had a firm grip on the submarine. Fleet technology and tactics appeared sound. Defeating the submarine was simply a matter of asset management. But one naval constituency began to have second thoughts about the mission's continued utility. Carrier aviators participated in ASW missions to demonstrate the flexibility of naval aviation and ingratiate aviators to senior navy leaders. By the mid-1930s, aviators began to reconsider the importance of the mission to their future. At the critique following Fleet Problem Sixteen in May 1935, the comments of Lt. Cdr. F. B. Stump, senior squadron commander on USS *Saratoga,* reflected the changing attitudes of aviators. Stump acknowledged that the employment of his squadrons in antisubmarine warfare was appropriate for the exercise. But he also cautioned that the principal purpose of carrier aviation should not be forgotten. Its primary task, he asserted, "must be to take the offense against enemy carriers and light vessels."[31] Senior aviators echoed Stump's observations. Vice Adm. Frederick Horne argued following Fleet Problem Eighteen that the integration of carrier aircraft in the fleet's antisubmarine screen detracted from the carrier's offensive mission. "The *offensive* aircraft complements," he contended, "do not lend themselves to *defensive* missions."[32]

The employment of carrier aircraft in antisubmarine warfare in the fleet problems presented an early opportunity for naval aviation. Detecting and attacking submarines from the air helped to expand aviation doctrine. But the arrival of fast carriers, with aircraft capable of projecting power well beyond the range of ships' guns, stirred aviators' own Mahanian ambitions. Submarines became less attractive, particularly when larger and more prestigious targets were available. Tying aircraft to a protective screen became as egregious as tying the carrier to the battle line. Aviators did not wholly reject their role in antisubmarine warfare, but their comments suggest that when it came to hunting submarines, fleet carriers might be more gainfully employed.

CINCUS Joseph Mason Reeves could no more dismiss the submarine in 1935 than his predecessors could in the 1920s. His plan implemented the available technology and tactical measures to defeat the submarine. But from a strategic standpoint, Reeves simply validated the long-held conception of the submarine as more of an irritant than an obstacle to sea control. Warfare simulation downplayed the submarine as a grave strategic threat. The submarine was managed tactically. ASW technology and lessons, many drawn from the previous war, were applied to reinforce the confidence by line officers in their ability to contain the submarine.

Conclusion: The Limits of Simulation

The navy did not neglect antisubmarine warfare. Technological and tactical measures, many learned from the first Battle of the Atlantic, were incorporated into the fleet problems of the interwar years. Exercise fleet commanders and their staffs demonstrated a healthy respect for the subsurface enemy and proved willing to exploit all tools available to defeat it, even if it necessitated at times using those tools defensively.

Where the navy did fall short was in its stubborn refusal to consider the submarine as a strategic threat. The fleet problems defined antisubmarine warfare as simply the tactical means to the greater strategic end of sea control. Within this conceptual framework, submarines were relegated as nothing more than an irritant.

The "Mahanization" of antisubmarine warfare was reinforced through simulation. And therein lay the problem. Critical fallacies in simulation informed expectations. The fleet problems nurtured a false sense of security. Naval officers expected that substantial resources would be available for antisubmarine operations. Central to the fiction was the destroyer. The fleet problems set a precarious standard. In a future war, convoys would be ringed by bands of armed escorts. Exercise fleets were consistently supplied with appreciable numbers of destroyers for escort, even if that meant conjuring up ships that did not exist. During the March 1925 problem, twenty-four destroyers were assigned to the Blue fleet commander, as well as an additional thirty "constructive" destroyers. The opposing fleet was assigned twenty-nine.[33] Destroyers made up over 50 percent of the White fleet in Fleet Problem Sixteen ten years later, while twenty-nine of the sixty-seven ships assigned to the opposing fleet were destroyers and destroyer minesweepers.[34] The abundance of assets, both real and imaginary, may have soothed the strategic dilemmas of exercise fleet commanders. But in practical terms, the tendency to exaggerate in the fleet problems left officers with a false notion of their preparedness.

The fleet problems also ignored the lessons of World War I when it came to the complexity of convoy operations. The process of forming and moving a convoy was slow and tedious. Enormous coordination was required to round up civilian merchant ships. Integrating foreign-owned ships added another significant complication. Operations at sea were no less difficult. Antisubmarine escorts were at the mercy of the ships they were protecting. The convoy proceeded only at the speed of the slowest ship. Formation integrity was challenging for ships that normally travel independently. Things got even dicier at the convoy's destination. Extensive coordination was again required to prioritize entry into port, resulting in ships being stacked up outside and extremely vulnerable to attack.[35]

The fleet problems anticipated none of these contingencies. Instead, the exercises instilled a belief that a convoy was a convoy, whether comprised of civilian merchants or navy logistics ships. Both would operate like any other well-oiled fleet maneuver. Security and logistical problems were pragmatic reasons for excluding civilian merchants from the exercises. But the fleet problems failed to compensate for the omissions. Exercise planners instead relied upon imagination to fill out their convoys. In Fleet Problem Two, for example, the number of simulated auxiliaries numbered seventy ships. The convoy in Fleet Problem Four was composed of one hundred actual and imaginary support ships. The battleship *Utah* played the role of merchant ships during the 1939 exercise. Naval officers acknowledged *Utah* as a problem with their simulation. The battleship was characterized as a "high type of convoy." There was a "vast difference between the fine fast troop convoys of a few capable units and the miscellaneous convoys made up of what was left."[36] Unfortunately, that acknowledgement was set against sixteen years of prior experiences. The prevailing attitude was that the convoy could be integrated into fleet strategy and tactics. The possibility that the imperatives of the convoy would drive fleet operations, which had happened in the Atlantic in World War I, was not addressed.

The final and perhaps most critical shortcoming was the neglect of any scenario testing the vulnerability of U.S. waters to attack from submarines. Exercise planners were not blind to the possibility of a future enemy appearing off U.S. shores. Fleet Problem Fourteen, held in February 1933, was designed specifically to test navy mobilization plans against an enemy operating close to the United States. The threat, however, was not from submarines but Japanese carrier-based aircraft. It was the more likely hazard, given the navy's Pacific orientation. Any inclination towards an Atlantic scenario would have been deemed unnecessary. It was also the more likely scenario within the context of the navy's sea-control doctrine. Submarines were instruments of blockade but only after a fleet achieved control of the sea.

There was plenty of room in the bottle for antisubmarine warfare. The problem was that the concept was never blended into the sea-control elixir. Naval officers applied their Mahanian perspectives to a necessary evil. The convoy was envisioned as an extension of the fleet. Its defensive requirements were acknowledged only as means to a greater offensive end. Sea control remained the fleet's priority. Submarines would not deter the fleet from its envisioned sea-control mission. But the reality orchestrated in the fleet problems concealed chinks in the navy's doctrinal armor. The Mahanization of antisubmarine warfare prevented officers from fully recognizing just how tenuous their doctrine was. Theirs was a blinkered concentration on what they believed was an inevitable war in the Pacific. The implications were enormous. The oversight contributed to Adolphus Andrews's embarrassment in 1940 and left him staggering in 1942.

Some day we will recognize that a Navy is not merely ships. Then, you Marines will come into your own. It may take a war to do it.

Admiral Y

CHAPTER 6

A Strategic Afterthought

The Fleet Problems and Amphibious Warfare

Admiral Y was not some prescient navy flag officer writing behind the veil of anonymity but a fictional character fashioned by Brig. Gen. John H. Russell in 1933.[1] Russell, who was the assistant commandant of the U.S. Marine Corps, submitted to the *Marine Corps Gazette* a story of a chance meeting between a marine "Brigadier General X" and retired "Admiral Y" at the Army-Navy Club. In the ensuing conversation, the admiral took the opportunity to offer his Naval Academy classmate some suggestions on how best to "sell the Corps" to the navy.

Marines, Admiral Y observed, needed to do a better job of selling to line officers the need to seize and defend advance bases. He pointed to Britain's web of global bases as evidence that a navy's strength was based on more than the number of ships it possessed. Admiral Y then made a remarkable comparison. Islands were like warships. The seizing and holding of advanced bases was no different than having additional warships in an area. Finally, the admiral pointed out that the Marine Corps and navy had something very much in common when it came to amphibious warfare. A larger Marine Corps, with a coherent doctrine for conducting amphibious operations, would keep the army out of the picture.

Russell's allegory could be interpreted as a wake-up call to his fellow marines. The future of the Corps lay in amphibious operations. But all would be for naught if the fleet ignored the strategic importance of advanced bases. It is also likely that Russell was employing a bit of reverse psychology. The article was addressed to naval officers as well. Implied in Admiral Y's grasp of amphibious warfare was an implied criticism of the navy. The fleet had yet to appreciate the strategic significance of seizing and holding advanced bases.

Two themes tend to dominate U.S. Marine Corps' experience during the interwar period. Official histories celebrate the development of amphibious warfare doctrine as the work of visionaries. Their efforts saved the Corps from absorption into the army. The doctrine they produced contributed significantly to victory in the Pacific during World War II. Scholarly works examine the doctrinal process within the context of modern organizational theory. By seizing upon a specialized mission, marines acquired resources essential to the organization's existence. Amphibious warfare doctrine additionally elevated the Corps to a level of strategic sophistication that rivaled the senior services. Finally, the doctrinal process offered a medium for strengthening the organization's cultural identity. Refining amphibious warfare into a formal doctrine "matured" the Corps' technical proficiency, managerial capability, structural boundaries, and its ability to adapt to external threats.[2]

While official and new military histories are careful to include the navy, both have left open for discussion an important issue raised by General Russell. The assistant commandant was frustrated with the navy. He was not so much concerned that the fleet would ignore the tactical support required for amphibious warfare. What did bother him was the navy's failure to acknowledge the importance of advanced bases to sea control. In his fictional account, Russell's admiral understood that marines were like warships. In truth, line officers proved less than willing to broaden their perspectives so liberally. They tolerated the concept of amphibious operations as a necessary facet of a future war. Warfare simulation addressed the tactical problems associated with amphibious assaults. But from a strategic perspective, the navy kept the marines at arm's length. Amphibious warfare was an afterthought to the navy's sea-control mission.

The Great War made marines celebrities and contributed to the Corps' image as an elite fighting force. But the war also brought home some important lessons. The 41 officers and 1,114 enlisted men killed in combat offered a stark introduction to modern war. Marines gained experience in infantry-artillery coordination, aviation, battlefield communications, field staff operations, and even cooperation with the army. And though their advanced base force mission had not been put to the test, they experienced in France what they had crudely simulated on Culebra. They learned the strategic necessity, and tactical difficulty, of assaulting an entrenched enemy.[3]

It proved difficult, however, to translate wartime popularity into consolidation of the advanced base force mission. Gone was any semblance of a European threat. Germany was defeated. Rapprochement with Britain was a foregone conclusion.[4] Japan loomed as the most likely enemy. The Japanese had opportunistically seized Germany's island possessions in the central Pacific. But they had also fought with the Allies. Finally, the Senate's politically inspired rejection of the Versailles Treaty sent an unambiguous signal. The United States was tired of entangling international alliances and the quagmires that followed. The 1922 Washington Naval Conference was evidence of America's desire to be left alone.

The Marine Corps also faced significant challenges at home. Demobilization, and a penurious president and congress, meant that further development of the advanced base force concept would be done on a shoestring. Traditional missions would compete for meager funding. Competition also arose from professional constituencies within the officer corps. Many marines looked to duty in China and the Banana Republics as the Corps' destiny. Others viewed the war in Europe as the model for the future. And there remained within the ranks the lingering influence of "Old Corps" marines. The drinking and carousing might have added to the romantic aura of the service, but such behavior was also a handicap to the Corps' image as a serious, professional organization.[5]

A final obstacle was continued navy indifference. A revised landing force manual published in 1921 aimed specifically to bring U.S. Navy procedures into accordance with revised army infantry drill regulations. Only forty-two of the seven hundred pages in the manual were devoted to landing force operations. Marines were again subordinated to line officers. Landing operations remained scripted affairs, more parade than actual military operation. The defensive flavor of the manual reflected the navy's conditional commitment to the possibility of an opposed landing. If the ships covering the landing force could not reduce enemy defenses, the manual recommended looking for a safer place to land.[6]

It was in this maelstrom that Maj. Gen. John A. Lejeune, commandant of the Marine Corps, found himself. He was commissioned from the Naval Academy in 1888, a time when U.S. Marine Corps officers were drawn predominantly from civilian society or the enlisted ranks. In 1909 Lejeune became the second marine to attend the Army War College. He commanded one of the two advanced base force regiments during the Culebra exercise in 1913. Lejeune's reputation had grown so much that he was given serious consideration as commandant in 1913—while only a lieutenant colonel.[7]

Lejeune's tenure as commandant began on June 30, 1920. His mission became the future existence of the Corps. Two important premises conditioned his agenda. The first was that the destiny of the Corps was closely intertwined with the fleet. Land operations in the Caribbean and China were important responsibilities, but building roads in Haiti or protecting the embassy in Peking also kept the Corps out of the navy's sight. To lean too far in the direction of the army's land warfare mission would only serve to alienate naval officers. Much like their aviator counterparts, marines had to go to sea "on the back of the fleet." So Lejeune steered a Mahanian course. The mission of the fleet was to "gain command of the sea and hold it." Marines supported the fleet by helping to facilitate the sea-control mission. Expeditionary forces would conduct "minor shore operations" as the fleet moved to the theater of operations. Once sea control was established, the army could then invade and occupy the enemy's territory.[8]

Associating the Corps more closely with the fleet than with ground warfare was an act of pragmatism. But also influencing Lejeune's vision was the prospect of an Orange war. Japan's acquisition of the Caroline and Marshall Islands and plans for extensive naval construction following World War I fueled the imaginations of navy and marine officers. Efforts to create regional stability through disarmament did little to diminish their vision of war in the Pacific. One particularly inspired imagination belonged to Maj. Earl H. "Pete" Ellis. Ellis enlisted in the Marines in 1900 and received a commission two years later. While much of his career was spent in overseas expeditionary duty, Ellis did manage a tour at the Naval War College. He later served as Lejeune's adjutant during World War I and was made the intelligence director of Commandant Lejeune's division of plans and training.[9]

In July 1921 Ellis prepared a report that emphasized the strategic relevance of the amphibious mission. Entitled "Advanced Base Operations in Micronesia," the document was a blueprint for Marine Corps participation in a future Pacific war. Ellis hypothesized a worst-case scenario. Japan would initiate war but would conserve the bulk of her navy in the western Pacific. Her regional dominance would lead to the loss of the Philippines and Guam. Hawaii would be left as the navy's westernmost base. Any movement of the fleet west from Hawaii would be subject to attrition attacks from Japanese naval and air units operating from her central Pacific Mandates in the Marshall and Caroline island chains. The U.S. fleet would enter the western Pacific weakened and without an advanced base of supply.[10]

Ellis believed that the linchpin of any successful Pacific strategy lay in the Marshalls and Carolines, and he was convinced that their reduction was "practically imperative." But Ellis was also a realist. Extensive fleet operations in close proximity to the atolls would be extremely risky. Advocating such a strategy would no doubt hit a nerve among line officers, whose Mahanian vision was focused exclusively on the western Pacific. Ellis offered a compromise. He deferred in principle to the Mahanian canon. A decisive fleet action would still decide the war in the Pacific. But the reduction of the central Pacific atolls, he also argued, was necessary to protect the battle fleet as it advanced to its western Pacific destiny. Ellis proposed that the fleet use marine brigades to seize and hold temporary bases in the Marshalls. With the Marshalls in navy hands, the fleet would move next against selected targets in the Carolines and the Marianas, including Guam.[11] Ellis went even further to assuage navy sensitivities. "Any operations preliminary to a fleet action," he asserted, "must be carried out by the minimum naval forces and those of least value in fleet action. Marine forces of reduction, occupation and defense must be of such strength and composition as to require the least possible naval support."[12]

Ellis accompanied his strategic overview with a meticulous analysis of the requirements for successful amphibious operations. Included in his report was an extensive description of the geography of the region, including the physical characteristics of the atolls. He described in great detail various aspects of the amphibious operations: reconnaissance of landing sites, use of feints and dawn landings, disembarkation, boat formations, the composition of the landing force, naval gunfire and air support, and even the use of poison gas.[13] Such detail was necessary if amphibious operations were to be taken seriously. But just as important, Ellis's tactical overview conceptually aligned marines with their navy counterparts. He was careful not to ruffle navy feathers by insisting that amphibious operations were integral to the sea-control mission. Instead, Ellis gave marines relevance by appealing to the navy's Mahanian standards. Ellis' worst-case scenario presumed opposition at the beach. Amphibious landings were meant to be offensive operations.

With Ellis providing operational legitimacy for the amphibious warfare mission, Lejeune began a campaign to sell it to a broad constituency. He mollified congressional budget hawks by using marine labor for base improvement projects. Lejeune engaged the public with innovative training demonstrations. Quantico marines engaged in modern tactical exercises at Civil War battlefield sites, such as the Wilderness, Gettysburg, New Market, and Antietam. Lejeune also used his membership on the General Board to gain formal acceptance of the mission. He successfully lobbied his navy colleagues to formally add the "primary war mission" to supply a "mobile force to accompany the Fleet for operations on shore in support of the fleet."[14] Within his organization, Lejeune used his position as commandant to consolidate the Corps around the amphibious warfare mission. He reorganized and expanded his headquarters to embody a more formal staff system. Divisions of operations and training, personnel, education, and recruiting were created. Lejeune also transformed the Corps educational infrastructure. The Marine Corps School of Application was expanded into a three-tiered education system of an entry-level course for junior officers, a course for company-grade officers, and one for field-grade officers. In 1923 Lejeune formalized the transformation when he directed that the Advanced Base Force be renamed the "Marine Expeditionary Force."[15]

Marines could point to the changes as a harbinger of better days ahead. The Corps had been resurrected from death in 1798. It weathered the transition from sail to steam, staved off attacks from antagonistic naval officers, and avoided absorption by the army. In the process, marines discovered a viable mission. Amphibious operations fit within the framework of modern naval war. The mission supported the navy's increasing focus on the Pacific. The advanced base force concept created the initial momentum towards the amphibious warfare mission. Ellis gave the concept an offensive emphasis, and Lejeune constructed an intellectual infrastructure to nurture it. Even the geopolitical landscape appeared to bear out the sensibility of Lejeune's agenda. The termination of the Anglo-Japanese Alliance of 1902 during the Washington Naval Conference in 1922 made Ellis's report look prophetic.

Marines had made progress, but their future was hardly secure. The amphibious warfare organization was supported on paper. Doctrine, however, had yet to be formalized. The few opportunities to exercise in Culebra were principally tactical in nature. Lejeune's organizational initiatives were too new to produce any formal doctrine. Perhaps the greatest blow was the loss of Pete Ellis. His mysterious death, while on an intelligence-gathering mission in the atolls, left the Corps without its chief visionary.[16]

The Early Fleet Problems: Orchestrating the Obvious

In Ellis's absence, the Corps needed an opportunity to demonstrate the strategic relevance of its mission. The opportunity presented itself in January 1924 with Fleet Problem Three. The exercise was developed to test the ability of the fleet to transit the Panama Canal under wartime conditions. Control of the Caribbean was the strategic objective. On January 14, 1924, a Blue Pacific fleet under Adm. Samuel S. Robison was at anchor on the Pacific side of the canal. His assignment was to safely move his forces through the canal and join up with a "constructive" Blue Atlantic fleet en route to the Caribbean. Opposing Robison was a Black fleet, assigned to destroy the canal prior to the Blue fleet's transit or to destroy the Blue fleet as it entered the Caribbean.[17]

The scenario was written ostensibly to reflect a future war with England. The opposing fleets reflected the tonnage ratios for battleships established by the Washington Naval Conference. Both navies were relatively equal in the total number of battleships. The preponderance of Blue's battleship strength lay in the Pacific, while twelve of Black's eighteen dreadnoughts were located in British ports. Specific references to Black possessions such as Halifax, Trinidad, and Bermuda also gave the exercise a Red emphasis.[18]

And yet, while exercise planners designed Fleet Problem Three to address a Red threat, there was also a decidedly Orange flavor to the exercise. One indication of a broader agenda was the fact that the exercise was sandwiched between two fleet problems with an Orange orientation. Fleet Problem Two had simulated the advance by the fleet across the Pacific. Fleet Problem Four would represent the final phase of an Orange war. The second key was Panama. In Fleet Problem Two the canal represented Manila. Its description in Fleet Problem Three, as a "titularly independent republic, dominated and protected by Blue government," could just as easily have been used to characterize the Philippines. The use of army defense forces in the exercise was a further indication that the scenario could be applied to the Pacific. The implication was that the fleet would arrive in the Philippines before the Japanese could take them. The analogy to Orange was not lost on Robison. The fleet problem, he remarked, "forecast the strategy of our most probable enemy in the Pacific." Black's possessions in the Caribbean, the admiral reasoned, could as easily represent Japan's situation in the western Pacific. If Blue had a strategic advantage, it was that its preponderant naval strength in the Pacific would allow for immediate offensive operations.[19]

During Fleet Problem Three, the newly designated Marine Expeditionary Force was introduced into strategic simulation. On January 2, eighty-nine officers and sixteen hundred marines, under the command of Brig. Gen. Eli Cole, embarked in the transport *Henderson* for the journey to Panama. The marines spent the two-week transit preparing for the exercise. They received instruction in a variety of tactical aspects associated with amphibious operations. Field orders were developed. Troops practiced embarking and disembarking from small boats. During the evening of January 16 instruction stopped, and operations began. Marines boarded small boats under the cover of warships. By one-thirty the next morning, they were pushing to the beach. The boats were divided into three columns and sent toward their objective at Fort Randolph, a shore defense outpost on Margarita Island, which defended the Atlantic side of the canal.[20]

The marines ran into problems from the outset. The second and third waves of boats had difficulty navigating in the dark. They also could not locate the beachmaster, who was with the first wave on the island. General Cole embarked in a speedboat, found a naval officer who could assist, rounded up his errant troops, and sent them off to their objective.[21] At five forty in the morning they finally landed on the island and assaulted Fort Randolph. Within thirty minutes they had captured the whole island, taking over one hundred prisoners. The force also took the submarine base and naval air station at Coco Solo, capturing an additional seven hundred prisoners, forty-seven airplanes, six submarines, one collier, and one airplane tender. At about eight in the morning, the chief umpire informed General Cole that hostilities on land had ceased and that the exercise was over.[22]

General Cole identified several valuable tactical lessons from the exercise, from adding more beachmasters to suggestions for improvement in loading and embarking in small boats. Maj. Holland M. Smith, who as an assistant umpire had observed the operation, was more effusive in his assessment. "The problem," he observed, "has conclusively shown that a Marine Expeditionary force is a powerful weapon for any Commander in Chief engaged in any such operation, that such an Expeditionary Force is an integral part of the Fleet, and that this Force should be carefully trained as any other integral part of the Fleet."[23]

Smith's suggestion, that amphibious operations should be considered integral to the sea-control mission, ignored an important detail. General Cole's marines were on the wrong side in the war. The expeditionary force was part of Adm. Nulton McCully's Black fleet. Its mission was to assist McCully's naval forces in the destruction of the canal. Cole's men were nothing more than role players in CINCUS Robert Coontz's script. The star of the show was the Blue fleet. Planning documents conveyed Robison's indifference to Cole's force. In his "Estimate of the Situation" for the problem, he dismissed the importance of an amphibious assault on the canal. The principal threat, Robison believed, would come from the heavy guns of Black battleships and attacks from aircraft. A landing might be attempted but only if primary attacks failed. Robison's after-action report was equally dismissive. It made no mention of the amphibious assault on Fort Randolph. In fact, it seems that Robison wanted nothing to do with land operations during the problem. Prior to the exercise, he had reached an agreement with the commanding general of the Panama Canal Department. The land defense of the canal was designated as a "paramount interest to the Army." When Robison had moved enough of his ships through the canal to significantly challenge the Black fleet, then he would assume the responsibility for the defense of the canal.[24]

Robison's indifference to the contribution of the marines was shared by others on his staff. His aviation commander sarcastically characterized the capture of the Coco Solo air station as so "peacefully if not peaceably done that no one hardly knew of it." A single marine was noticed rushing onto the airfield, but his claims that he had destroyed the hangars and parked aircraft were met with skepticism. "You know," the chief aviator remarked, "no one would pay very much attention to a single Marine running around."[25] Even the umpires for the exercise seemed unimpressed. They attributed the marines' success to deficiencies within the army's defense force. The garrison was too small both to man the fixed defenses and to respond to a landing force. The disposition of the troops had also been poorly planned. And in a particularly stinging criticism, the umpires concluded that the army lacked initiative. Had its forces only counterattacked, "a more logical solution could have been rendered."[26]

The umpires did acknowledge in their report that more study should be given to landing expeditionary forces. But that recommendation was the fifty-fourth of sixty items listed and was directed specifically at the tactical problems experienced during the landing. It is not surprising that General Cole's postexercise remarks did not match the enthusiasm of Major Smith. His summary of the exercise consisted of two sentences. Marines were given a mission by the commander-in-chief. They executed the mission.[27]

Adm. Samuel S. Robison, Blue fleet commander for Fleet Problem Three, displayed the indifference to the contribution of U.S. Marines operating with the Black fleet that reflected the navy's early belief that amphibious warfare was not integral to Mahanian sea control. Courtesy U.S. Naval Institute.

The marines demonstrated in Fleet Problem Three that amphibious operations might have a role to play in the navy's sea-control mission. They had seized key defensive positions that would have aided the Black fleet's mission of harassing Robison's transit through the canal. Robison's indifference to their efforts was troubling. But he would not be able to discount them in the next exercise. Fleet Problem Four was drafted specifically to assess marine contribution to an Orange war. The scenario devised by CICNUS Robert Coontz, who assumed command of the Blue fleet for the exercise, represented the final phase of the envisioned Pacific war. The fleet had arrived at the Philippines intact at the conclusion of Fleet Problem Two. Manila was now a main operating base. The fleet's chain of supply was deemed secure. The final step, according to Coontz, would be an offensive campaign to secure an advanced base within five hundred miles of Japan. From there the fleet would operate against Japan's seaborne commerce. If the opportunity presented itself, the battle fleet would engage the Japanese in a decisive battle.[28]

Coontz transformed the geography of the Caribbean to represent the western Pacific. The island of Martinique was turned into the Japanese city of Sasebo. Trinidad was made into Kure. Haiti became China. Puerto Rico represented Okinawa, the main island in the Bonins chain. The Blue fleet's objective was Culebra, the small island off Puerto Rico, which had been first used as a training prop in 1903.[29]

In his report to the chief of naval operations, Coontz made it perfectly clear that "the crux of the whole problem is in the seizing of the base."[30] But exactly how that mission fit into the overall strategic picture was open to question. Coontz placed overall responsibility for the operation in the hands of navy flag officer Montgomery Meigs Taylor. What is interesting is that the marines were assigned to Taylor as part of his "Control Force." While it might be inferred from its name that the Control Force was to achieve sea control, its mission was exactly the opposite. The U.S. fleet was organized functionally. The Battle Fleet, as its name implied, was the chief instrument in the Mahanian sea-control paradigm. It was the only force capable of securing sea control in a decisive engagement with an enemy fleet of capital ships. Only after sea control had been achieved would the Control Force of submarines, destroyers, and marines commence their work. Even Taylor, who was in overall command of the amphibious operation, recognized and accepted his subordinate role. "The Estimate of the Commander in Chief," Taylor acknowledged, "stresses the need for expediting as much as possible the seizure of the base in order that the Fleet may be freed from its escort duties and free to operate against the enemy fleet."[31]

To his credit, Coontz kept the focus of the exercise on the amphibious operation. To ensure that Blue would not be distracted from the exercise objectives, the Black fleet was made up primarily of destroyers and submarines. The Marine Expeditionary Force was divided in half. General Cole commanded the marines who would conduct the assault. A relatively equal number of marines under Col. Dion Williams were assigned to the Black fleet for the defense of Culebra. General Cole developed a comprehensive "Estimate of the Situation," which included a detailed assessment of Culebra, the opposing force's most probable intentions, and Cole's own tactics for the assault.[32]

In the early morning of January 31 the Blue fleet arrived off Puerto Rico. The transport *Henderson* anchored two miles off the intended landing site. A small group of marines embarked in small motor launches and landed on Culebra to make an initial reconnaissance of the prospective landing sites. At dawn additional reconnaissance forces landed, covered by the guns of Taylor's Control Force, which included the battleships *Arkansas, Florida,* and *Utah.*[33]

The main landings, scheduled for the morning of February 1, experienced early difficulties. Lights from commercial vessels confused the officers in charge of the landing craft, resulting in the intermingling of the waves of assault boats. Cole personally interjected himself into the situation and by six in the morning successfully got his troops ashore. For the remainder of the early morning Cole's assault force pushed its way beyond the beach. By eight forty-five, when hostilities were called to a halt, Blue marines claimed the high ground beyond the beachhead.[34]

The marines learned many important lessons during the exercise. The detailed planning for a successful night operation was validated. Coordination of naval gunfire needed work. Once again the beachmaster was shown to be a critical part of any amphibious operation. More detailed planning in embarkation procedures was needed. The navy was dangerously short of transports. Cole estimated that *Henderson* was manned (including sailors and marines) at 65 percent beyond its personnel capacity. Finally, the general observed the deficient state of landing craft. The current navy motor-sailing launches were inadequate for shore landings. During the exercise marines experimented with a modified British motor launch, which from its appearance was called a "beetle-boat." The vessel, Cole acknowledged, was a step in the right direction. But the beetle's size limited the number of landing craft that *Henderson* could carry. When loaded down with troops and equipment, it proved sluggish during the landing.[35]

Where General Cole fell short in his assessment of the fleet problem, however, was in its strategic significance. At no point in his report did he share his views on the contribution marines made to the war in general. Perhaps the overwhelming number of tactical problems precluded any discussion of the strategic value of the amphibious mission. The consequence of Cole's silence, unfortunately, was that judgment of the value of the amphibious mission was left to the navy. Admiral Taylor was so disappointed with the exercise "that the signal ending the problem was read by me with profound relief." He did not completely disavow the utility of amphibious landings, but the tone of his report lacked enthusiasm. The most damning assessment was made by CINCUS. Taking a cue from the Control Force commander's report, Coontz provided a pessimistic appraisal to the CNO. The exercise pointed out that the time required for an opposed landing "accentuated the great hazard attendant upon the whole undertaking." The amphibious mission only served to keep the escorting warships within close proximity to the enemy, subjecting them to continuous harassment. The whole affair of seizing a defended base was too hazardous, he concluded, unless the enemy fleet had been first destroyed or contained.[36]

The navy's attitude was a foregone conclusion, even before marines embarked on *Henderson* for Fleet Problem Three. The postwar world and Washington Naval Conference had stimulated the thinking of marines. To them, amphibious operations appeared a snug fit in the navy's Pacific strategy. But the employment of marines in a Pacific war was not accepted by all. Naval officers viewed amphibious operations as a distraction from sea control. Criticism arose from outside the naval service as well. Governor general of the Philippines Gen. Leonard Wood did not particularly care for a strategy that implied his soldiers would not hold out against the Japanese.[37] Critical to the success of amphibious warfare doctrine, though, were officers such as CINCUS Robert Coontz and Samuel Robison in senior positions in the fleet. They believed that the fleet's speedy advance across the Pacific would counter opposition by the Japanese from their central Pacific bases. The marines might be needed during the final phase of an Orange war, but the key to victory was sea control in the western Pacific. Coontz dashed any likelihood for acceptance of amphibious warfare within the navy's sea-control mission. The fleet, not marines, would secure the seas.

Out of the Abyss Comes a Doctrine: 1925–34

Marines faded from the landscape of strategic exercises following the 1924 fleet problems. Between 1925 and 1932 they participated in a few exercises with the U.S. Army, called "Grand Joint Army and Navy Exercises." Yet the events failed to live up to their billing. In April 1925, for example, marines participated in a joint landing exercise with the army in Hawaii. But the 1,500 troops, simulating a 42,000-man landing force, relegated the operation to a headquarters-level exercise. The Joint Army-Navy Board recommended to the secretaries of the navy and war that no exercise be conducted in 1926, since the fleet was going to the Canal Zone, site of two previous joint maneuvers. The last of the Grand Joint Exercises was held in Hawaii in February 1932. A force of 600 soldiers, 700 marines, and 101 pack animals represented an army and marine expeditionary force of two divisions. At 6:35 A.M. on February 12, lead elements of the Army 3rd Division landed on Oahu, followed shortly by the Marine's 1st Division. By two in the afternoon the landings had been completed. Ninety minutes later, the umpires, judging that "nothing more of benefit was to be derived from continuing the operation," terminated Grand Joint Exercise Number Four.[38]

There were some practical reasons for the increasing absence of marines from warfare simulation. The Corps was no less immune from the Coolidge and Hoover peace-through-penury program than was the navy. In 1922 the Corps numbered 19,500 men. Six years later that number had fallen to less than 17,000. Marines would not see their numbers rise to their statutory peacetime strength of 24,000 until late in the 1930s. But while Marine Corps' budgets stagnated, marines were still viewed as the principal tool of nonprovocative U.S. intervention. To their commitments in the Caribbean was added an expedition to Nicaragua in 1927. And in China, the spillover from war between nationalists and warlords led to a significant increase in marine presence.[39]

Despite these obstacles, Lejeune's agenda of reforming the Corps was slowly bearing fruit. Fullam's influence on navy attitudes was beginning to wane. Rear Adm. William Veazie Pratt, responding to a June 1924 *Proceedings* article written by former commandant George Barnett, concluded that "without a doubt the most efficient body of men that can be landed on shore quickly to meet an emergency are the Marines."[40] The Fullamite lobby continued to weaken throughout the decade. In 1927 the navy finally invited the Marine Corps to participate in the revision of its landing forces manual. Navy interest in amphibious warfare remained circumspect. Only seventeen pages were devoted to landing operations. But interestingly, the manual's writers proved willing to turn over greater responsibilities to the marines. They even acknowledged the advantages of the "special training of Marine officers and men" in landings ashore.[41] Even the army appeared ready to formally recognize the amphibious warfare mission and to anoint the marines as solely responsible. In a 1927 document entitled "Joint Action of the Army and Navy," the Joint Army-Navy Board gave the Corps the wartime responsibility for the seizure of advanced bases, as well as for military operations that were part of a naval campaign.[42]

The 1927 decision of the Joint Board did not yield anything in the way of extra funding or increases in Marine Corps personnel. But it did appear to nurture momentum toward the development of a formal doctrine of amphibious warfare. Movement began in the pages of professional journals.

Surprisingly, one of the first articles to address the issue in *The Marine Corps Gazette* was from a naval officer. In September 1929 Lt. Cdr. E. W. Broadbent addressed the relationship between the fleet's mission and the necessity for advanced bases. Broadbent remained loyal to the Mahanian sea-control paradigm. The principal objective of the fleet was the enemy's fleet. But Broadbent also challenged chauvinistic naval officers who dismissed the importance of amphibious operations. Advanced bases, he contended, were essential to sustain a fleet on the strategic offensive. Hinting at an Orange war scenario, Broadbent implied in his article that enemy bases could neither be ignored nor reduced by the guns of the fleet. Only through "assault from the sea," he concluded, could a heavily defended base be secured.[43]

To Broadbent's words were added audacious arguments from marines. In 1931 Lt. Col. Walter Hill had the gall to suggest that the amphibious-warfare mission and the navy's sea-control mission were not separate *but integrated.* Hill acknowledged that the ultimate mission of gaining control of the sea could only be assured with the destruction of an enemy's main fleet. But a naval expedition, Hill argued, should be conceived as a campaign and not a single operation. He suggested that the seizure of bases by marines was an integral component of local sea-control operations. Local sea control prevented the enemy from acting against an advancing expeditionary naval force before it reached its destination.[44] The heresy continued. Col. E. B. Miller took the navy to task in 1932, accusing its senior officers of "accepting the MARINE CORPS as a matter of fact." In an effort to educate his navy brethren, Miller pointed out to them that the sea-control mission pivoted on the amphibious-warfare mission. Relying on a single weapon to destroy the enemy fleet, he cautioned, was folly. Miller directed his criticism specifically to navy strategy and training. The service, he observed sarcastically, may have a plan "stuck away in the secret archives." But having a plan did not ensure successful operations. What were needed were appropriations, manpower, and practice.[45]

In 1932 all three of Miller's recommendations were out of the question. The navy's indifference was overshadowed by reduced budgets stemming from the Great Depression. Marines would have to take their destiny in their own hands. Their first initiative was to ensure the Corps' institutional autonomy. In August 1933 Asst. Commandant John H. Russell recommended to the commandant that the Marine Expeditionary Force be renamed the "Fleet Marine Force." On December 7 navy secretary Claude Swanson signed General Order 241, which established the Fleet Marine Force. Added to the title change were more substantive responsibilities. The organization retained the same form as the old expeditionary force, but the Fleet Marine Force was now specifically assigned to CINCUS, with a specific mission for landing operations. The commandant was directed as well to ensure that the FMF would be kept in readiness to support the fleet and not detailed to support traditional Marine Corps responsibilities.[46]

The official history of the Marine Corps characterized General Order 241 as the "Magna Carta" of the Fleet Marine Force. Marines remained autonomous but were also formally associated with the fleet. The order also assured that army agitation to absorb the Corps would come to an end, at least for the time being.[47] The organizational initiative was followed by more significant developments. FDR's "Good Neighbor Policy" in Central America implied that the future of small wars was tenuous.[48] As a result, Marine Corps Schools Command began shifting its curriculum away from army-related topics and focusing more on the amphibious mission. In October 1933 the commandant of the Marine Corps ordered the suspension of the curriculum at the Marine Corps Schools. Staff and students were directed to focus their studies towards the development of an amphibious warfare manual.[49]

The fruit of their effort, the *Tentative Manual for Landing Operations,* was presented to the commandant in January 1934. The prevalent theme of the manual was the uniqueness of the amphibious-warfare mission. Individual sections provided comprehensive requirements for successful amphibious operations. Command relationships were structured to avert controversy with the navy and avoid provoking the army. The manual directed that amphibious landings were part of a naval campaign, with CINCUS in charge. It approached naval gunfire support so as to ease the inherent fear of sailors to engage shore fortifications. Air support was emphasized to ensure adequate reconnaissance of the landing site, force protection, and coordination of activity between sea and shore. The manual proposed the creation of embarkation and debarkation teams to ensure that effective combat power was placed on the beach. The beachmaster was given increased responsibilities to ensure that enough space was made on shore for subsequent waves of heavier-armed troops. Finally, the manual emphasized and articulated the concept of "combat loading," under the direction of a qualified transport quartermaster, to ensure that marines on the beach were adequately supplied.[50]

While Colonel Miller and his colleagues might not have been completely satisfied with the progress made by 1934, the road ahead looked good. John Lejeune's agenda appeared to have worked. The navy seemed to accept its role of protecting the Corps' autonomy. And for the first time, marines had a formally articulated explanation of their mission. The only remaining issue was practice. Creating the impression that amphibious warfare and sea control were integrated was one thing, but to be taken seriously, marines had to get back into strategic warfare simulation.

Warfare Simulation in the 1930s: Fleet Problems and Fleet Landing Exercises

It appeared that 1934 had all the makings of a breakthrough year for the Marine Corps. Marines had adopted amphibious warfare as their raison d'être and had codified the mission in published doctrine. The navy's vision of war in the Pacific was becoming more amenable to the amphibious mission. Even the navy's leadership appeared to be in the marines' camp. *The Tentative Manual for Landing Operations* was approved by the CNO late in 1934 and was specified as the guide for both the navy and Marine Corps in conducting opposed landings.[51]

Organizational and administrative reforms leaned toward the integration of amphibious warfare into the sea-control mission. But those initiatives were internal to the Marine Corps. In the realm of operational warfare simulation, marines still remained an afterthought. The navy's indifference to the strategic implications of amphibious warfare continued. Fleet Problem Thirteen, held in March 1932, simulated the advance of a U.S. fleet from Hawaii westward. The strategic map was flipped to allow the Blue fleet commander the choice of three atoll chains simulated by Puget Sound, San Francisco, and Magdalena Bay near San Diego. Despite harassment from enemy forces, the Blue fleet successfully made its way across the Pacific to its destination at Magdalena Bay.[52]

The 1932 exercise illustrated an important shift toward the strategic vision offered by Ellis in 1921. It emphasized the viability of local sea-control operations. But the exercise also failed Ellis. The Marine Expeditionary Force did not physically participate in the fleet problem. Imaginary marines were embarked on simulated transports to sail with the fleet from Hawaii. The exercise was terminated as the Blue fleet closed its objective. The implied lesson was that as long as the fleet reached its destination, follow-on operations would be relatively uncomplicated.

The inclusion of actual marines two years later did little to alter navy attitudes. Fleet Problem Fifteen was planned as a sea-control exercise to be held in the Caribbean in May 1934. The scenario appeared to be an opportunity for the reorganized Fleet Marine Force to prove its even newer doctrine of amphibious warfare. The exercise was almost a complete reenactment of the

1924 fleet problems. A Blue U.S. fleet, including the Fleet Marine Force, was staged in the Canal Zone. A Gray fleet had assembled in the eastern Caribbean and reinforced its bases at Culebra, St. Thomas, and San Juan. A constructive Gray fleet was expected to be in the area within the month. Control of the Caribbean was the strategic objective. Marines had good reason to be optimistic. CINCUS Frank Schofield acknowledged that the only way for the Blue fleet to achieve its objective was to recapture one of the more important Gray bases prior to the arrival of the second Gray fleet. The Fleet Marine Force was to be used to secure an advanced base in Culebra.[53]

The Fleet Marine Force's participation in the exercise implied that it was integral to sea control. In reality, however, marines could just as well have stayed home. In fact, the director of fleet training implied as much prior to the exercise, when he advised the CNO that it was "questionable whether the importance of Marine Corps participation is sufficient to the problem to warrant the expenditure of funds."[54] The problem itself was conducted within the strict parameters of the navy's sea-control mission. The Blue fleet fought its way across the Caribbean against very stiff opposition. Gray destroyers and cruisers inflicted significant damage on seven Blue battleships and its two fleet carriers. On May 5 Gray destroyers successfully penetrated Blue's protective screen and attacked several of the constructive troop transports. By May 8, the Gray fleet commander decided that his adversary had been weakened enough to commit his capital ships in a decisive battle. In the ensuing twilight engagement, Blue battleships were continuously hit, three were sunk, and transports sustained additional damage.[55]

The marines on the transport *Henderson* were spectators. Their landing on Culebra at the conclusion of the exercise was anticlimactic. The battleships assigned to provide them covering fire had been pulled away for the engagement with the main Gray fleet. The loss made little difference, as the landings were made without opposition. The entire amphibious phase of the exercise was so scripted that the chief umpire ignored the proceedings.[56]

CINCUS reported that his "primary effort" in the fleet problem had been to "introduce realism into Fleet tactics and to simulate the operations of actual war as closely as this could be done." Schofield went on to assert that artificialities in the exercise had been reduced to a minimum. "If some remain," he concluded, "it is because the only way to eliminate them is to have a war instead of tactical exercises."[57] The at-sea aspects of the exercise appeared to bear out Schofield's assertions. From the standpoint of the marines, however, his comments rang hollow. One thousand troops had represented a force ten times that size. The only real transport used was

Henderson. Tenders, destroyers, and imaginary ships represented the others. The landing on Culebra was intended to be part of the strategic design for sea control in the Caribbean. What transpired was nothing more than a tactical maneuver, overshadowed by the allure of naval operations.

In May 1935 the scene was changed to the Pacific. For the first time, an Orange scenario was actually going to focus on an atoll west of Hawaii. Fleet Problem Sixteen was a multifaceted problem that simulated a more cautious approach to the Orange strategy. The fleet exercised from the U.S. west coast north to the Aleutians and west to Hawaii and Midway. The first phase, begun on April 29, simulated the mobilization of a White fleet from its west coast ports against submarine opposition. On May 3 the White fleet advanced from the west coast to Hawaii with a concurrent advance and occupation of Midway. Following a brief stop in Hawaii, the White fleet began the third phase of the exercise. Representing a step in an overseas advance, the White fleet was assigned the objective of transiting to Midway. Keeping close to the cautionary script, Black submarines, destroyers, and land-based aircraft would harass the simulated U.S. fleet during its movement west. The White fleet commander was provided two options to achieve a decisive strategic advantage. He could capture Midway by an amphibious landing, or he could engage the awaiting Black fleet in battle. The Black fleet commander was given similar strategic options. He could either prevent Midway's capture or defeat the White fleet to win the campaign.[58]

For the seven hundred marines participating in the fleet problem, the scenario appeared another opportunity for the navy to recognize the strategic value of amphibious operations. For the first time they would land on a Pacific atoll. Marines would not only play the assaulting force in phase two but also act as Midway's defenders in phase three. Finally, the island had been deemed critically important to both the White and Black fleets' strategic objectives. It would be impossible to ignore amphibious warfare, which appeared to occupy the center of the strategic stage. Fleet Problem Sixteen posed a strategic reality that the navy could not dismiss. The scenario implied that amphibious warfare was not ancillary to the navy's sea-control mission. It was integral to it. The Fleet Marine Force was similarly not an aggregate of sea-going soldiers but a weapons system analogous to a capital ship.

What the marines failed to appreciate was that verisimilitude was multifaceted. To them, seizing islands was analogous to sinking ships. Naval officers did not share that vision. And it was the fleet's vision that mattered. So once again, marines became a strategic sideshow. The west coast Fleet Marine Force disembarked from the battleship *Utah*, the only vessel the navy had available as a transport, and went ashore unopposed on Midway on May 11, 1935. For the next ten days they made extensive preparations for a rigorous defense of the island. But all of their work went for naught. While they sat on Midway and waited, the White fleet commander opted for a naval engagement with the Black fleet.[59]

In his postexercise report, CINCUS Joseph Mason Reeves remarked that the "great desirability of practice in joint operations with the Fleet Marine Force was given great emphasis." Brig. Gen. Charles Lyman disagreed. Lyman had commanded the Fleet Marine Force during the 1934 fleet problem. It was obvious from his postexercise comments that his patience with the navy had run its course. It was a "sad commentary," Lyman observed, that the only transportation the navy could provide was a "defunct old battleship." He went on to characterize the time spent on Midway as monotonous. In between "sweating and freezing," the only break in the tedium was a brief air attack from planes of Adm. Thomas Hart's White cruiser force.[60] Lyman saved his most critical comments for his concluding remarks. He cautioned his colleagues not to ignore the strategic importance of seizing advanced bases. Midway, he predicted, was someday going to be strategically important. The next war would not be like the last. "We cannot expect the Almighty to always be on our side and when the proper moment comes to deliver a base to us." As the father of a naval officer, and with another son headed to the Naval Academy, Lyman assured his audience that the navy's concerns were his concerns. His comments were not meant to "sell the Marines or the Fleet Marine Force." Rather, his intention was to emphasize the complexity of amphibious operations and their value to the navy's sea-control mission.[61]

Lyman's comments for the most part fell on deaf ears. Reeves's chief of staff put the amphibious warfare mission in the proper Mahanian context. "The capture and occupation of an island atoll against opposition," he observed, was "a practical problem which can only be solved by joint training."[62] It was these comments, and not Lyman's, that appeared to have had far-reaching consequences. From the standpoint of strategic simulation, the navy and Marine Corps parted ways. After 1934, subsequent fleet problems relied predominantly on simulated marines in the scenarios.[63] For their part, marines shifted their concentration to tactical exercises on Culebra or San Clemente Island on the west coast. Dubbed "Fleet Landing Exercises," or "FLEX's," these yearly exercises refined critical facets of the amphibious-warfare mission. Landings up to the regimental level were conducted. Naval gunfire support procedures were given greater scrutiny. The army participated in the landings during FLEX 3 in 1937, an exercise that also verified

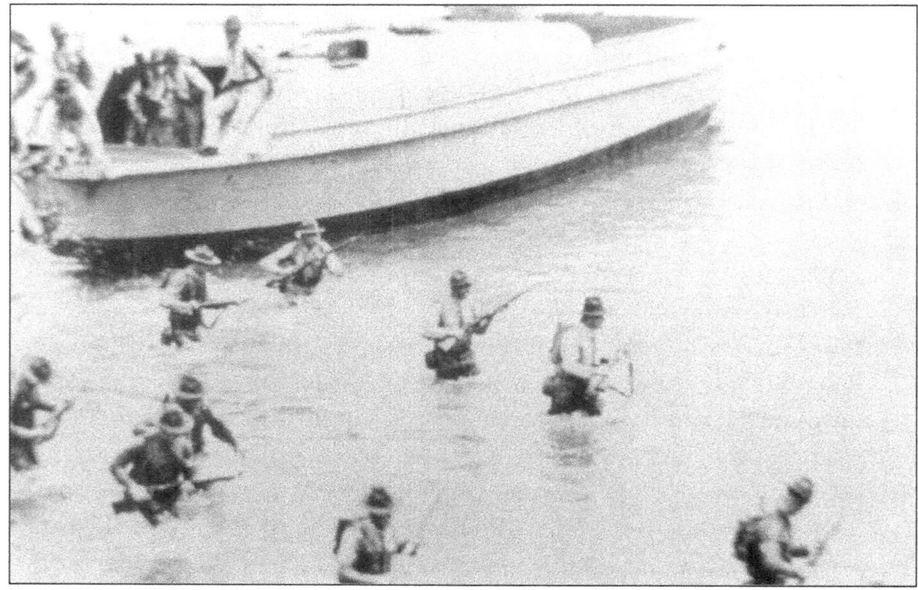

U.S. Marine Corps amphibious warfare exercise in the early 1930s. While the Marine Corps made great strides developing the concept of amphibious assaults, this photo of marines awkwardly disembarking illustrates that the navy was not ready to fully integrate the seizure of advance bases into its warfare doctrine. Courtesy U.S. Naval Institute.

again the unsuitability of navy small boats as landing craft.[64] The marines learned many valuable lessons in their FLEX's, but a critical distinction remained between Fleet Marine Force simulation and its navy counterpart. While the fleet worked out strategic *problems*, amphibious warfare was practiced in Fleet Landing *Exercises*. The difference was more than semantic.

Conclusion

In 1938 the navy once again appeared ready to embrace amphibious warfare. The *Landing-Force Manual, United States Navy* for that year stipulated that marines would compose the entire landing force whenever their numbers were adequate. The manual also acknowledged that the landing force could be commanded either by a navy flag officer or his U.S. Marine Corps equivalent.[65] The CNO took an additional step that appeared to further affirm the importance of the Corps. The *Tentative Manual for Landing Operations*, the Marine Bible since 1934, was incorporated into the navy's war fighting doctrine as *Fleet Tactical Publication 167*.

Placing a blue binder on a green doctrine, however, proved nothing more than a symbolic gesture. The navy's narrow comprehension of amphibious warfare, reinforced in its strategic exercises, left too many issues unresolved. The complexity of command relationships was never explored fully. All agreed that CINCUS held overall responsibility for an amphibious operation, but simulation failed to address the likelihood of friction between subordinate fleet commanders and Fleet Marine Force generals. Issues of tactical importance also lay dormant. The navy still owned only two transports specifically designed to carry the Fleet Marine Force. The Bureau of Construction and Repair was also stalling on a suitable landing craft. Its engineers preferred their own designs, despite lobbying by marines for Andrew Higgins's promising prototype. Naval gunfire support was another aspect given only cursory attention. The navy acknowledged the importance of covering the amphibious assault from the sea, but the fleet problems never delved beyond basic requirements. The fleet's commitment was offset by its continued reliance on flat trajectories, armor-piercing shells, and "neutralization" of enemy resistance.[66]

The path taken by the Marine Corps during the interwar years was in many respects similar to that of naval aviators. Both organizations sought legitimacy by integrating their highly specialized skills within the traditional missions of the parent organization. Marines and aviators employed a campaign strategy of forwarding their agendas without antagonizing navy leadership. Both succeeded in gaining the navy's protection from corporate raiders in the army and air corps. But while aviators successfully positioned themselves for entry into the sea-control mission, marines remained outside the bottle, looking in. By the end of the 1930s warfare simulation had demonstrated the relevance of airplanes to sea control. Battleship admirals considered the aircraft carrier a capital ship. The aircraft-dropped bomb was likened to the shell fired from a naval gun. The same officers proved incapable of making the conceptual leap to the marine rifleman. At least for the foreseeable future, amphibious warfare remained a strategic afterthought. Admiral Y, or rather General Russell, was right. It would probably take a war to bring the navy around.

Well, when we get our Navy,
what are we going to do with it?

Alfred Thayer Mahan,
Naval War College address, September 1892

CHAPTER 7

Re-examining Mahan

The Fleet Problems and Sea Control

On May 2, 1794, 49 Royal Navy warships, including 34 ships of the line, put to sea from their anchorages at Spithead. Under the command of Lord Richard Howe, the fleet's mission was to intercept a convoy of some 130 French cargo ships loaded with American grain. The convoy was so important to the French government that it instructed the fleet at Brest to put to sea immediately to protect the vital cargo as it approached Europe.[1]

Howe was faced with competing objectives. His primary mission was to intercept the convoy. But he could not ignore the French Navy. Howe decided to divide his fleet. A detachment of 8 ships of the line was sent to the west to search for the convoy. Howe and the remainder of the fleet would remain closer to Europe and watch for the French Navy. A reconnaissance of Brest on May 19 confirmed Howe's suspicions when he discovered that the French fleet had sailed. He ran across the French nine days later and after several days of maneuvering to gain an advantageous position converged his ships on the French line.[2]

The ensuing action, known simply as the Battle of the First of June, was a decisive victory for the Royal Navy. At the end of the action the French fleet of 26 ships of the line had been reduced to 12 serviceable warships. To Capt. Alfred Thayer Mahan, who narrated events in *The Influence of Sea Power upon the French Revolution and Empire, 1793–1812,* Howe's actions exemplified the importance of sea control. Although Howe's primary objective was the French convoy, in Mahan's judgment the subsequent sailing of the Brest fleet had altered the strategic landscape. Of the two objectives, Mahan argued that "fighting the French fleet was indisputably the more important, and was doubtless considered by Howe, in accordance with the usual British naval policy, which aimed at the destruction of the enemy's organized forces afloat." Mahan was less direct when it came to explaining events in the larger strategic context. He could not ignore the fact that the convoy had reached port intact. The "principal object" of the French fleet had been achieved. Mahan added, though, that the price had been a "great naval disaster."[3]

Almost 150 years later, Vice Adm. Adolphus Andrews faced a similar situation in Fleet Problem Twenty. At the direction of Franklin D. Roosevelt, the chief of naval operations instructed CINCUS Claude C. Bloch to hold the exercise in the Caribbean. The CNO additionally "suggested" that Bloch devise a scenario that would examine the navy's response to an attempt by a "European axis" nation to extend its influence to South America. Bloch responded by developing a problem in which a fascist White government had decided to lend military aid and advisors to a sympathetic revolutionary movement in a Green South American country. A convoy of three White merchants, escorted by a fleet of warships, was dispatched to aid the rebels. In response the country of Black, representing the United States, ordered a portion of its Pacific fleet into the Caribbean, with the expressed intention of preventing the White convoy from reaching its destination.[4]

To Adolphus Andrews, commanding the Black fleet, the political consequences of the White convoy reaching port were made perfectly clear. Its arrival would certainly lead to the overthrow of the constitutional government of Green, providing fascism a foothold in the Western Hemisphere. Yet Andrews was also provided confusing strategic guidance. His principal objective was to intercept the White convoy and prevent it from reaching its destination. But Andrews was also instructed to gain "command of the vital sea-areas" off the Green coast. Finally, he was to prepare an advanced base in the Caribbean to allow continued fleet operations against White. Adding to these seemingly competing objectives, CINCUS also advised that in the event of war the destruction of the White fleet was "paramount, as its successful operation in the Lesser Antilles, or westward, threatens our vital lines of communication to the Canal Zone and elsewhere."[5]

Although notations in the margin of the operations order indicate that Andrews recognized the strategic quandary he was in, he nevertheless adopted a course of action similar to the one taken by Lord Howe against the French.[6] Andrews concluded that the presence of the White fleet had transformed the general objective of intercepting the convoy to one of attaining sea control. A detachment of cruisers from his Black fleet, assisted by land-based aircraft, would be sent to search for and destroy the White convoy. The remainder of the fleet would "destroy the White First Fleet by decisive engagement."[7]

Unfortunately for Andrews, history did not repeat. Although his cruiser detachment located the White merchants, the warships were attacked by aircraft from the White carrier *Enterprise* and prevented from closing to within gun range. Andrews also had fleet carriers, but he opted to keep them close to his battleships rather than assist in the search for the convoy. The chief umpire of the exercise subsequently judged that the convoy had arrived safely at its destination. Worse yet, the anticipated battle for sea control never came to pass. The exercise ended before the battle could be fought. Had Mahan been alive in 1940, he might have had difficultly explaining events. For unlike its French counterpart in 1794, the White fleet had not only achieved its principal objective but had averted the great naval disaster.[8]

Though Andrews failed to achieve the two most important objectives assigned to him, he adamantly defended his strategy during the postexercise critique. He acknowledged that the White convoy was critical to the initial success of the insurgency. But Andrews contended that destroying the White fleet first was still the correct solution to the strategic problem. Even though the first convoy got through, he argued that achieving sea control would have made future attempts to supply the insurgents impossible. The fact that he had not brought his strategy to a successful conclusion was not his fault. He had simply run out of time.[9]

Andrews did not lose the war because of artificialities in warfare simulation. It was his unconditional acceptance of Mahan's sea-control doctrine that had failed him. In the late nineteenth century Mahan crafted a pragmatic argument for the employment of naval force that resonated long after his death in December 1914. But what seemed so evident in theory proved to be more complicated in practice. The introduction of modern weapons in the fleet problems complicated Mahan's historicist-based doctrine. As Adolphus

Andrews learned, what worked in 1794 would require some modification to accommodate naval warfare in 1939.

Sea Control and the Early Fleet Problems

The peace treaty ending World War I eliminated the necessity for a war plan against Germany. As for war against Britain, planning resumed soon after the Washington Naval Conference in 1922. Although a joint army-navy war portfolio was not completed until 1930, the plan retained many elements of its prewar predecessor. Military planners envisioned that the British would reinforce Canada (Crimson) as a precursor to an invasion of the United States. Ancillary operations would be conducted against U.S. possessions in the Caribbean and western Pacific. The bulk of the Royal Navy would stand ready somewhere in the Atlantic, waiting to pounce on the numerically inferior U.S. fleet. The solution arrived at by the Joint Army-Navy Board reflected the differing strategic perspectives of the two services. Army planners believed that an invasion from Canada could be best prevented by rapid U.S. mobilization and an invasion of Canada. Navy planners were skeptical. They feared that the army's vision of a Red war would commit the fleet to an unwinnable naval battle. The navy only partially acquiesced. It showed its support by planning to concentrate a force in the Atlantic. Decisive fleet action, however, would be fought only under conditions favorable to the navy. It was not Canada but Britain's possessions in the West Indies that navy planners believed would be strategically decisive in a Red war.[10]

The likelihood that a Red war was possible has been the subject of some debate.[11] Naval records correlate the new skepticism of its officers. One of the fundamental assumptions for a war with England was the importance of Canada. Army planners envisioned that the British would attempt to reinforce their North American possession as a precursor to an invasion of the United States. The U.S. Navy would concentrate in the western Atlantic in order to prevent a British reinforcement of Canada. The problem is that not one fleet problem dealt with this contingency. The navy also never carried out a fleet problem in the western Atlantic. Some of the exercises did deal with strategic problems in the Caribbean.[12] Only five of the problems, however, could be interpreted as Red scenarios, and none of those appeared after 1934. Neither was an Atlantic scenario acted out in any of the Caribbean exercises. Exercise planners were very adept in reconfiguring one geographic area to meet the scenario requirements of another.[13] Many of the Pacific fleet problems, for example, particularly those that simulated operations in the western Pacific, necessitated that planners configure the geography so that the eastern Pacific represented the western Pacific. Much of this was done because of both scheduling and logistic constraints, with fuel usage being a primary concern. But the Caribbean was never redrawn to represent the Atlantic vision of War Plan Red.

The navy's neglect of War Plan Red in its fleet problems was an implied acceptance of British hegemony in the Atlantic dating back to the nineteenth century.[14] The fact that the navy's newer battleships were concentrated on the U.S. west coast, far from any Atlantic scenario, was a more practical demonstration that service interests lay elsewhere.[15] There is another subtle indication from the fleet problems of the navy's skepticism of war with Britain. Winter exercises in the Caribbean afforded significant training opportunities for ships stationed in Norfolk, Brooklyn, or San Francisco. But the Caribbean was also where the fleet played. In 1923, for example, Atlantic and Pacific forces arrived at Panama on February 17. Fleet Problem One lasted from the nineteenth to the twenty-fourth. Following the exercise, units broke up to conduct tactical exercises, overhaul, and visit liberty ports in the region.[16] Fleet Problem Ten was particularly instructive. The 1930 scenario presented to the Black (Britain) and Blue (U.S.) fleet commanders by Adm. William V. Pratt, commander-in-chief, U.S. fleet, required a dispersed U.S. fleet to concentrate and prevent a British force from establishing sea control in the Caribbean. For the nine days prior to the beginning of the exercise, however, both Black and Blue fleets were enjoying themselves in West Indies and Caribbean liberty ports, many of them British possessions.[17]

When retired navy captain Dudley Knox argued that "British aggression against America was possible on an important scale," his rhetoric was no more realistic than the plans being made in the War and Navy Departments.[18] The exercises in the Caribbean failed to follow Washington's scripts because the navy did not seriously believe war with Britain was likely. By the end of the 1930s, even rhetorical animosity between the two was unrealistic. The rise of European fascism and Japanese adventurism posed threats to both Britain and the United States, threats that could be managed only through some sort of collaboration.[19]

While War Plan Red seemed to have more abstract utility, in the western Pacific reaches naval officers saw a more credible adversary and the possibility of a real war at sea. While the guiding principles of War Plan Orange remained intact after World War I, two competing schools of thought emerged to vie for control of the details of Pacific strategy. One group of officers viewed speed as the key to a Pacific war. Called "Thrusters" by Edward Miller, these naval officers envisioned the fleet massing quickly and immediately steaming across the Pacific. A north-central route could take advantage of the U.S.-held islands of Midway and Wake, leading to an advanced base at Guam. From Guam, the fleet would rush to the Philippines to rescue its beleaguered defenders. If Manila had fallen, a base would be established in the southern islands of the archipelago. Interdiction of Japanese trade in the region would begin immediately, followed soon thereafter by a climactic fleet engagement that would seal the fate of Japan.[20]

Arguing against the "through ticket" strategy were naval officers who advocated a slower pace. A direct thrust across the Pacific, they believed, would leave the fleet in such poor material condition that it might suffer the same fate that befell the Russians in the straits of Tsushima in 1905. Instead, "Cautionaries" emphasized a progressive trans-Pacific campaign. They argued that the fleet could best be supplied and protected by establishing a series of bases as it moved west. Cautionaries neither de-emphasized the importance of the Philippines, nor rejected the notion of a decisive engagement with the Japanese fleet. A long war, they argued, while perhaps not palatable to the American public, was nevertheless essential to victory in the Pacific.[21]

Formal planning for an Orange war resumed shortly after World War I. The international picture following the war initially favored a more cautious approach to the Pacific. The Versailles Treaty granted the Japanese a mandate to island chains that lay athwart the route the fleet would take to Guam or the Philippines. Three years later, the world's major naval powers signed a series of naval treaties in Washington. The treaties banned new battleship construction for ten years, restricted tonnages on existing battleships between the United States, Britain, and Japan to a 5:5:3 ratio, respectively, and prohibited the fortification of possessions held by all signatories in the western Pacific.

When the CNO and secretary of the navy approved an "Estimate of the Situation Blue-Orange" in September 1922, the U.S. Navy held only a slight advantage over the Japanese in capital ships. Moreover, the probability of the fleet crossing the Pacific unscathed appeared low. The navy's first plan therefore adopted a cautionary approach. Following mobilization, the fleet would steam west some two thousand miles to the Marshall Islands, where an advanced base would be established on the island of Eniwetok. From the Marshalls, the fleet would advance next to the Carolines and seize Truk. The final contest for sea control in the western Pacific would not begin until Truk was made ready to support the fleet, some six months after initial mobilization.[22]

The reign of the Cautionaries over war planning proved short-lived, however. The bone of contention was the Philippines. Criticism of the 1922 plan emanated from outside the service. Former army chief of staff and current governor-general of the Philippines Leonard Wood charged that the navy plan would sacrifice the islands to caution.[23] Wood's criticism resonated with Adms. Samuel Robison and Robert Coontz, advocates of the Thruster school who also occupied the navy's two most powerful positions within Washington. Coontz was CNO when the Cautionary strategy was introduced in September 1922. But events soon after indicate that his support was lukewarm. He delayed approving the Blue-Orange estimate until March 1923. Two months later Samuel Robison, the director of the War Plans Division, submitted a memorandum modifying the 1922 Blue-Orange estimate, which was approved by the CNO a scant thirty-one days after it had been submitted.[24]

The changes were so poorly incorporated into the previous Blue-Orange estimate to make it look as if a schizophrenic had written the war plan. The document retained enough of the old plan to make a cogent argument for a progressive advance across the Pacific, but the intentions of Robison and Coontz and their opinion of the Cautionary strategy were clear when it came to the Philippines. In the original estimate, war planners characterized the Philippines as having "great advantages as an assembling point for our forces in the Western Pacific." Coontz and Robison added urgency to the plan. After the change was incorporated, the archipelago was now characterized as having "great strategic and economic importance." For the fleet they constituted "the most important naval position in the Western Pacific. Their retention by us is of the utmost importance."[25] A cautious advance, they argued, would therefore be a "long and laborious undertaking." Operating in the vicinity of the Mandates would also place the fleet, particularly the battleships, in close proximity to Japanese submarines. Finally, the admirals argued that a progressive advance delayed the decisive engagement in the western Pacific, which was in their minds the true mission of the fleet.[26]

The Mandates were therefore to be ignored. The fleet would sail directly to the Philippines, a strategy that Coontz admitted was bold but would be less costly than a deliberate war, which he believed would only give the Japanese time to "stiffen their resistance."[27] Coontz moved from CNO to CINCUS in August 1923, but he took his Thruster plan with him and incorporated it into the fleet's upcoming exercises with little interference from Washington. Although CNO Adm. Edward Eberle had established a special committee to prepare plans for the fleet problems scheduled for 1924, its members were instructed "not to trespass on the prerogative of the Commander-in-Chief, and also not to dictate to the Commander-in-Chief the details of training."[28]

Why did the CNO direct his staff to proceed so cautiously? One would think that the navy's senior line officer would provide formal direction to CINCUS on the details of a major naval exercise. The reason is that the position of CNO was never given the level of control that its advocates had hoped for. Fearing the "Prussification" of the service, Josephus Daniels had used his influence in Congress to have the enabling legislation for a general staff watered down. The CNO was given authority for plans and operations, but he could not issue orders without the secretary's signature, nor was he given control over the navy's powerful bureaus. Finally, the CNO's ex officio status on the General Board made him essentially one among equals. Daniels was adamant that the CNO was not to become a navy version of Helmuth von Moltke. Instead, the service's senior officer would be wedded to civilian leadership, a "loyal servant of the administration," rather than an autonomous commander.[29]

By tying the CNO so closely to civilian leadership, the distinction between sea and shore command became acute. Operational commanders could never be sure if the CNO was serving the fleet's best interests or was bowing to the whims of the current administration.[30] Secondly, by restraining the CNO's control over the bureaus, the General Board, and CINCUS, Daniels dispersed power amongst the navy's individual fiefdoms.

The message conveyed was that while the chief of naval operations might be in charge of the navy, it was CINCUS who would fight the war. Coontz took advantage of the relationship and used Fleet Problems Two and Four to extirpate caution from Pacific strategy. As a consequence, the exercises represented different phases of the "through ticket" to Manila. In Fleet Problem Two, Coontz, playing the commander of the Blue (U.S.) fleet, decided to establish "at the earliest possible date Blue sea power in the South Pacific." An advanced base was to be established in the area. And while Coontz implied that there might be flexibility in deciding where to go, he offered the not-so-subtle suggestion that Ingles Bay (representing Manila) was the best available site for such a base. "The Blue Army and Navy have agreed," to quote from Coontz's instructions, "that the promptest possible reinforcement of Ingles Bay is of great military and naval importance."[31]

The crucible of warfare simulation emerged as a way to examine sea control in a modern context. But the fleet problems also served to sustain naval officers' conviction on the nature of strategy. "As practical individuals,"

In 1924 Adm. Robert Coontz used Fleet Problem Two to extirpate caution from the navy's envisioned war plan with Japan by orchestrating his Blue fleet's transit from the U.S. west coast to Panama without enemy opposition. Courtesy U.S. Naval Institute.

naval historian Clark Reynolds writes, "sailors throughout history have not generally had the time or the inclination to deal with the theoretical aspects of their work. They are ship drivers, not philosophers."[32] The fleet problems bear out Reynolds's observations. The navy distinguished its at-sea endeavors from similar exercises at the war college. In Newport, students played "war games." At sea, however, officers worked out "fleet problems."[33]

Commentaries drawn from the exercises reflected the belief that strategy was more than an intellectual pursuit. CINCUS Adm. Hilary Jones concluded at the end of the first fleet problem that "book knowledge, while desirable and necessary, does not ensure efficient practical operations." Adm. Harris Laning made similar observations twelve years later. The purpose of naval strategy, he remarked during the critique of Fleet Problem Sixteen, was to "place ships in position where with their weapons they can destroy the enemy." Adm. Claude C. Bloch was even more direct in his comments following the

1937 exercise. "In the final analysis," observed Bloch, "there is only one school of application for the strategist, and that school is the sea."[34]

Naval officers during the interwar years were not Clausewitzian theorists. As cast-offs from the policy-making process, they had no incentive to spend time pondering the nature of war. Politicians would decide the if and why of war. The navy had only to fight. And the sea was the whetstone of strategy, not a classroom or game board.

And in the early postwar period the navy held firm to traditional convictions. Coontz's application of the Thruster strategy implied that debate on the merits of a decisive engagement in the western Pacific was moot. Exercises held between 1925 and 1928 similarly sidestepped close examination of sea control. There were certainly valuable lessons learned in these early exercises. Submarines were deemed too slow to keep up during the envisioned transit across the Pacific. A fleet cruising disposition was developed to protect it from the submarine threat. USS *Langley* offered hints of the utility of carrier aviation. Important strategic and tactical issues were identified. But the emphasis of early simulation was how to get the fleet to its destination intact. Not one of the first eight exercises examined how the decisive battle would be accomplished. The oversight was not unintentional. At issue in the 1920s was not the navy's fear that sea control was no longer relevant. Quite the opposite was going on. Naval officers were confident that the genie of technology was bottled up. As long as the battleships arrived in fighting form, sea control would naturally follow. There appeared to be no urgency to modify the doctrine.

Fleet Problems in the 1930s: The Genie Escapes

It is understandable why Mahan rejected the notion that weapons influenced strategy. His argument was founded entirely on a historical period largely devoid of technological innovation. But he was also concerned that the pace of technological change in his own time might subordinate strategy to tactics. Sea control offered order, stability, and control. The doctrine appeared to have its desired effect on at least one type of new weapon. By the end of the decade naval officers could argue that the underwater dimension of naval warfare constituted no threat to the canon. Fleet commanders in exercises became increasingly comfortable using their own submarines against enemy warships. Somewhat paradoxically, they also appeared confident that enemy submarines would not deter the fleet from its sea-control mission. In the April 1928 exercise, for instance, Blue fleet commander Adm. Louis de

Steiger successfully evaded an Orange force of submarines and cruisers on a transit from the U.S. west coast to Hawaii. De Steiger had his faster ships tow vessels incapable of sustaining the twelve-knot transit speed. Additionally, the admiral employed an antisubmarine screen of concentric rings of escorts extending twelve miles from his battleships. Finally, anticipating that his opponent would place his forces along the shortest route, de Steiger selected a more southerly course.[35]

The early fleet problems shaped a perception that the concept of a fleet submarine was flawed. De Steiger's success reinforced the corollary to the idea. If U.S. submarines could not keep up with the fleet, then certainly enemy submarines could be avoided as well. And if enemy submarines could not be avoided, then they would have to fight through rings of destroyers and aircraft. Underwater warfare technology appeared safely bottled up and for the present posed no threat to sea-control doctrine.

The problem was that there were two genies in the bottle. During the 1920s naval aviators avoided prophesy and focused instead on the practical aspects of flying at sea. Given that the first carrier was a converted collier that made only fourteen knots and carried only fourteen airplanes, humility seemed the order of the day. Battleship admirals accepted naval aviation as an auxiliary to the sea-control mission. Airplanes would help search for the enemy, defend the fleet from enemy air attack, and spot for the battleships during the climactic naval engagement.

Naval officers molded naval aviation to fit comfortably within the sea-control paradigm. Like Mahan, they were confident that technological change would not alter their conception of naval warfare. Their confidence was actually complacency, which in the 1930s was shaken by the second genie. In 1928 *Langley* was joined by two fleet carriers capable of speeds exceeding the fastest battleship and carrying seventy-two aircraft. Technological innovations also produced airplanes capable of dropping bombs on a moving target with exceptional accuracy. Warfare simulation married the new technology to an operational setting. While the notion of using airplanes in an attack role had been practiced as far back as Fleet Problem One, the incidences failed to generate much enthusiasm in postexercise critiques. Adm. William Pratt's decision to detach *Saratoga* from the protection of the Black fleet and conduct a dawn air attack on the Panama Canal during Fleet Problem Nine shook the old order and incited CINCUS Adm. Henry Wiley's criticism in his postexercise remarks. "The decision of Commander Black to detach SARATOGA and the OMAHA from his striking force," CINCUS observed, "was a move which placed this valuable carrier unit in a position of grave peril." At any point during the operation the opposing fleet might have discovered the carrier and easily overpowered the single cruiser Pratt had dragged along for protection. In Wiley's opinion, aviation had proven only that it had "found its place in the Fleet." When CINCUS concluded that nothing in the exercise altered his conviction that the battleship was "the final arbiter of Naval destiny," certainly the ghost of Mahan smiled.[36]

Pratt's use of aviation in Fleet Problem Nine was truly significant. He had detached a portion of his fleet beyond the protection of the battleships. He had also disrupted the choreography of sea control. The first objective was not the opposing fleet but the canal. And yet Pratt failed to shake Wiley's faith in sea control. That is because Wiley did not judge Pratt's actions as revolutionary but as merely radical. A revolutionary act would have to be explained. A radical maneuver could be easily dismissed. Pratt did not help his cause. Soon after launching its planes, *Saratoga* was engaged by enemy battleships and judged sunk by an observer who was also a naval aviator. Pratt's comments following the exercise were also problematic. In his opinion, accomplishing the strategic objective of destroying the canal justified his actions, even if that meant losing the carrier. Pratt added that *Saratoga* had been attacked while recovering her planes. Had it been actual war, he would have moved the carrier beyond the range of the surface threat and sacrificed his returning planes.[37]

Wiley's response to Pratt's accomplishment appeared to favor orthodoxy. But in May 1929 William Veazie Pratt became CINCUS. The radical was now in charge of fleet training. Pratt responded by putting sea control to the test in the spring and summer of 1930. Fleet Problems Ten and Eleven were held in the Caribbean. The venue implied war with Britain, but the geography could have just as easily suited a western Pacific scenario. Both exercises were designed as contests for sea control. Opposing fleet commanders had the full array of naval weapons for their use. There is no indication that Pratt used his position as CINCUS to influence the strategies developed by the fleet commanders or to orchestrate the exercises beyond developing the initial scenarios. As it turned out, he did not have to.

The stark contrast in perspectives between the opposing fleet commanders in Fleet Problem Ten suited Pratt's designs. Blue fleet commander Louis Nulton, representing the United States, adhered to the canon. He decided to "seek the enemy fleet for a decisive battle." Anticipating that his opponent would adopt an identical course of action, Nulton choreographed events to lead to the climactic engagement. Submarines would proceed independently and harass the opposing fleet. Cruisers would scout for the enemy fleet

Black fleet commander in Fleet Problem Nine, Adm. William Veazie Pratt detached his aircraft carrier USS Saratoga *to execute a surprise attack on the Panama Canal. Pratt's real contribution to changing navy attitudes, however, came as CINCUS during Fleet Problem Ten, when he chastised Blue fleet commander Adm. Louis Nulton for his overly conservative use of naval aviation. Courtesy U.S. Naval Institute.*

and protect the battleships from light surface forces. Nulton's two carriers, stationed close to the battleships, would defend against air attack, scout for the enemy carrier, and spot for Blue battleships. Destroyers would conduct a torpedo attack on the enemy battleships to coincide with the first salvo from Nulton's own battle line.[38]

History seemed to be on Nulton's side. He had developed a plan that in his mind had been validated over centuries. His strict order of events, culminating in a decisive engagement, was both orderly and economical. The plan epitomized naval efficiency. But on March 14 Nulton experienced the one factor that complicated sea control. Instead of the much-anticipated gun engagement, what occurred instead were waves of dive bombers attacking Nulton's carriers and battleships. Black fleet commander Adm. William C. Cole ignored tradition, detached his carrier from his main body, and ordered it to locate and attack the Blue fleet.[39]

Mahan admitted that at times a fleet commander might intentionally send his ships pell-mell against the enemy in an uncontrollable naval action known as a melee. He cautioned, however, that it was a phenomenon in which "skill was reduced to a minimum, and is not the best that can be done with the elaborate and mighty weapons of this age."[40] But what Mahan objected to in 1890, and Nulton failed to comprehend forty years later, were the implications of new weapons. Aviation challenged the notion that order in battle was the most efficient and economical means of achieving sea control. The sudden appearance of dive bombers overhead introduced a destabilizing aspect on warfare that could not be ignored. Nulton himself admitted during the postexercise critique that events on March 14 had proceeded with "astounding rapidity." And if airplanes could be unleashed against capital ships, how might that affect the economy of the decisive battle? Fleet Problem Ten addressed both issues. Cole had demonstrated that technology made the melee relevant in modern naval warfare. Even though Black and Blue fleet battleships did manage a gun engagement at the end of the exercise, the event was anticlimactic and hardly decisive. Umpires concluded that only one ship on each side had been reduced to a sinking condition.[41]

The moment was not lost on Pratt. Nulton's actions were an indictment on old ways of thinking. The objective of the exercise had been to secure use of the Caribbean. To CINCUS, Nulton ignored the broad objective and instead focused on the specific mission of destroying the opposing fleet. Neither fleet had been given a decisive advantage in strength, a point Pratt made clear in his criticism of the Blue fleet commander. In his view, Nulton had "no better than an even chance" of winning a decisive battle, an opinion that appeared to have been born out by the exercise.[42]

The lessons of the exercise were not ignored during Fleet Problem Eleven the following month. The only significant change to the scenario was the absence of Nulton, who was elevated to the position of chief observer for the exercise. But while the scenario remained the same, it was obvious that the previous exercise had a noticeable effect on the perspectives of the opposing fleet commanders. Although they did not discount the possibility of a battleship engagement, neither fleet commander viewed decisive battle alone as the most prudent use of force to obtain the assigned objectives.

Admiral Cole, who had surprised Nulton in the previous exercise and was now in command of the Blue fleet, determined that the best course of action to prevent the Black fleet from gaining control of the Caribbean was to make life miserable for his adversary. Consequently, the possibility of a major engagement was not an immediate priority. Instead, Cole would keep his Blue fleet concentrated, use his aircraft to attack the Black fleet at extended ranges, and only commit his fleet when it was obvious that he had an overwhelming advantage. Vice Adm. Lucius Bostwick, Cole's opponent in the exercise, was equally careful. He also decided not to plunge headfirst into a decisive naval engagement. An advanced task force would seize a base in the Haiti-Cuba-Jamaica area. Once secure in the area, more units of the Black fleet would arrive to strengthen Bostwick's position in the region.[43]

The thinking of both admirals was validated when plans were placed into action on April 14. Operations for the next four days were dominated by engagements between cruisers, carrier and land-based aircraft, and submarines. A final engagement between Blue and Black battleships, which occurred on April 18, lasted only one hour and thirty-five minutes. But ardent Mahanians would have been disappointed by the final results. No clear winner in the engagement was identified. And unlike the Glorious First of June, which was fought solely by ships of the line, aircraft, submarines, destroyers, and cruisers continued to engage the battleships, as they were engaging each other.[44]

William Pratt recognized the implications of technology. As CINCUS he used warfare simulation to demonstrate to his subordinates that new weapons disrupted the choreography inherent in traditional notions of sea control. Not every naval officer, however, was as receptive to the changes technology might bring. Rear Adm. Jehu V. Chase, Pratt's relief as CINCUS in September 1930, appeared intent on returning the navy to its roots. One month after assuming command, Chase submitted to *Proceedings* his perspective on the appropriate use of the fleet. He reaffirmed that battleships were still the "backbone of the fleet." All other ships were designed to protect them from attack and to assist them in accomplishing their purpose of destroying enemy battleships.[45] Implied in the article was that not every naval officer had been converted by aviation. There could be inferred a hint of anxiety as well. The Mahanian *Weltanschauung* (world view) rejected technology as a determining factor in naval strategy. In the crucible of warfare simulation, however, fleet commanders were learning just the opposite. Airplanes were emerging as an irritant to sea-control purists. Naval officers were beginning to learn the consequences of one-dimensional thinking as naval warfare was evolving into multiple dimensions.

The implications of technology did more than complicate the procedural coherence of sea control. Modern weapons challenged the relationship between naval warfare and geography. To Mahan geography was one of several important criteria for determining whether a nation could become a sea power. When it came to advancing the sea-control argument, however, landmasses were not considered major obstacles. British control of Gibraltar, for example, certainly impeded France's ability to move naval forces between the Atlantic and Mediterranean. But in an age when weather controlled ship movements and gun ranges were measured in hundreds of yards, even a strategically situated rock like Gibraltar did not prevent the French from escaping to the open sea. And as the French Navy learned in Aboukir Bay and Nelson demonstrated at Copenhagen, geography could just as easily be a strategic liability.

Mahanian sea-control doctrine favored a geo-strategic vision in which naval adversaries were separated by a large swath of open ocean. The vision seemed to point to Britain as the most appropriate sea power to fight. There was only one problem. The increasingly cordial relations between the two Atlantic powers, culminating in an alliance during World War I, made war with Britain unlikely. A more realistic adversary lay in the most western extremes of the Pacific, where, unlike the Atlantic, the ocean between the United States and Japan was dotted with dozens of island chains. The navy initially solved the geo-strategic problem without compromising its doctrine. War planners placed their faith in the speed of the fleet. A fast transit, they believed, would impede Japanese interdiction operations from her island possessions in the central Pacific.

The Thruster vision of War Plan Orange transformed the geography of the Pacific to fit the conceptual parameters of the navy's sea-control doctrine. The plan emphasized efficiency. Intermediate island chains were erased to make the great battle for sea control in the western Pacific possible. Planners did not neglect the likelihood of opposition as the fleet moved across the Pacific. But they framed Japanese naval operations to conform to Mahan's notion of economy. The Japanese were expected to attrite the U.S. fleet using light forces, such as destroyers, cruisers, and submarines. They would not commit their capital ships to a fleet action until the U.S. fleet had reached the western Pacific.[46]

So long as the threat was limited to submarines and surface ships the U.S. Navy's commitment to sea control could be argued as sound. The problem was that planners and fleet commanders failed to fully appreciate the pace of technological change going on around them. It would not be enemy submarines but airplanes that made the geography of the Pacific relevant. Ships could not outrun aircraft. The increasing capabilities of long-range patrol airplanes made evasion equally difficult. A more startling dimension of aviation was being demonstrated through simulation. As Fleet Problems Nine, Ten, and Eleven illustrated, aircraft were becoming more effective tools for attacking surface ships.

Events overseas pointed to darkening skies in the western Pacific. Japan annexed Manchuria in September 1931 and attacked Shanghai the following year. In 1933 Japan left the League of Nations yet refused to relinquish control of the Mandates. These alarming developments were made more ominous for navy planners by the army's apparent change of heart over the fate of the Philippines. Gen. Stanley Embick, director of the Army War Plans Division, labeled the "through ticket" vision of Orange "an act of madness." Embick believed that the Japanese, no longer restrained by the League, would move quickly to fortify their island possessions and threaten the flank of a trans-Pacific advance. The fleet, he warned, could get to the western Pacific either quickly or in one piece. It could not accomplish both simultaneously.[47]

Naval officers increasingly began to share Embick's concern. It was not long after the introduction of the fleet carrier and dive bomber that a conceptual comparison to the Pacific islands and airplanes was integrated into War Plan Orange. Plan O-1 Orange, also known as the "Royal Road," ended Thruster control over Pacific strategy by arguing that aviation made the central Pacific islands relevant. "The increasing range of aircraft and the advanced preparation of adequate and well defended airfields," planners cautioned, "will steadily extend to seaward the area into which BLUE Fleet may not penetrate without being subject to serious attack from shore based air forces." To add urgency they estimated that Japan already had suitable sites in the Marshalls, Carolines, and Marianas and would soon have twenty-five-hundred army and navy aircraft. The navy could no longer ignore the Mandates. The fleet would have to fight its way across the Pacific.[48]

Interestingly, aspects of a revised Orange plan were being incorporated into the navy's strategic exercises even before the "Royal Road" was written. The March 1932 fleet problem, for example, examined the movement of the fleet, accompanied by a constructive expeditionary force, to seize an intermediate island base simulated by designated sites along the U.S. west coast. But as no opposition forces had been positioned ashore, the exercise was of limited value beyond the transit phase. Naval officers needed a more realistic setting to test the relationship between Orange and their sea-control doctrine. The solution pointed to Midway. The atoll was only eleven hundred miles from Hawaii and within the cruising radius of the fleet, yet distant enough to offer a reasonable simulation of an overseas transit. Additionally, several smaller atolls along the way were suitable for use by advanced detachments of seaplanes. And if for no other than symbolic reasons, Midway was at least in the general direction the navy intended on heading.

The use of an actual Pacific atoll in simulation provided a catalyst for thinking beyond the rigid framework of Mahanian sea-control doctrine. CINCUS Joseph Mason Reeves, the first naval aviator to command the U.S. fleet, made Midway the centerpiece of the scenario for Fleet Problem Sixteen in May 1935. The exercise was formulated to examine the advance of a White (U.S.) fleet across the Pacific against attrition attacks from a Black (Japan) fleet, culminating in the seizure of an advanced base by the White fleet. The White fleet held a ten to six advantage in battleships over the Black fleet and had two fleet carriers to Black's one. Black held a distinctive advantage in submarines (nineteen to six), and had forty-five shore-based aircraft assigned to the defense of Midway. In order to induce the opposing fleets

Adm. Joseph Mason Reeves (front row, center), an early pioneer in the development of naval aviation, was William Pratt's air commander in Fleet Problem Nine and advised employing USS Saratoga *as an independent task force to attack the Panama Canal. As the first naval aviator to become CINCUS, he made Midway the centerpiece for Fleet Problem Fifteen, providing an early catalyst for thinking beyond the rigid framework of Mahanian sea-control doctrine. Courtesy U.S. Naval Institute.*

to action, Reeves provided both commanders two similar objectives from which to choose. Decision would be achieved by either the capture/defense of Midway or defeat of the opposing fleet.[49]

Reeves intended to accomplish what CINCUS William Pratt had done in Fleet Problem Ten. An anomaly was intentionally introduced to complicate the strategic thinking of the fleet commanders. On both occasions the anomaly was the air weapon. In 1930 Pratt used carrier aviation to test his fleet commanders. Five years later Reeves placed forty-five airplanes on Midway and turned the island into an aircraft carrier. Yet while Louis Nulton had shown no inclination to budge beyond the comfortable confines of Mahan, his counterpart demonstrated a more liberated appreciation of multidimensional warfare. Adm. Harris Laning decided that the reduction and seizure of Midway outweighed an attempt to initially induce the Black fleet to decisive battle.[50]

Whether Laning read Mahan extensively is unknown. It appears from his plan that he understood Mahan's axiom that history was the wellspring of strategy. The difference was that Laning ignored the age of sail and instead developed a strategy based on the contemporary history of modern naval warfare. Upon departing Pearl Harbor on May 15, Laning immediately divided his fleet into three parts. A cruiser division was dispatched at top speed to Midway to conduct a nighttime attack with its embarked aircraft. A carrier task force was sent towards Midway by a northern route to locate and attrite the opposing Black fleet. Laning, with his own main body of battleships, constructive transports, and the carrier *Saratoga,* slipped to the south and west to avoid detection by Black long-range aircraft.[51]

The plan worked to near perfection. The cruisers arrived off Midway after dark on May 16 and launched their aircraft in the moonlight just after midnight. The chief umpire judged that the attack resulted in the destruction of twenty-four of the forty-five Black aircraft, with the loss of only three White planes. Laning's invasion force arrived in the vicinity of Midway four days later. During the late afternoon of May 21 his fleet beat off an air attack from the remaining Midway-based aircraft and during the night defended the transports against attacks from destroyers and cruisers. Laning achieved his strategic objective by getting his constructive amphibious force safely to Midway. Only his carrier task force failed in their mission to find and attack the Black fleet.[52]

The exercise ended just as the Black and White battleships began to engage one another on the morning of May 22. CINCUS subsequently judged the action as irrelevant. The loss of a patrol plane the previous night forced

Reeves to redirect all air operations to search for the missing crew. In his opinion the removal of the air component made the remainder of the exercise inconclusive.[53] What had been made relevant in the exercise, however, was how aviation was making geography relevant to the sea-control process. Fleet Problem Sixteen became the template for future exercises held in the Pacific. In May 1937 Adm. Claude Bloch appropriated much of Laning's script to achieve his objective of securing a fleet base on the Hawaiian island of Oahu during Fleet Problem Eighteen. Two separate carrier task forces were used this time to reduce enemy defenses at Midway and at a smaller atoll closer to Hawaii. Bloch, like Laning, successfully achieved the objective for the exercise. But while Laning had reached Midway with his main forces relatively unscathed, Bloch's experience was far more demanding. His main body of battleships, fleet carriers, and transports was engaged nearly continuously by the enemy. Shore-based aircraft and submarines began harassing his fleet shortly after the exercise began on May 5. Enemy carrier aircraft joined in the following day. On May 8 Bloch had to fend off simultaneous attacks from cruisers, dive bombers, land-based aircraft, submarines, and battleships. Enemy dive bombers conducted one more attack on Bloch as he neared his destination before CINCUS signaled that the exercise had ended.[54]

Bloch estimated that in the four-day fight his fleet had damaged or destroyed three of four enemy battleships, its only fleet carrier, nineteen of twenty destroyers, between six and eight submarines, and numerous aircraft. As to his own force, he believed that he had lost only two light cruisers, three destroyers, three of twelve transports, and only one of his three fleet carriers. He also pointed out that his fleet had successfully established a fleet base at Lahaina. Bloch went on to identify several valuable lessons that he had learned, such as the positioning of his fleet carriers, use of independent task forces, and capabilities of shore-based patrol aircraft. His comments show that the exercise also shaped the way he thought from a doctrinal perspective. Bloch did not conceptualize his experience in strictly Mahanian terms. He did not dismiss the importance of engaging the enemy's naval forces. But neither did he explain events within the strict choreography of the sea-control canon. The notion of inducing his opponent to a decisive engagement is nowhere to be found in Bloch's comments.[55] His experience in simulation pointed out a conceptual problem that Mahan would not have been able to answer. What was a commander to do when battle no longer mattered?

The significance of the revised Orange plan was not that it reflected a complete break with Mahan's concept of sea control. In fact, the plan reinforced key aspects of his doctrine. The navy's mission was still to achieve sea control in the western Pacific. Destroying the Japanese fleet remained the fleet's principal objective. The opportunity for a decisive engagement was implied in the plan. And once sea control had been achieved, an economic blockade would be imposed on Japan. What the "Royal Road" added to the navy's conception of future war, which Mahan's vision lacked, was sophistication and depth. It was not enough, the planners argued, to establish a presence in the western Pacific. The fleet had to be able to sustain offensive operations. This broader definition of presence required the establishment of a base that would not have to rely on the fleet for its defense. It also demanded a supply line that could exist with little demand on fleet escorts. Finally, presence meant that when the decisive engagement occurred, be it three days or three months after the fleet entered the western Pacific, the navy would be in superior fighting strength.[56]

Technology made the Mandates essential to the Pacific strategy. Within the island chains were suitable locations for fleet anchorages. Removing the Japanese would further result in a reasonably secure supply line back to the United States, reducing the need for extensive escort. The anticipated amphibious operations were additionally viewed as opportunities for "fine training for the stiffer operations" that would be undertaken later in the war. Finally, naval officers learned that the progressive approach was aggressive but in a sensible and careful way. They employed very un-Nelson-like language to distance themselves from the Thruster strategy. The advantages of the previous plan, they pointed out, were "more glamorous than real. It is certainly not the methodical and soundest course for a stronger belligerent." A progressive advance through the Mandates, they concluded, would not force the fleet to "accept unsound risks and trust to chance."[57]

In Mahan's mind the path towards gaining control of the sea was orderly and had distinct breakpoints. But the culminating point was always a decisive engagement. Technology, principally in the form of aviation, blurred the distinctions. Bloch and his colleagues were not abandoning sea control. Destroying the enemy's naval forces remained the principal objective. But it was becoming increasingly clear that the objective could not be attained as efficiently as Mahan suggested. Technology was having a dramatic effect on doctrine. Though naval officers might desire a decisive battleship engagement, modern weapons were making it difficult to achieve. War at sea was becoming less about one specific fight and more about fighting.

In April 1940 Adm. Adolphus Andrews was given one final opportunity to distinguish himself as a fleet commander. Despite the fact that a real war was being waged in Europe, President Roosevelt "suggested" in a meeting with CNO Harold Stark that the 1940 fleet problem be held in the Pacific. FDR additionally desired that the fleet operate as far to the southwest as was practicable, though the CNO inferred from the discussion that the final decision on the geographic parameters of the exercises would be left to CINCUS.[58]

After giving careful consideration to the president's desires, CINCUS Adm. J. O. Richardson decided that fuel constraints made operations far from Hawaii impractical. Instead, he incorporated FDR's vision into the scenario leading up to the exercise. The Philippines were in Purple (Japanese) hands. On April 8 war was declared between Purple and Maroon, a maritime power in the eastern Pacific. The following day it was learned that a Purple expeditionary force, accompanied by a large fleet, had departed its base in Manila. On April 16 the Maroon radio station on Wake reported the approach of a Purple landing force before it went off the air.[59] CINCUS advised Maroon fleet commander Andrews that he should assume the most probable intention of Purple was to seize an advanced base in the Hawaiian Islands. Andrews was further warned that the enemy would also attempt to eliminate U.S. forces occupying the small atolls leading to the main islands. Richardson instructed the Maroon fleet commander to "destroy units of the PURPLE Fleet in order to prevent seizure of advanced base at Lahaina by PURPLE."[60]

The predominant influence on Andrews's thinking was evident as he formulated the mission in his "Estimate of the Situation." He inferred from his orders that CINCUS had assigned him the "task" of destroying Purple fleet units in order to achieve the "purpose" of preventing the seizure of Lahaina. But what did CINCUS mean by "Purple fleet units"? Andrews deduced that his "purpose" was to achieve sea control. He further considered the landing forces as not constituting part of his "task," which made attacking the transports an "insufficient" means of achieving his principal objective. In his judgment the purpose of his fleet was to engage and destroy the enemy fleet. He therefore decided to concentrate his ships in the vicinity of Lahaina, interpose his forces between the enemy and the anticipated landing site, and engage the Purple fleet in a decisive day engagement. Once the major elements of the enemy fleet had been destroyed, Andrews anticipated that his forces would then chase down and destroy the transports.[61]

Mahan would have approved of the plan. Unfortunately, it failed. Purple fleet commander Adm. Charles P. Snyder had no intention of following the script. Snyder instead used his capital ships to protect his transports. He would engage Maroon forces only when necessary to drive them away from the transports. Snyder's strategy worked. His forces arrived intact in the vicinity of Lahaina Roads on the night of April 23. Awaiting him was Andrews's Maroon fleet. What confronted Andrews, however, was not what he anticipated. Snyder had divided his fleet. Interposed between Andrews and the Purple main body lay a covering force of cruisers and destroyers. Both fleets' battleships managed to converge to within gun range in the final hours of the exercise. The engagement, however, was of little consequence. Snyder's expeditionary force had reached its destination.[62]

Andrews's failure to achieve decisive results during Fleet Problem Twenty-One did not mean that Mahan was obsolete. His sea-control canon had provided the navy with a conceptual bridge between the age of sail and the age of steam. The doctrine sustained organizational continuity for decades, offered answers when operational experiences were lacking, and shielded the navy from its detractors. But while naval officers in general clearly understood what Mahan said, a growing number recognized that history had not ended with the age of sail. It was easy for Mahan, whose focus was entirely on the past, to reject the notion that weapons would influence doctrine. Naval officers, however, could not so casually dismiss the present. The implications of technology, even in the artificial environment of warfare simulation, could not be ignored.

Even one of Mahan's most ardent supporters recognized the changing environment. One year after his biography of Mahan was published, Capt. W. D. Puleston attempted to place the technological genie in context. In a *Proceedings* article entitled, "A Re-examination of Mahan's Concept of Sea Power," Puleston admitted that it was time for a "dispassionate" re-examination of Mahan's ideas. "With the increasing improvement of aviation," he wrote, "it is not impossible that the relative positions of air and surface will be reversed; aviation may become our major weapon and the fleet only a sustaining member like the Army." But Puleston was adamant that technology had not made Mahan irrelevant. The most that might happen was that one type of weapon would replace another. The historical foundation of Mahanian doctrine, he argued, was still pertinent. The employment of naval force to deny an enemy access to the sea remained valid. Puleston went so far as to speculate that Mahan would not only have approved of aviation but would have enthusiastically incorporated airplanes into his sea-control doctrine in operations against the enemy's navy.[63] Puleston was right in the sense that the name on the bottle remained the same. What he did not understand, unlike a growing number of his colleagues, was how new ingredients were changing the elixir inside.

CHAPTER 8

Conclusion

Between 1923 and 1940, the U.S. Navy conducted major fleet exercises designed to allow senior officers to work through strategic issues in an operational setting. The exercises, known as fleet problems, were intended to simulate conditions of a future war. Yet they often reflected an inexact view of the world, vied with political reality, and cast doubts on many of the navy's most cherished principles. Despite these limitations, warfare simulation became an important medium for organizational learning and reform. Operational experiences exposed naval officers to the interdependence between technology and doctrine. Time-honored beliefs on the proper use of naval forces were adapted to accommodate modern weapons.

Given that much of the historical literature on the United States has characterized the interwar navy as slavishly devoted to Mahan, it is interesting that naval officers felt compelled to conduct strategically oriented exercises at all. The international climate was certainly not conducive to officers positing a future war. World opinion, led by the United States, assigned much of the blame for World War I to the existence of the large battle fleets Mahan and his colleagues had endorsed. Diplomats opted for disarmament to avoid repeating the past. But naval arms control did little to alter the mindset of U.S. naval officers. Ironically, diplomats achieved with arms limitation what Woodrow Wilson had pledged through naval construction in 1916. The U.S. Navy had become, at least on paper, second to none. Even the apparent indifference of civilian policy makers to naval matters following the Washington Naval Conference had a bright side. Naval officers were free to think and plan with little interference.

Left to its own devices, the navy devised annual exercises designed to refine its vision of a future war and test the mettle of its senior leaders. Critics of the interwar navy would argue that the fleet problems were just the operational extension of the navy's doctrinal myopia. Naval officers were too wedded to a vision of decisive engagements between battleships to realize the full potential of new weapons. Those criticisms seem valid, particularly as the first fleet problems do not appear especially innovative. Fleet Problem One tested the defenses of the Panama Canal with a single airplane, hardly a challenge to the Mahanian canon. Fleet Problems Two through Four reinforced the conviction that victory in a future war with Japan would be decided by a decisive naval battle in the western Pacific. Exercises from 1925 to 1928 focused principally on scouting, submarine, and antisubmarine warfare. At issue in most of these exercises was the importance of getting the battleships to the fight intact. Airplanes and submarines were accordingly employed to fit within the Mahanian paradigm. Enemy submarines came to be viewed as a credible but manageable threat. Marines were deemed necessary, but not critical to, the sea-control mission. Though decisive engagements were anticipated in many of these early problems, none actually transpired. Naval officers might have been disappointed, but the absence of climactic battleship fights did not upset what they thought was a reasonably sound doctrine.

To conclude that there was nothing new going on in these initial exercises, however, ignores the dialectic that was emerging between doctrine and modern technology. Submarines proved too slow to be useful as the eyes of the fleet. Rather than abandon them to coastal defense, naval officers adapted them to use as independent attack platforms. Similarly, the early fleet problems demonstrated that carrier aviation, though in its crawling stage, could be used in other ways than just spotting for the battleships. Neither was the navy's geo-strategic vision immune to lessons learned in simulation. In stark contrast to the efforts of diplomats, naval officers decided that preparation for a future war was prudent. Japan appeared to them the most likely adversary. Arms control gave the U.S. fleet only a slight superiority over Japan's naval forces. U.S. Navy planners simply added imaginary ships in their exercises to fill out the fleet. During the 1920s the "through ticket" dominated planning for a future Pacific war. But even "thrusters" like Adm. Robert Coontz recognized that the supply and troop ships that slowed the fleet's transit could not be left unprotected. And a slower transit across the Pacific intimated that islands, and the Japanese aircraft and submarines that would operate from them, might indeed be significant.

The early fleet problems might have reinforced much of what Mahan believed a navy was meant to do. But warfare simulation also left the door ajar for different approaches, should conditions warrant. In 1929 during Fleet Problem Nine, Adm. William Veazie Pratt used dive bombers from the new fleet carrier *Saratoga* to attack the Panama Canal. The fact that Pratt used airpower to achieve his objective was not novel. Edward Eberle had used the same strategy in 1923. What was new was that Pratt had sent his fast carrier well beyond the protection of his battleships. It was a plan that only aviators might have appreciated, which is perhaps why CINCUS Henry Wiley played down Pratt's accomplishment. What Wiley could not so easily dismiss was that the Mahanian canon had been modified to conform to the capabilities of a new technology. Worse yet, new thinking had come not from aviators but from a battleship sailor.

The incorporation of fast carriers and dive bombers in exercises after Fleet Problem Nine sharpened the doctrinal dialectic created by the earlier fleet problems. Succeeding problems contributed to a new synthesis envisioning how a modern naval war might be waged. In the 1930 exercise, carrier-based dive bombers disrupted the choreography of Adm. Louis Nulton's plan for decisive engagement between battleships. Independent carrier task forces became common fixtures in subsequent exercises, and admirals proved increasingly willing to use airpower against capital ships. More capable aircraft began stretching the dimensions of naval warfare beyond what had been experienced with submarines. Critics of the express version of War Plan Orange took notice. The 1932 fleet problem, run by CINCUS Frank Schofield, was a simplified version of a cautious advance across the Pacific. Two years later, officers in the War Plans Division articulated what had been suggested by simulation: airplanes made geography relevant. By the 1937 exercise, naval officers were simulating a Pacific war fought in an area bounded by the U.S. west coast, the Aleutian Islands, Hawaii, and Midway. Carrier task forces, dive bombers, marine expeditionary forces, independent submarine striking groups, and antisubmarine screens were woven into exercises that participants believed to be both realistic and instructive.

The fleet problems offered invaluable learning opportunities for naval officers. Planners developed exercises incorporating actual naval vessels in an operational setting. The scenarios that they fashioned became increasingly sophisticated and complex. Senior officers developed strategic plans, put them into action at sea, and experienced success and failure. Subordinate commanders not only gained insight into the thinking of senior navy leadership but also compared those thoughts with actual experiences. Finally, junior officers who attended the postexercise critiques were exposed to dimensions of naval warfare hidden from them in their watch stations on the bridge or in the cockpit. The officers who fought in World War II were not accidents of history, nor were they a new generation of Young Turks. Much of their behavior in actual combat was conditioned by experiences gained from nearly two decades of practice.

Warfare simulation proved to be an extremely important tool in the development of the navy during the interwar years. Still, the fleet problems did not prepare the navy for every contingency it would face in war. Navy planners, for example, concentrated on war in the Pacific and, with the exception of Fleet Problem Twenty, neglected the Atlantic. Artificialities inherent in simulation also left important issues unresolved. Naval officers retained their belief that antisubmarine warfare was little more than a problem of tactics and resources. They consequently disregarded in their exercises the complexity of a convoy composed of both civilian merchants and warships. The navy similarly held little regard for the strategic importance of amphibious warfare. Marines became increasingly important as Cautionaries assumed control of Pacific war planning. But that concern failed to rise to a commensurate level in the fleet problems. Whether or not marines actually participated did not seem to matter. Finally, the confrontation of Mahan with modern technology did not lead to the wholesale conversion of the naval officer corps. Many senior officers retained a stubborn allegiance to the canon, even when their failures in fleet problems, such as Louis Nulton in 1930 and Adolphus Andrews in 1939 and 1940, demonstrated the consequences of relying too much on the past for answers to present-day problems.

The fleet problems did not provide as much clarity as naval officers desired. Many grasped the implications of modern technology for doctrine. Others ignored lessons that appeared to challenge long-held notions. The differing receptions demonstrate that the interwar navy does not fit any theoretical model of organizational transformation neatly. By its nature, warfare simulation could not answer every question with precision. The fleet problems envisioned events contrary to the efforts of diplomats. Submarines and airplanes challenged conventional wisdom, yet enough limitations were evident in the new technologies to merit caution. Fleet commanders had to reconcile their desire to directly control operations with weapons that operated beyond the visual horizon. The fleet problems were not perfect representations of reality, but they did succeed in demonstrating the consequences of conformist thinking. Officers learned how complex naval warfare could be, and as a result they developed a reasonable sense of where and how the next war would be fought.

Much of what was learned was put into practice when the anticipated war appeared imminent. Planners, for instance, conjured up a Red (British) threat in the exercises held in the Caribbean. Yet they understood all along that Britain was more a diplomatic problem than a potential military adversary. CNO William Leahy hinted as much in the general outline he provided to CINCUS for Fleet Problem Twenty. In the scenario for the exercise, he wrote that "a masterly diplomatic arrangement" had occurred, which accomplished "the transfer of the Bahamas, Jamaica, and Trinidad to the United States in exchange for our cancellation of the British War debt."[1] A little more than eighteen months after the exercise, the United States exchanged fifty destroyers for basing rights in Newfoundland, Bermuda, and many British possessions in the Caribbean.

Control of the Caribbean was achieved without firing a shot. The same could not be said of the other two theaters in the navy's geopolitical vision. By the end of 1941 the navy supported a national strategy of Germany-first. Yet the presence in the Pacific fleet of the majority of the navy's battleships and aircraft carriers demonstrated that the fleet's focus was on Japan. The Destroyers for Bases Agreement in September 1940 sent an even clearer signal. The principal guarantor of security in the Atlantic was the Royal Navy. At least in one respect the navy's strategic indifference to the Atlantic was validated. By the time the United States entered World War II, the Royal Navy had all but eliminated the German and Italian surface navies. But the fleet problems also helped to blinker naval officers to the prospect that the Germans might interpret sea control differently than they did. Yates Stirling had warned back in 1919 that the submarine complicated traditional notions of sea control. Navy planners failed to integrate Stirling's ideas into their exercises. As a result, the German strategy of sea denial reappeared, much to the navy's surprise and consternation, off the eastern seaboard in the form of U-boats in January 1942.

To see the connection between the fleet problems and the U-boat crisis one has only to look at the person responsible for defending the eastern seaboard. Adm. Adolphus Andrews had not distinguished himself as a fleet commander in the final two exercises. His subsequent assignment as commander of the Eastern Sea Frontier reflected the navy's confidence that the war would not reach American shores. When the U-boats did make their appearance, Andrews went to the solution he was most comfortable with. Trained to view antisubmarine warfare as a managerial problem best addressed by heavily escorted convoys, he concluded that a poorly escorted convoy was worse than none. Leaving merchant vessels to ply the East and Gulf coasts individually and unprotected, Andrews assigned the few ships and aircraft at his disposal to seek out and destroy U-boats. Adm. Ernest King, who held positions as both CNO and COMINCH and whose focus was on Europe and Japan, deferred to his subordinate commander.

Adm. J. O. Richardson, Adm. Claude C. Bloch, Adm. Adolphus Andrews, and Vice Adm. Charles P. Snyder (left to right). Admiral Andrews, as a fleet commander in Fleet Problems Twenty and Twenty-one, lost to his opponent due to his unconditional acceptance of Mahan's sea-control doctrine. Andrews illustrates that while not all naval officers were willing to give up Mahan, success in strategic exercises became increasingly tied to a commander's ability to adapt Mahanian doctrine to incorporate new weapons. Admiral Snyder was Andrews's adversary in Fleet Problem Twenty-one. Courtesy U.S. Naval Institute.

The navy's geopolitical miscalculation that the British were in charge of Atlantic security, combined with its indifference to the submarine as a strategic threat, made the first months of the second Battle of the Atlantic costly in both lives and material. In this respect warfare simulation did not serve Admirals Andrews and King well, as the blinkered perceptions of both officers were nurtured in the fleet problems. Yet by its nature, simulation cannot completely reveal the exigencies of combat. Nor are its limitations always clear. Yet the underlying premise, that the submarine threat could be managed, was born out over time. The navy bears responsibility for mismanaging the early stages of the campaign, but naval officers also proved capable of modifying their perspectives to accommodate the changed environment. Coastal convoys were adopted in April 1942. By fall, U.S. Army Air Corps bombers, outfitted with radar, floodlights, and air-dropped depth charges, were being employed as long-range convoy escorts, while bombers flying from British bases were acting on ULTRA intercepts of U-boats transiting the Bay of Biscay. In the spring of 1943 escort carriers were providing protection in the hard-to-reach stretches of the mid-Atlantic. Overseeing theater-wide antisubmarine operations was an organization completely devoid of ships and aircraft, the Tenth Fleet. By May 1943 the combined effects of technology, organization, and tactics were reducing the effectiveness of the U-boats. The Battle of the Atlantic would continue until the end of the war, but the key to winning was not the development of a new strategy. Naval officers modified their preconceived notions, rolled up their sleeves, and respected underwater warfare.

Although warfare simulation contributed to the navy's early problems in the Atlantic, the fleet problems did a much better job revealing how modern weapons would affect a Pacific war. Naval officers had become comfortable with the concept of independent submarine operations as a result of the exercises. The Pearl Harbor disaster certainly simplified CNO Harold Stark's order to wage an unrestricted naval campaign against Japan. Blaming the submarine community's slow and sluggish response on a constrained peacetime training regimen, however, overlooks the freedom in which they operated in the fleet problems. More importantly, the criticism ignores the psychological strains on submarine commanders ordered to operate in Japanese-held waters with little, if any, support west of Pearl Harbor. Submarines eventually proved to be an important tool in the Pacific theater, supporting diverse missions from intelligence-gathering and rescuing downed pilots to attacking Japanese warships. And as Lt. Hyman Rickover predicted, international law proved no match for utilitarian necessity. U.S. submarines took advantage of Japan's deficient antisubmarine warfare forces and ravaged its commerce.[2] Yet while submarines did not decide sea control in the Pacific, they nevertheless made a contribution arguably as integral to final victory as the navy's surface and air forces. Having learned how to operate independent of the fleet, submarine crews demonstrated that sea control and commerce warfare not only complemented each other but could also be performed simultaneously.

While naval officers did not hesitate to employ underwater warfare to achieve their aims in the Pacific, the technology upon which victory ultimately rested was carrier aviation. The fleet problems revealed over time that carrier-based aircraft could not only operate beyond the protection of battleships but were capable of inflicting great harm on an enemy's surface forces. Fleet commanders, many of whom had spent their careers on battleships, became less constrained by tradition and more inclined to employ carriers in the role assumed to belong exclusively to the battleship. Pearl Harbor might have made the aircraft carrier a de facto replacement for the battleship as the "backbone of the fleet," but the fact that within six months of the disaster the navy achieved a significant victory with its carriers at Midway, an engagement commanded by battleship sailor Raymond Spruance, suggests that the seeds for an air navy were sown well before December 7, 1941.

Warfare simulation married modern weapons to a pragmatic vision of how the great Pacific war would be fought. Navy planners still envisioned some type of major engagement in the western Pacific. Yet over time they learned that technology and geography complicated Mahan's claim that sea control could be achieved so efficiently. The fleet problems increasingly reinforced the need for a progressive advance using Pacific atolls as forward bases. The fleet followed the script to success, with one glaring exception. Navy hesitance to fully integrate Marine Corps amphibious warfare doctrine into the fleet problems contributed to the muddled features of early amphibious operations. The problems experienced during the Guadalcanal operation in the fall of 1942 were the product of Ernest King's haphazard and indifferent approach to amphibious warfare, a mindset established during the interwar period.[3] The decision to attack Tarawa one year later was also conditioned by the navy's limited experiences in prewar exercises. The importance of these small atolls was perhaps not so much their position athwart the central Pacific advance but rather the experience they provided for naval officers who lacked confidence in amphibious operations. For CINCPAC Chester Nimitz, mistakes made in the Gilberts would be less damaging than a setback in the Marshalls, which would have given southwest Pacific commander Gen.

Douglas MacArthur increased leverage for his own campaign to liberate the Philippines.

If there was one underlying theme, though, that connected the two great naval theaters of World War II, it was sea control. Alfred Thayer Mahan had bequeathed to the modern navy a warfare doctrine derived from battles fought with great sailing ships. The canon of decisive engagements between concentrated fleets of modern battleships appealed to officers of the new steel navy, particularly when their own history offered little precedent. But unlike Mahan, who rejected all but the force of history in shaping doctrine, naval officers recognized that they could not ignore the implications of the present. The introduction of new weapons had a decidedly telling effect on sea control. Naval officers learned that they could modify or reject aspects of the canon to accommodate technology without compromising its most fundamental principle.

Fading fast, for example, was the notion that sea control in the age of three-dimensional warfare could be choreographed to a single, decisive battle. The so-called "Battle of the Atlantic" ignores the scope, duration, and nearly continuous efforts expended to defeat the U-boats. While the navy eventually reduced the effectiveness of U-boats, the submarine menace persisted until the end of the war. In the Pacific, airplanes and submarines made geography strategically relevant. As a consequence amphibious warfare eventually became part of the sea-control process and naval operations less independent of events on land. Decisive battle might have been on the minds of men like Halsey, Spruance, and Nimitz. But in a campaign of nearly continuous fighting, pragmatism prevailed over nostalgic desires to relive Trafalgar.

Nor could naval officers restrict the definition of a capital ship. From a visual perspective the long guns of a battleship might appear more impressive than a fleet carrier with aircraft on its deck. But when it was shown in exercises, and demonstrated in combat, that airplanes could sink ships at far greater distances than a battleship, naval officers came to treat aircraft carriers as capital ships.

Finally, the fleet problems loosened the grip of Mahan's maxim that technology had no effect on strategy. In the Atlantic, naval officers initially remained loyal to orthodox views. But they adapted to the U-boat threat and wound up devoting a disproportionate effort to a technology long considered a nuisance. Airplanes turned Pacific atolls into fixed aircraft carriers, making any notion of a rapid transit to the western Pacific a polite fiction. And when Japanese and American naval forces did engage, more often than not the fighting was carried out well beyond the range of shipboard guns and the direct control of the fleet commander. Carrier aviation made the melee not only possible but also an efficient way of fighting a naval war.

All of this seemed to imply that Mahan was no longer relevant. In fact, just the opposite was the case. Naval officers might have recognized how technology had complicated the orchestration of the single, decisive battle or that there might be more than one type of capital ship. But the premise of sea control, that the principal objective of a navy was an enemy's navy, remained intact. In the 1920s and 1930s sea control insulated the navy from disarmament enthusiasts, frugal politicians, and the U.S. Army. Within the service, the doctrine was a binding agent that permitted the navy to flex its muscles in new ways while keeping the body intact. The message became even more relevant in the crucible of war. The enemy fleets encountered in World War II were not entirely what Mahan had envisioned or exactly what the navy practiced against in peacetime. But naval officers, no matter what their warfare specialty, retained their commitment to Mahan's core belief. Though different weapons might be used, the enemy's naval forces remained the principal focus. Warfare simulation stimulated thinking beyond the rigid framework erected by Mahan and taught peacetime naval officers lessons that would prove invaluable in war.

APPENDIX

Chiefs of Naval Operations and Commanders-in-Chief, U.S. Fleet, 1919–42

Chiefs of Naval Operations

Robert Coontz (November 1919–July 1923)
Edward Eberle (July 1923–November 1927)
Charles F. Hughes (November 1927–September 1930)
William V. Pratt (September 1930–June 1933)
William Standley (January 1933–January 1937)
William Leahy (January 1937–August 1939)
Harold Stark (August 1939–March 1942)

Commanders-in-Chief, U.S. Fleet

Hilary P. Jones (December 1922–August 1923)
Robert Coontz (August 1923–October 1925)
Samuel S. Robison (October 1925–September 1926)
Charles F. Hughes (September 1926–November 1927)
Henry Wiley (November 1927–May 1929)
William V. Pratt (May 1929–September 1930)
Jehu V. Chase (September 1930–September 1931)
Frank Schofield (September 1931–August 1932)
Richard Leigh (August 1932–June 1933)
David Sellers (June 1933–June 1934)
Joseph M. Reeves (June 1934–June 1936)
Arthur Hepburn (June 1936–January 1938)
Claude C. Bloch (January 1938–January 1940)
J. O. Richardson (January 1940–February 1941)

Note: Lists compiled from *Register of Commissioned and Warrant Officers of the United States Navy and Marine Corps.* The register is a yearly publication, providing the current position and seniority of active-duty commissioned officers in the navy and Marine Corps. Stephen Roskill, *Naval Policy between the Wars,* 1:572–73. Charles F. Hughes and William V. Pratt are the only two officers to have ascended from CINCUS to CNO. Robert Coontz was the only officer to have moved from CNO to CINCUS. William Pratt was the only officer to have held the presidency of the Naval War College and either CINCUS or CNO.

NOTES

Chapter 1. Introduction

1. Commander-in-chief, U.S. fleet, report to the secretary of the navy, Aug. 28, 1924, "Annual Report of the Commander in Chief, U.S. Fleet—1 July 1923 to 30 June 1924," 1–4, *Annual Reports of Fleets and Task Forces of the U.S. Navy, 1920–1941*, microfilm, roll 4 (hereafter cited as *Annual Reports*). For most of the interwar period the U.S. fleet was organized into four major functional divisions. The "battle fleet," home-ported on the U.S. west coast, was comprised principally of the navy's battleships and aircraft carriers. As its name implied, navy leaders envisioned it as the principal means of achieving sea control. Assisting the battle fleet would be the "scouting fleet." Assigned to east coast ports, its cruisers and shore-based aircraft would be employed to seek out an enemy fleet and shape the naval engagement that would decide sea control. The battle fleet and scouting fleet commanders acted as opposing fleet commanders for the majority of the fleet problems. Once sea control was achieved, the "control force," comprised of destroyers, submarines, and Marine Corps expeditionary forces, would sustain it by blockading the enemy's ports and seizing bases for further fleet operations. Finally, the "fleet base force" (also known as the "fleet train") provided logistic support for the fleet.

2. "Introduction," *Records Relating to United States Navy Fleet Problems I to XXII, 1923–1941* (Washington, D.C.: National Archives and Records Service, 1974), microfilm, roll 1, 1–3 (hereafter cited as *Records*).

3. "Battle Fleet Organizational Order No. 1—23," Jan. 1, 1923, in commander-in-chief, U.S. fleet, report to secretary of the navy, July 1, 1923, "Annual Report of the Commander in Chief, U.S. Fleet 1 July 1922 to 30 June 1923," *Annual Reports*, roll 4; Ronald H. Spector, *At War at Sea: Sailors and Naval Combat in the Twentieth Century*, 134. The navy spent most of the interwar period in port. The prohibitive cost of fuel and ammunition limited major training opportunities to annual periods of "fleet concentration." In 1923, for example, the fleet concentration period lasted from February 10 to March 30. Fleet Problem One took place in the Caribbean February 19–24, leaving the remainder of the period to tactical exercises, overhaul, fleet athletic activities, and port visits. Outside of the fleet concentration period, sailors, for the most part, enjoyed a five-day workweek.

4. George W. Baer, *One Hundred Years of Sea Power*, 143; George W. Baer, "U.S. Naval Strategy, 1890–1945," *Naval War College Review* 44, no. 1 (winter 1991): 25; Ronald H. Spector, *Eagle against the Sun*, 482–83; Peter Padfield, *War beneath the Sea*, 30–31; Robert L. O'Connell, *Sacred Vessels*, 7, 281–90; William M. McBride, *Technological Change and the United States Navy*, 1–7; William M. McBride, "Challenging a Strategic

Paradigm: Aviation and the U.S. Navy Special Policy Board of 1924," in *Readings in American Naval Heritage*, ed. Department of History, United States Naval Academy, 132. Baer compares the rise of the aircraft carrier and submarine in World War II to a biological theory originally developed by Stephen J. Gould called "punctuated equilibrium," in which a "slow operational evolution" is "accelerated in a matter of hours into a huge strategic leap." The attack on Pearl Harbor "catapulted" the carrier into its role in the Pacific, and the submarine was "instantly redefined" as a weapon of unrestricted warfare. Baer implies that the focus of naval officers on December 6, 1941, was not far removed from the theories of Mahan half a century earlier. Traditional notions were simply overcome by events the following day.

Ronald Spector argues that submarine training during the interwar years emphasized caution. Safety restrictions, such as operating on the surface at night, were imposed on submarine captains. Violations resulted in a severe "dressing-down." Peter Padfield presents a similar interpretation in *War beneath the Sea*. Submarine commanding officers, he maintains, were ill-prepared for the conditions they would face in the Pacific in World War II. Submarines were prohibited from acting independently in exercises. Commanding officers were reprimanded when their boats were detected during simulated attacks. Padfield contends that such training restrictions instilled a cautious attitude within the submarine community, which contributed to the relief of nearly one-third of its commanding officers in the early stages of the war.

Another aspect of the interwar period that has focused the attention of historians is the influence of technology on navy policy. Particular interest has been directed toward the battleship. In *Sacred Vessels*, Robert O'Connell argues that naval officers suffered a myopic attachment to these capital ships. Battleships, he claims, "represented a way of life, they were the core of the naval soul, and for that reason their occupants clung to them with remarkable tenacity." O'Connell believes that this overwhelming attachment led naval officers to dismiss new technologies, such as submarines and aircraft. William McBride makes a similar claim that the technological-strategic paradigm constructed around the battleship inhibited the development of technological "anomalies." His analysis of the navy's 1924 Special Policy Board picks up on O'Connell's theme of doctrinal myopia. Secretary of the Navy Curtis Wilbur directed the Navy General Board to investigate the future capabilities of aircraft. This committee, McBride concludes, was so heavily stacked with battleship officers that naval aviation would have to wait until "the majority of the artifacts of the battleship strategy were destroyed at Pearl Harbor in 1941."

5. John Keegan, *The First World War*, 257–74. The naval encounter between the British Grand Fleet and German High Seas fleet occurred in the North Sea between May 31 and June 1, 1916. With sixty-four dreadnoughts, pre-dreadnoughts, and battlecruisers engaged in the action (in addition to a great number of cruisers, destroyers, and submarines), the battle is known as the largest naval encounter in history. Jutland's reputation as the most studied and controversial naval battle, however, stems from arguments over its ambiguous results. Germans claimed victory (which they named "the victory of the Skagerrak") because the High Seas fleet sank fifteen Royal Navy ships, including three of its newest battlecruisers, as opposed to German losses of two capital ships, ten smaller warships, and 2,551 men. Royal Navy officers claimed a strategic victory, as the Kaiser's fleet remained bottled up in the North Sea. But the enduring

perception of many Britons that the grand fleet had failed to achieve decisive results (Winston Churchill is said to have described Adm. Sir John Jellicoe, who commanded the fleet at Jutland, as the only man who could lose an entire war in a day) has contributed to the enduring controversy over the battle. "The inconclusiveness of the event," Keegan observed, "has continued to haunt the mind of the Royal Navy ever since."

Although somewhat dated, the most comprehensive narrative of Jutland is found in Arthur Marder's *From the Dreadnought to Scapa Flow*, vol. 2, *The War Years*, and vol. 3, *Jutland and After*. Although criticized for a lack of explanatory depth, Marder's work does provide an excellent assessment of the strategic perspectives of Royal Navy officers prior to the war, as well as a thorough and detailed description of the event.

6. Elting Morison, *Men, Machines, and Modern Times*, 98–122. Morison describes the reaction of senior officers to the frigate *Wampanoag*, a coal-burning ship designed after the Civil War. Despite its reputation as the fastest warship of the day, senior officers considered the frigate an expensive luxury, and further construction was cancelled. Morison argues that the navy's cultural attachment to the tradition of sail, which held steam propulsion technology as a "destructive energy in their society," doomed the *Wampanoag*.

There may, however, be more than one dimension to the definition of the term "conservative," particularly when applied to a military organization. In *Railroads and Rifles*, Dennis Showalter offered such an interpretation. Military institutions, Showalter argued, face a particular dilemma of dealing with changing circumstances without compromising their inherent responsibility for state security. The delays of incorporating a technological innovation such as the Dreyse needle gun, for example, could also be explained as a "legitimate reluctance to trust public safety to anything not thoroughly proved and tested." Bernard Brodie offered a similar argument on the relationship between naval technology and strategy in *Sea Power in the Machine Age*. While acknowledging that aviation and submarines could not be ignored in strategic algorithms, Brodie cautioned that their potential had yet to be fully realized.

One final point merits mention. Any discussion of the relationship between technology and the U.S. Navy during the interwar period cannot ignore the context of international disarmament initiatives. The navy was prohibited by a series of naval treaties from building battleships for fifteen years and restricted to a maximum of 135,000 tons in carrier construction. Additionally, while no consensus between the naval powers could be reached in the area of limiting submarine construction, language in the Washington Treaty of 1922 and London Naval Treaty of 1930 confined submarine operations to the restrictions imposed by nineteenth-century Prize Law, which required submarines to surface and ensure the safety of both crew and passengers before sinking an unarmed merchant ship.

7. An informative analysis of early warfare simulation can be found in Arden Bucholz's *Moltke, Schlieffen, and Prussian War Planning*. While Bucholz's primary purpose is to explain the growth of the German general staff within the framework of organizational theory, he identified war-gaming as one of four integral components within the general staff. The Prussian staff officer was exposed to warfare simulation in a sequence that began with board-type war games played at the Kriegsacadamie, staff rides while attached to an operational staff, and large field exercises known as Kaisermanover. While Bucholz contends that much of what went on during the

early Kaisermanover was superficial pomp and circumstance, with the expansion of the general staff in the late nineteenth century the exercises took on a more practical value. The 1907 exercises, for example, tested the integration of railroad transportation, aircraft, telephone, and wireless telegraphy. The 1910 maneuvers placed seventy-four battalions of infantry, sixty-nine artillery battalions, and fifty-eight cavalry squadrons in the field.

On the naval side, Theodore Ropp points out in *The Development of a Modern Navy* (ed. Stephen S. Roberts), early attempts by Britain to use at-sea exercises to test countermeasures to French torpedo boats. For the most part, though, the early exercises of both the Prussians and British were geographically limited in scope and focused predominantly on tactical issues.

8. Warren I. Cohen, *Empire without Tears*. Cohen challenges the notion of U.S. isolation during the interwar years.

9. Carl Von Clausewitz, *On War*, ed. Michael Howard and Peter Paret, 122.

10. Graham T. Allison, *Essence of Decision*. Allison used the Cuban Missile Crisis to introduce Organizational Behavior Theory as a model for analyzing crisis-level decision making. His work offered one of the first challenges to traditionally held conceptions of policy makers acting as a single "rational actor," whose decisions could be viewed as calculated solutions to particular strategic problems.

11. Irving Britton Holley, *Ideas and Weapons*; John Howard Morrow, *The Great War in the Air*.

12. Barry R. Posen, *The Sources of Military Doctrine*, 7–105; Stephen Peter Rosen, "Military Effectiveness: Why Society Matters," *International Security* 19, no. 4 (spring 1995): 5–31; Tami Davis Biddle, *Rhetoric and Reality in Air Warfare*; David E. Johnson, *Fast Tanks and Heavy Bombers*.

13. Barbara Levitt and James G. March, "Organizational Learning," *Annual Review of Sociology* 14 (1988): 319–40.

14. Ronald H. Spector, *Professors of War*, 35–37, 71–80; Michael Vlahos, "Wargaming, an Enforcer of Strategic Realism: 1919–1942," *Naval War College Review* 39 (Mar.–Apr. 1986): 7–22.

15. Phillips Payson O'Brien, ed., *Technology and Naval Combat in the Twentieth Century and Beyond*, vi–xiii.

16. Edward Hallett Carr, *What Is History?* 35.

17. Lawrence J. Korb, "Threat from a budget destroyer," *Raleigh News and Observer*, Jan. 17, 2001, editorial page.

Chapter 2. The Origins and Persistence of Mahanian Doctrine

1. Henry L. Stimson, *On Active Service in Peace and War*, 506.

2. Philip A. Crowl, "Alfred Thayer Mahan: The Naval Historian," in *Makers of Modern Strategy*, ed. Peter Paret, 446–47; Allan Westcott, ed., *Mahan on Naval Warfare*, 360–61.

3. Crowl, "Alfred Thayer Mahan," 446–48.

4. Alfred Thayer Mahan, *The Influence of Sea Power upon History, 1660–1783*. The Dover edition is a slightly altered republication of the 1894 edition of the work, originally published by Little, Brown, and Company, Boston, in 1890; Alfred Thayer

Mahan, *The Influence of Sea Power upon the French Revolution and Empire*; Alfred Thayer Mahan, *The Life of Nelson, the Embodiment of the Sea Power of Great Britain*; Alfred Thayer Mahan, *Sea Power in Its Relations to the War of 1812*.

5. Mahan, *Influence of Sea Power upon History*, 25–90.

6. Ibid., 13–28.

7. Ibid., 25–27; Westcott, ed., *Mahan on Naval Warfare*, 1–15.

8. Mahan, *Influence of Sea Power upon History*, 107–33; E. B. Potter, ed., *Sea Power*, 18; Joseph Allen, *Battles of the British Navy*, vol. 1, 384–85; Sir Julian Corbett, ed., *Fighting Instructions, 1530–1816*. During the age of sail a warship was "rated," or classified, according to the number of guns it carried. Ship ratings therefore indirectly determined the ship's principal mission. First-, second-, and third-rate ships, for example, carried between seventy and one hundred guns. These were the ships identified to fight major naval battles. Potter uses the phrase "fit to be tied in the line" to demonstrate the derivation of the term "ships of the line" but fails to specifically cite the originator of the phrase. (A close reading of Sir Julian Corbett's collection of the Royal Navy's Fighting Instructions also failed to turn up the phrase.) Potter also makes the point that while Britain built a number of sixty-four-gun ships, which technically could be considered a ship of the line, he argues that they proved to be too small and saw little service in the line. Joseph Allen's collection of Royal Navy battles offers supporting evidence. During the Battle of the First of June 1794 (discussed in chapter 8), the ships of the line under Adm. Richard Howe of the Royal Navy included three of one hundred guns, four of ninety-eight, two eighty-gunned ships, and sixteen carrying seventy-four guns.

Fourth-rate ships, which carried around fifty guns, were principally used as flagships, as well as offering an economical means of providing presence during peacetime, when it was often necessary to "lay up" the larger warships. The fifth- and six-rate ships, the last in the system, were more commonly known as frigates. Carrying between thirty-two and thirty-eight guns, these were the most versatile of the rated warships. They served a multitude of functions, such as scouting, carrying messages to and from the flagship, enforcing blockades, and commerce raiding. Below the rated ships were naval vessels of smaller size, known as sloops, brigs, and schooners. These ships were limited by their size to a single gun deck and were used primarily as commerce raiders and for operations close to shore.

9. Mahan, *Influence of Sea Power upon History*, 173–78.

10. Ibid., 286–90, 302–307.

11. Ibid., 314–24.

12. Ibid., 105, 173–78, 286–88.

13. Ibid., 505–40. Mahan resolved the paradox by ignoring events on land. He instead emphasized the conflict as "purely a maritime war" in which Britain had failed to decisively defeat the French navy.

14. Ibid., 193–98.

15. Ibid., 132–38.

16. Ropp, *Development of a Modern Navy*, v–vii, 3–5, 157–65.

17. Alex Roland, *Underwater Warfare in the Age of Sail*, 1–16, 156–82.

18. Ropp, *Development of a Modern Navy*, 157–66.

19. Mahan, *Influence of Sea Power upon History*, 111.

20. Ibid., 9–10.

21. Ibid., 132–38, 193–97.

22. Mahan, *Influence of Sea Power upon the French Revolution and Empire*, 1:220–29, 256–86.

23. Mahan, *Life of Nelson*, 2:90–99; Mahan, *Influence of Sea Power upon the French Revolution and Empire*, 2:44–52. While it is clear whom Mahan was praising, it is less clear exactly what he was praising. Nelson had argued against the enterprise. In his mind the Russian Baltic fleet should have been the objective. During the battle Nelson also disregarded an order from Sir Hyde-Parker, his commander-in-chief. Parker, who was well distant from the fighting, became increasingly anxious about Nelson's progress. A signal was sent to discontinue the attack. It is alleged that upon being informed of the signal, Nelson placed his glass to his blind eye (he had been blinded in the right eye during a landing on the Corsican town of Calvi in 1794) and replied to his flag captain, "You know, Foley, I have only one eye. I have a right to be blind, sometimes. I do not see the signal."

Mahan's interpretation of events is instructive. He judged the attack on Copenhagen as overly conservative and an imprudent use of naval force. Mahan was convinced that Nelson, whose genius provided a "clear discernment of the decisive features of a military situation," was right. Nelson, therefore, could be absolved from his apparent disobedience, for in Mahan's view his only fault was that he "had lifted and carried on his shoulders the dead weight of his superior," which in Mahan's mind had prevented the British fleet from demonstrating the true nature of sea control. And yet, it appears that attacking Copenhagen was successful. Hyde-Parker's conservative plan succeeded in securing a promise from the Danes not to interfere with British commerce in the Baltic. The Russian fleet likewise showed no inclination after the attack on Copenhagen to challenge the Royal Navy at sea. Sea control was attained, it appears, not by naval battle, but by projecting power ashore.

24. Mahan, *Influence of Sea Power upon the French Revolution and Empire*, 2:119–90; Mahan, *Life of Nelson*, 2:339–46.

25. Mahan, *Life of Nelson*, 2:369–98; Mahan, *Influence of Sea Power upon the French Revolution and Empire*, 2:119–26, 184–96.

26. Mahan, *Influence of Sea Power upon the French Revolution and Empire*, 2:199–203, 221–34.

27. Ibid., 199–218, 272–91, 402–11.

28. Ibid., 406–11.

29. Westcott, ed., *Mahan on Naval Warfare*, 8–15. Mahan's belief that command decision-making skills could be developed through intellectual pursuits is a major theme in Jon Sumida's *Inventing Grand Strategy and Teaching Command*.

30. Mahan, *Life of Nelson*, 1:312, 2:323–24.

31. Potter, *Sea Power*, 160–61; Peter Karsten, *The Naval Aristocracy*; Robert Seager II, "Ten Years before Mahan: The Unofficial Case for the New Navy, 1889–1890," *The Mississippi Valley Historical Review* 40, no. 3 (Dec. 1953): 491–93.

32. William McAdoo, "The Navy and the Nation," U.S. Naval Institute *Proceedings* 20, no. 2 (1894): 401–22.

33. Ibid., 401.

34. Richard Wainwright (lieutenant commander, USN), "Our Naval Power," U.S. Naval Institute *Proceedings* 24, no. 1 (Mar. 1898): 39–87.

35. Ibid.

36. Spector, *Professors of War*, 71–102.

37. Alfred Thayer Mahan, *Lessons of the War with Spain*, 47–59.

38. Bradley A. Fiske (commander, USN), "American Naval Policy," U.S. Naval Institute *Proceedings* 31, no. 1 (Mar. 1905): 2–34.

39. W. W. Kimball (commander, USN), "Submarine Boats," U.S. Naval Institute *Proceedings* 27, no. 4 (Dec. 1901): 739–46; Lawrence Spear, "Submarine Torpedo Boats: Past, Present and Future," U.S. Naval Institute *Proceedings* 28, no. 4 (Dec. 1902): 1000–13; A. B. Hoff (lieutenant, USN), "The Submarine as an Enemy," U.S. Naval Institute *Proceedings* 31, no. 2 (June 1905): 384–99.

40. Clark Reynolds, *Admiral John H. Towers*.

41. Westcott, ed., *Mahan on Naval Warfare*, 258–75; Alfred Thayer Mahan, "Reflections, Historic and Other, Suggested by the Battle of the Sea of Japan," U.S. Naval Institute *Proceedings* 32, no. 7 (June 1906): 447–63; Richard Wainwright (captain, USN), "The Battle of the Sea of Japan," U.S. Naval Institute *Proceedings* 31, no. 4 (Dec. 1905): 779–805; Bradley A. Fiske (commander, USN), "Why Togo Won," U.S. Naval Institute *Proceedings* 31, no. 4 (Dec. 1905): 807–809. Wainwright pointed to the superiority of Japanese ships and criticized the Russians for their lack of training. Fiske emphasized the advantage of experience. Togo's superiority in maneuvering and gunnery, he concluded, was the result of a fleet that had spent a great deal of time operating together.

42. W. H. Beehler (commodore, USN), "The Navy and Coast Defense," U.S. Naval Institute *Proceedings* 35, no. 2 (June 1909): 343–81.

43. Spector, *Professors of War*, 102.

44. Frank J. Merli, *The* Alabama, *British Neutrality, and the American Civil War*, ed. David M. Fahey. Queen Victoria's Neutrality Proclamation of 1861 prohibited the sale or transfer of military equipment to either belligerent during the war. Yet Confederate naval agent James Bulloch was successful in purchasing an English-built merchant ship that became CSS Alabama, the Confederacy's most successful commerce raider. Merli's excellent work softens previously held notions of conspiracy by senior British officials. Yet he does not succeed in completely exonerating London from responsibility for obvious violations of the neutrality law.

45. Michael Vlahos, *The Blue Sword*, 99–102.

46. Ibid; Sumida, *Inventing Grand Strategy and Teaching Command*, 82–92.

47. Vincent Davis, *The Admirals' Lobby*, 129.

48. Edward S. Miller, *War Plan Orange*, 21–36.

49. William F. Fullam (lieutenant, USN), "The Organization, Training and Discipline of the Navy Personnel as Viewed from the Ship," U.S. Naval Institute *Proceedings* 22, no. 1 (1896): 83–116.

50. Dirk A. Ballendorf and Merrill L. Bartlett, *Pete Ellis*, 25–27.

51. Graham A. Cosmas and Jack Shulimson, "The Culebra Maneuver and the Creation of the U.S. Marine Corps' Advanced Base Force," in *Assault from the Sea*, ed. Merrill L. Bartlett, 121–41; Kenneth J. Clifford, *Progress and Purpose*, 7–11; Alan R. Millett, *Semper Fidelis*, 273; Raymond G. O'Connor, "The U.S. Marines in the 20th Century: Amphibious Warfare and Doctrinal Debates," *Military Affairs* 38, no. 3 (Oct. 1974): 97–98; Eli K. Cole (lieutenant colonel, USMC), "The Necessity to the Naval

Service of an Adequate Marine Corps," U.S. Naval Institute *Proceedings* 40, no. 5 (Sept.–Oct. 1914): 1395–1401. Exercises were first held on the Puerto Rican island of Culebra in 1903. During the exercise, naval officers pressed marines into performing shipboard duties and interfered with their work on the island. The following year Gen. Leonard Wood, governor general of the Philippines, complained that marine exercises in Subic Bay were an intrusion on the army's mission and a conspiracy by the navy to take over the defense of America's western Pacific holdings. In 1914 the marines returned to Culebra for one final exercise before World War I. The exercise was designed to simulate the defense of an advanced base from a possible German incursion in the Caribbean. Marines from the newly established Advanced Base Force went ashore January 9 and commenced defensive preparations. An assaulting force, composed of sailors and marines from Atlantic fleet warships, attacked on the January 21. Navy umpires judged that the defensive measures taken by the marines successfully thwarted the landing.

52. Robert G. Albion, *Makers of Naval Policy*, 1798–1947, ed. Rowena Reed, 354–56.

53. "Alfred Thayer Mahan, in Memoriam," U.S. Naval Institute *Proceedings* 41, no. 1 (Jan.–Feb. 1915): 1–9.

54. Dudley W. Knox (commander, USN), "The General Problem of Naval Warfare," U.S. Naval Institute *Proceedings* 42, no. 1 (Jan.–Feb. 1916): 23–47.

55. Holloway H. Frost (ensign, USN), "The Problem of Firing at a Fleet Under Way with Long Range Torpedoes," U.S. Naval Institute *Proceedings* 39, no. 2 (June 1913): 681.

56. Lyman A. Cotton (captain, USN), "Commerce Destroying in War," U.S. Naval Institute *Proceedings* 45, no. 9 (Sept. 1919): 1495–1517. Cotton placed a motto under the title of the article that read, "Easy methods; inconsiderable results"; Cotton, "Unrestricted Commerce Destroying," U.S. Naval Institute *Proceedings* 45, no. 9 (Sept. 1919): 1517–1527.

57. Richard Compton-Hall, *Submarines and the War at Sea*, 277; C. S. McDowell (captain, USN), "Anti-submarine Work during the World War," Washington, D.C.: National Archives and Records Service, 1977, 17–32. McDowell's report is an unpublished typescript, originally produced in December 1919; report of Capt. Frank W. Schofield, USN, Oct. 12, 1917, "Sound Detection," *Hearings before the General Board of the U.S. Navy, 1917–1950*, roll 1, frames 390–97; report of Maj. R. A. Milliken, U.S. Army, Jan. 18, 1918, untitled, *Hearings before the General Board*, roll 1, frames 83–93; Archibald Douglas Turnbull, *History of United States Naval Aviation*, 81–150; Kenneth Whiting (lieutenant, USN), "Aeronautics, January 16, 1918," *Hearings before the General Board*, roll 1, frames 61–75; report of Commanders A. W. Johnson and J. K. Taussig to the General Board, Dec. 4, 1917, "Anti-submarine Warfare," *Hearings before the General Board*, roll 1, frames 685–705

58. Yates Stirling (commander, USN), "The Submarine," U.S. Naval Institute *Proceedings* 43, no. 7 (July 1917): 1371–90; Bradley A. Fiske (rear admiral, USN), "Air Power," U.S. Naval Institute *Proceedings* 43, no. 8 (Aug. 1917): 1701–1705.

59. Holloway H. Frost (lieutenant commander, USN), "The Results and Effects of the Battle of Jutland," U.S. Naval Institute *Proceedings* 47, no. 9 (Sept. 1921): 1335–54.

60. Lee P. Warren (lieutenant commander, USN), "The Battleship Still Supreme," *The World's Work* (Apr. 1921): 556–60.

61. Ibid., 559.

Chapter 3. The Airpower Pragmatists

1. William Mitchell (brigadier general, USA), "Has the Airplane Made the Battleship Obsolete?" *The World's Work*, Apr. 1921, 550–56. The citation is the title section of the article, which accounts for the awkward sentence structure.

2. Commander-in-chief, U.S. fleet, "Report on Fleet Problem One, February 1923," 84, *Records*, roll 1.

3. Ibid., 77.

4. Ibid., 75.

5. Ibid., 78, 82.

6. Ibid., 75, 84.

7. Ibid., 140.

8. McBride, *Technological Change and the United States Navy*, 4–7, 111.

9. Reynolds, *Admiral John H Towers*, 108–23.

10. Robin Higham, "Airpower in World War One, 1914–1918," in *The War in the Air*, 1914–1994, ed. Alan Stephens, 8–13. Two additional works offer competing interpretations of the early formation of airpower doctrine. I. B. Holley's *Ideas and Weapons*, points to the U.S. Army's stumbling efforts to build a credible air component. John Howard Morrow offers a different perspective in *The Great War in the Air*. His comparative analysis implies that innovation in military aviation, and the close proximity between pilots on the front and aircraft manufacturers in the rear, outpaced efforts to develop coherent doctrine.

11. William F. Trimble, *Admiral William A. Moffett*, 71.

12. Charles M. Melhorn, *Two-Block Fox*, 32–36; Turnbull, *History of United States Naval Aviation*, 150–64.

13. Thomas Wildenberg, "In Support of the Battle Line: Gunnery's Influence on the Development of Carrier Aviation in the U.S. Navy," *Journal of Military History* 65, no. 3 (July 2001): 699–70; Reynolds, *Admiral John H. Towers*, 127–62.

14. David MacIsaac, "Voices from the Central Blue: The Air Power Theorists," in *Makers of Modern Strategy*, ed. Peter Paret, 625.

15. Alan Stephens, "The True Believers: Airpower between the Wars," in *The War in the Air, 1914–1994*, ed. Alan Stephens, 29–30, 40.

16. Burke Davis, *The Billy Mitchell Affair*, 11–27.

17. Ibid., 28–45.

18. Giulio Douhet, *The Command of the Air*, trans. Dino Ferrari, 3–33; Stephens, "The True Believers," 30–35.

19. William Mitchell, *Winged Defense*, xv–xvii, 7–8, 9, 10, 14, 120–33, 218–20.

20. Stephens, "The True Believers," 38–39.

21. Albion, *Makers of Naval Policy*, 368–77.

22. U.S. Navy General Board Hearing on March 5, 1919, "Development of Naval Aviation," 12–13, *Hearings before the General Board*, roll 2, frames 158–80.

23. Albion, *Makers of Naval Policy*, 368; Melhorn, Two-Block Fox, 58–59.

24. Melhorn, *Two-Block Fox*, 60–61; Turnbull, *History of United States Naval Aviation*, 192–94.

25. Melhorn, *Two-Block Fox*, 60–73; Turnbull, *History of United States Naval Aviation*, 192–99; McBride, *Technological Change and the United States Navy*, 142.

26. Mitchell, *Winged Defense*, 73; O'Connell, *Sacred Vessels*, 259–60.

27. Melhorn, *Two-Block Fox*, 66–69, 76, 80; Turnbull, *History of United States Naval Aviation*, 68–71, 76–80.

28. Paolo E. Coletta and Bernarr B. Coletta, *Admiral William Moffett and U.S. Naval Aviation*, 20–25; Trimble, *Admiral William A. Moffett*, 137–38.

29. Trimble, *Admiral William A. Moffett*, 1–8; Albion, *Makers of Naval Policy*, 365.

30. Melhorn, *Two-Block Fox*, xi; Spector, *At War at Sea*, 144–45.

31. Trimble, *Admiral William A. Moffett*, 95–96.

32. Samuel Taylor Moore, *U.S. Airpower*, 79–80.

33. McBride, *Technological Change and the United States Navy*, 143–48, 150–51; Stephen Roskill, *Naval Policy between the Wars*, vol. 1, *The Period of Anglo-American Antagonism, 1919–1929*, 398–99. Officers providing testimony included the chiefs of the navy's bureaus, fleet commanders, officers from BUAER, and army officers (including Billy Mitchell). Civilian experts included MIT president S. W. Stratton, Johns Hopkins physicist J. S. Ames, MIT Aerodynamic Department chair E. P. Warner, and NACA members such as W. F. Durand of Stanford and George Lewis.

34. Commander-in-chief, U.S. fleet memorandum to CNO, Apr. 30, 1924, "United States Fleet Problem Number Four—Report on," 1, *Records*, roll 3.

35. Commander, scouting fleet memorandum to CINCUS, Feb. 12, 1924, "Fleet Problem No. 4—History of Operations," 7; "Remarks by Captain S.H.R. Doyle, U.S. Navy, (From time of arrival at rendezvous X until completion of Problem)," 1–3, *Records*, roll 3.

36. "Remarks by Captain S.H.R. Doyle," 3.

37. "United States Fleet Problem Number Four—Report on," 3; "Remarks by Captain S.H.R. Doyle," 1–3; "Annual Report of Aircraft Squadrons, Battle Fleet—1 July 1923 to 30 June 1924," 3–5, *Annual Reports*, roll 4; Commander Battle Force memorandum to CINCUS, May 21, 1936, "Annual Report of Commander Battle Force for the period 1 July 1935 to 24 June 1936," 15, *Annual Reports*, roll 10; Reynolds, *Admiral John H. Towers*, 198; Clark Reynolds, *The Fast Carriers*, 227–29.

38. Commander, Aircraft Squadrons, scouting fleet memorandum to CINCUS, Feb. 15, 1924, "Fleet Problem No. 4—Conference on—CALIFORNIA," *Records*, roll 3.

39. Frank W. Wead (lieutenant, USN), "Naval Aviation Today," U.S. Naval Institute *Proceedings* 50, no. 4 (Apr. 1924): 563.

40. Commander-in-chief, U.S. fleet memorandum to commander, scouting fleet, Oct. 20, 1924, "U.S. Fleet Problem Number five," *Records*, roll 3; commander-in-chief, U.S. fleet memorandum to commander-in-chief, battle fleet, Oct. 20, 1924, "U.S. Fleet Problem Number Five"; "Comment by Commander Aircraft Squadrons, Battle Fleet on Fleet Problem No. V March 2 to March 11, 1925," *Records*, roll 4.

41. Black Fleet Operation Order No. 1, Feb. 28, 1925, "Task Organization," *Records*, roll 4.

42. Commander-in-chief, battle fleet, confidential letter, Jan. 28, 1925, "Battle Fleet convoy Screening Formation," *Records*, roll 3; "Comment by Commander Aircraft Squadrons, Battle Fleet on Fleet Problem No. V," *Records*, roll 4.

43. Commander-in-chief, U.S. fleet memorandum to CNO, Mar. 14, 1926, "U.S. Fleet Problem No. 6—Report on"; "Estimate of the Situation by Commander Black Naval Forces," 3–5, *Records*, roll 7.

44. "Blue Estimate of the Situation—U.S. Fleet Problem VI," 10, *Records*, roll 7.

45. U.S. fleet, aircraft squadrons, battle fleet, "Chronological History," 23, *Records*, roll 7; Wildenberg, "In Support of the Battle Line," 705–13; Trimble, *Admiral William A. Moffett*, 199–200.

46. U.S. fleet, aircraft squadrons, battle fleet, "Fleet Problem Six Report of Operations," 1–5, *Records*, roll 7.

47. Commander aircraft squadrons memorandum, "Procedures in Handling Air Forces During Problem Six"; "Fleet Problem Six, Report of Operations,"4, *Records*, roll 7.

48. "Fleet Problem Six Report of Operations," 11.

49. Yates Stirling (captain, USN), "The Place of Aviation in the Organization for War," U.S. Naval Institute *Proceedings* 52, no. 6 (May 1926): 1103; Spector, *At War at Sea*, 142–43.

50. Melhorn, *Two-Block Fox*, 99–102.

51. "Annual Report of the Commander in Chief, U.S. Fleet for the period 3 October 1925 to 30 June 1926," 59, *Annual Reports*, roll 5.

52. Davis, *Billy Mitchell Affair*, 218–21, 281–88; MacIsaac, "Voices from the Central Blue," 625–35; Stephen L. McFarland and Wesley Phillips Newton, *To Command the Sky*, 26–29, 30–33.

53. Melhorn, *Two-Block Fox*, 97–98; Trimble, *Admiral William A. Moffett*, 175–81; McBride, *Technological Change and the U.S. Navy*, 150–52.

54. Spector, *At War at Sea*, 143–48; Trimble, *Admiral William A. Moffett*, 182–89, 199.

55. Thomas Wildenberg, *Destined for Glory*, 36–48; Francis H. Dean, *America's Navy and Marine Corps Airplanes*, 36–41.

56. David Hamer, *Bombers versus Battleships*, 20.

57. "Annual Report of the Commander-in-Chief, U.S. Fleet, for the period 8 November 1927 to 30 June 1928," 87, *Annual Reports*, roll 6.

58. Commander-in-chief, U.S. fleet memorandum to CNO, Mar. 18, 1929, "United States Fleet Problem IX—Report of the Commander-in-Chief, United States Fleet," 6–26, *Records*, roll 12.

59. "United States Fleet Problem IX—Report of the Commander-in-Chief, United States Fleet," 22, 130–31.

60. Ibid., 11, 22, 28.

61. Ibid., 103; "Statement on Fleet Problem Nine by Rear Admiral J. M. Reeves, USN," *Records*, roll 12.

62. "United States Fleet Problem IX—Report of the Commander-in-Chief, United States Fleet," 28; aircraft squadrons, battle fleet, letter, Jan. 23, 1929, "Umpire's Comments and Decisions," 1–6, *Records*, roll 12.

63. "United States Fleet Problem IX—Report of the Commander-in-Chief, United States Fleet," 29, 36.

64. Ibid., 29–30.

65. Bradley A. Fiske (rear admiral, USN), "Torpedo Plane and Bomber," U.S. Naval Institute *Proceedings* 48, no. 9 (Sept. 1922): 1475–78; "Annual Report of the Commander-in-Chief, United States Fleet, period 1 July, 1928 to 21 May, 1929," 59, *Annual Reports*, roll 7.

66. Commander-in-chief, U.S. fleet confidential letter no. 9—30, May 7, 1930, "Fleet Problem Ten," 1, *Records*, roll 13; Annex Baker to U.S. Fleet Operation Plan No. 3–36, "Assignment of Units U.S. Fleet for Fleet Problem XVII, Phase Two," *Records*, roll 21.

67. Trimble, *Admiral William A. Moffett*, 14.

68. Ibid., 257–58, 273–74; commander-in-chief, U.S. fleet memorandum, May 23, 1932, "Fleet Problem XIII," 15, *Records*, roll 14; commander-in-chief, U.S. fleet memorandum, June 1, 1934, "Report of Fleet Problem XV," 18, *Records*, roll 16.

69. U.S. fleet confidential letter no. 12—July 14, 1930, "Fleet Problem Eleven," 19–38, *Records*, roll 13.

70. Commander-in-chief, White fleet, "Fleet Problem XVI Estimate of the Situation," May 15, 1935, 1–25, *Records*, roll 19; commander aircraft, Base Force memorandum to CINCUS, June 5, 1937, "Fleet Problem XVIII—Comments and recommendations," 4, *Records*, roll 22; Miller, War Plan Orange, 234–44.

71. U.S. Navy General Board Discussion, Oct. 9, 1928, "Building Program of Aircraft for the Navy," *Hearings before the General Board*, roll 8, frames 309–13.

72. "Fleet Problem Ten," 8–11.

73. Ibid., 17, 29, 53.

74. Ibid., 43–46.

75. Ibid., 8–11, 64–66.

76. Hamer, *Bombers versus Battleships*, 41–50.

77. "Fleet Problem XIII," 6–9, 26–32.

78. "Fleet Problem XIII," 21, 32–33, 40.

79. J. C. Hubbard (lieutenant, USN), "Aviation and Control of the Sea," U.S. Naval Institute *Proceedings* 62, no. 1 (Jan. 1936): 33–38.

80. Commander-in-chief, U.S. fleet memorandum, Nov. 16, 1936, "Vessels Available for Fleet Problem 19 April to 30 May 1937," 1–3; Operation Order No. 5—Mar. 5, 1937, "Task Organization"; commander-in-chief, U.S. fleet confidential notice 1 CN-37, Mar. 12, 1937, "USF-10, Chapter VI, Temporary Changes in"; Annex Baker to U.S. fleet Operation Order No. 6, "General Plan of U.S. Fleet for Minor Joint Army and Navy Exercises 23–25 April 1937"; commander, Battle Force (commander, Black fleet) memorandum to CINCUS, May 11, 1937, "FPXVIII—Narrative of Events and track Charts,"1–8; commander, Midway Force, Black fleet memorandum to CINCUS, May 11, 1937, "Chronological Resume of Operations of Midway Force, Black Fleet, Fleet Problem XVIII"; commander aircraft, main body, Black fleet memorandum to CINCUS, May 11, 1937, "Chronological Resume of Operations of Aircraft, Main Body, Black Fleet during Fleet Problem XVIII," 1–28; commander aircraft, Base Force (commander, White Air Force) memorandum to CINCUS, May 12, 1937, "Track Charts—Narrative of Events; White Air Force, Fleet Problem XVIII," 1–29, all in *Records*, roll 22.

81. Commander, Battle Force (commander, Black fleet, Fleet Problem XVIII) memorandum to CINCUS, June 23, 1937, "Comments and recommendations on Fleet Problem XVIII," 1–8, *Records*, roll 22.

82. Commander-in-chief, U.S. fleet memorandum, May 7, 1938, "Exercise 74—Air Attack on Fleet," *Records*, roll 23.

1. Commander, Submarine Force, U.S. fleet memorandum, May 15, 1934, "Exercise M-General Comments," 7; "Commander, Battle Force, and chief umpire reports on Exercise L (BLUE and BROWN)," *Records*, roll 17.

2. O'Connell, *Sacred Vessels*, 281.

3. Spector, *Eagle against the Sun*, 130, 480–82.

4. Baer, "U.S. Naval Strategy; 1890–1945," 16.

5. *Conference on the Limitation of Armament: Washington, November 12, 1921–February 6, 1922*, 66, 448–60. The battleship issue was not without controversy. The French insisted on a fleet of ten battleships. Their demands not only exceeded the 175,000 tons Hughes intended for them to have, they were also well beyond what the French could reasonably afford to build. The Italians, suspicious of their principle rival in the Mediterranean, expressed the desire to maintain parity with the French. Hughes solved the impasse by simply going over the head of the French delegation. In a telegram to Aristide Briande, minister for foreign affairs, the secretary informed his counterpart of his emissary's demands. Briande responded that he would "instruct our delegates in the sense you desire."

6. Ibid., 486.

7. Ibid., 488.

8. Ibid., 596.

9. Ernest Andrade, "Submarine Policy in the United States Navy, 1919–1941," *Military Affairs* 35, no. 2 (1971): 55.

10. W. T. Mallison, *Studies in the Law of Naval Warfare*, 43; Roskill, *Naval Policy between the Wars*, 1:498–517.

11. U.S. Department of State, *London Naval Treaty of 1930*, 7, 13–16; Baer, *One Hundred Years of Sea Power*, 113; Stephen Roskill, *Naval Policy between the Wars*, vol. 2, *The Period of Reluctant Rearmament*, 37–71.

12. Stephen Pelz, *Race to Pearl Harbor*, 152–64.

13. U.S. Naval History Division, *Dictionary of American Naval Fighting Ships*, 6:177–78.

14. John D. Alden, *The Fleet Submarine in the U.S. Navy*, 5.

15. *Annual Reports of the Navy Department*, 1922 (Washington, D.C.: GPO, 1923), 345; *Annual Reports of the Navy Department*, 1923 (Washington, D.C.: GPO, 1924), 330.

16. "Report on Fleet Problem One, February 1923, 83–87," *Records*, roll 1.

17. "Report on Fleet Problem Number One, February 1923," 12, *Records*, roll 1.

18. "Extracts from the Report of Commander Submarine Division Nine, LCDR F. C. Sherman, in "Report on United States Fleet Problem Number One," 107, *Records*, roll 1.

19. "Extracts from Commander Battleship divisions, Battle Fleet," in "Report on Fleet Problem One," 87, *Records*, roll 1.

20. Ibid.

21. CINCUS memorandum to CNO, "Fleet Problem No. 5—Report on," 7; "CINCUS report, May 29, 1925 (enclosures a–g)," *Records*, roll 3.

22. Gary Weir, "The Search for an American Submarine Strategy and Design, 1916–1936," *Naval War College Review* 44, no. 1 (1991): 40–41.

23. CINCUS memorandum to CNO, Apr. 30, 1924, "United States Fleet Problem Number Four—Report on," *Records*, roll 3.

24. Commander, scouting fleet, memorandum to CINCUS, "Fleet Problem No. 4—History of Operations," 1–3, *Records*, roll 3.

25. "Estimate of the Situation, Fleet Problem No. Four, 1924," *Records*, roll 3.

26. R. H. English (lieutenant commander, USN), "Black Sea Operations," *Records*, roll 3.

27. CINCUS memorandum to CNO, Apr. 30, 1924, "United States Fleet Problem Number Four—Report on,"1–5, *Records*, roll 3. CINCUS recommendations following Fleet Problems Two, Four, Five, and Seven included the necessity for additional fleet submarines.

28. "U.S. Fleet Problem No. 5, Blue Estimate of the Situation," 11, *Records*, roll 3.

29. "Additional Estimate of the Situation Blue, U.S. Fleet Problem Five, Submitted by Rear Admiral M. M. Taylor, Commander Control force, United States Fleet," undated, *Records*, roll 3.

30. "Statement of Lieutenant (A. E.) King, U.S. Navy—Commanding U.S.S. S-11, Blue Fleet Critique—Fleet Problem No. 5," Mar. 14, 1925; "Remarks of Lieutenant H. L. Challenger, Commanding U.S.S. S-12 Blue Fleet (re: Critique Fleet Problem No. 5," Mar. 14, 1925, *Records*, roll 3.

31. CINCUS memorandum to CNO, "U.S. Fleet Problem Seven—Report on," 4, *Records*, roll 8. The new V-class "fleet" submarine was introduced in Fleet Problem Seven in 1927. Even though the boats enjoyed significant advantages over the S-boats, the new boats were used as trailers to slow-moving convoys, transmitting information to the fleet commander, and executing effective attacks. "While submarines are still weapons of opportunity," commented CINCUS Adm. Charles F. Hughes following the exercise, "the V-Boats are much more able to create that opportunity than any previous submarine we have experimented with."

32. "United States Fleet Problem XIV, Report of the Commander-in-Chief, United States Fleet, 20 April," *Records*, roll 15.

33. Commanding officer, USS *California*, memorandum, Feb. 25, 1923, "Notes and comments on Panama problem," *Records*, roll 1.

34. "Report on Fleet Problem Number 1, February 1923," 83, *Records*, roll 1.

35. "Summary and Comments on the Actual Operations, Summary of Actual Operations, Blue, Report on United States Fleet Problem Number One, February 1923," 82, *Records*, roll 1.

36. "U.S.S. *S-19* Unit Observer's Report," Mar. 12, 1927, *Records*, roll 8.

37. "U.S. Fleet Problem Number Two, Black Situation, March 3, 1924," 15, *Records*, roll 1.

38. "Blue Fleet Operation Order No. (x)-25, 28 February, 1925," *Records*, roll 3.

39. CINCUS memorandum to CNO, May 23, 1932, "United States Fleet Problem XIII, Report of the Commander-in-Chief, U.S. Fleet," *Records*, roll 14.

40. *Annual Reports of the Navy Department*, 1926 (Washington, D.C.: GPO, 1927), 68.

41. *Annual Reports of the Navy Department*, 1928 (Washington, D.C.: GPO, 1929), 2–3.

42. CINCUS memorandum to CNO, Sept. 16, 1935, "Commander-in-Chief, U.S. Fleet, Fleet Problem XVI—Report on," 32, *Records*, roll 18.

43. "Statement of Lieutenant (A. E.) King, U.S. Navy—Commanding U.S.S *S-11*, 14 March 1925," *Records*, roll 3.

44. "Report of Operation of Control Force, Fleet Problem No. 3," *Records*, roll 2.

45. Control force observer, USS Camden, report, "Ship and Unit Observer's reports—Fleet Problem #7, 16 March 1927," *Records*, roll 10.

46. CINCUS memorandum to CNO, June 2, 1934, "Report of Fleet Problem XV," 4–5, *Records*, roll 16.

47. CINCUS memorandum to CNO, "Submarine Torpedo Attack on Fleet—Exercise No. 77, Week 4–8 April, Fleet Problem XIX, report of," 3, *Records*, roll 24.

48. Ibid., 8.

49. CINCUS memorandum to CNO, Sept. 15, 1935, "Fleet Problem XVI—report on," 22, *Records*, roll 18.

50. "Remarks of Admiral Laning at Critique of Fleet Problem Sixteen," 1–2, *Records*, roll 18.

51. CINCUS report, Dec. 1935, "Employment of BLUE Submarines, ORANGE War," *Records of the Strategic Plans Division, Office of the Chief of Naval Operations and Predecessor Organizations*, microfilm, roll 22.

52. Ropp, *Development of a Modern Navy*, 348–52.

53. Annex A to U.S. Fleet Operations Order No. 3, "General Plan for Fleet Problem XIX and Annual Fleet Exercises, 15 March–30 April 1938, 3 January 1938," 8, *Records*, roll 24.

54. Dudley W. Knox, *The Eclipse of American Sea Power*, 67–82.

55. Yates Stirling (rear admiral, USN), "Naval Preparedness in the Pacific Area," U.S. Naval Institute *Proceedings* 60, no. 5 (May 1934): 606.

56. Richard Burns, "Regulating Submarine Warfare, 1921–1941: A Case Study in Arms Control and Limited War," *Military Affairs* 35, no. 2 (Apr. 1971): 56–62.

57. Ibid., 59.

58. Yates Stirling (rear admiral, USN), "Sea Power," U.S. Naval Institute *Proceedings*, 61, no. 6 (June 1935): 774.

59. H. G. Rickover (lieutenant, USN), "International Law and the Submarine," U.S. Naval Institute *Proceedings* 61, no. 9 (Sept. 1935): 1223.

60. Walter Anderson (captain, USN), "Submarines and Disarmament Conferences," U.S. Naval Institute *Proceedings*, 53, no. 1 (Jan. 1927): 69.

61. Miller, *War Plan Orange*, 320.

Chapter 5. Getting a Grip on the "Jellyfish"

1. Maroon fleet commander memorandum to CINCUS, Mar. 18, 1940, "Fleet Problem XXI Estimate of the Situation," 2, *Records*, roll 31.

2. Ibid., 26; Maroon Fleet Operations Plan No. 2, Apr. 10, 1940, "Task Organization," 1–3, *Records*, roll 31.

3. "Remarks by Admiral C. P. Snyder, U.S. Navy (Commander Purple Fleet) at Critique of Part IV, Fleet Problem XXI," May 6, 1940, *Records*, roll 36.

4. Maroon fleet commander memorandum to CINCUS, "Maroon Report of Part VI, Fleet Problem XXI," 5, *Records*, roll 33; remarks by Vice Adm. Adolphus An-

drews, commander, Maroon fleet, "Critique, Tuesday, 7 May, Part VI, Fleet Problem XXI Discussion and Comments General," 5, *Records*, roll 36.

5. C. D. Bekker, *Hitler's Naval War*, 309–10.

6. Chester W. Nimitz, *Triumph in the Atlantic*, 86. King changed the acronym from "CINCUS" to "COMINCH" shortly after taking command of the U.S. fleet. In the wake of the Pearl Harbor disaster, the pronunciation of the acronym, "sink-us," seemed to King defeatist.

7. Letter from commander, North Atlantic Naval Coastal Frontier (Eastern Sea Frontier) to commander-in-chief, U.S. fleet, "Status of Naval Forces, 22 December 1941"; memorandum, "Convoy for Protection of Coastwise Shipping Along Eastern Sea Frontier, 26 February 1942," cited in C. C. Felker, "Airpower on the Offensive; The U.S. Army Air Corps versus the U-Boats in the Bay of Biscay" (master's thesis, University of Alabama, Apr. 1992), 4–6; Dan Van der Vat, *The Atlantic Campaign*, 243–44.

8. R. A. Bowing, "The Negative Influence of Mahan on Antisubmarine Warfare," *Journal of Royal United Services Institute for Defense Studies* 122, no. 4 (1977): 55–56; Davis, *Admirals' Lobby*, 134–35; O'Connell, *Sacred Vessels*, 277; Montgomery Meigs, *Slide Rules and Submarines*, 6; Donald Macintyre, *The Battle of the Atlantic*, 139, 143; Alvin D. Coox, "Military Effectiveness of Armed Forces in the Interwar Period, 1919–1941," in *Military Effectiveness*, vol. 2, ed. Allan R. Millett and Williamson Murray, 265; Ronald Spector, "The Military Effectiveness of the U.S. Armed Forces, 1919–1939," in *Military Effectiveness*, 81–90; Ladislas Farago, *The Tenth Fleet*, 99; Paul Kemp, *Convoy Protection*, 12–13; Roskill, *Naval Policy between the Wars*, 2:227.

9. Fleet Problems Two (Jan. 1924), Four (Jan. 1924), Five (Mar. 1925), Six (Feb. 1926), Seven (Mar. 1927), Eight (Apr. 1928), Nine (Jan. 1929), Twelve (Feb. 1931), Thirteen (Mar. 1932), Sixteen (May 1935), Seventeen (Apr.–May 1936), Nineteen (Mar.–Apr. 1938), and Twenty-one (Apr.–May 1940).

10. Commander-in-chief, battle fleet memorandum to CNO, Feb. 1, 1924, "U.S. Fleet Problem No. 2: Report On," 7, *Records*, roll 1. The "Train" refers to fleet logistics ships.

11. Commander, fleet base force memorandum to CNO, Feb. 4, 1924, "Fleet Problem IV," *Records*, roll 3.

12. "United States Fleet Problem Number Five, Black Solution by Commander-in-Chief Battle Fleet, 21 January, 1925," 3, *Records*, roll 3.

13. Battle fleet confidential letter no. 1, Jan. 12, 1925, "Battle Fleet Zigzag Plans"; battle fleet confidential letter no. 2, Jan. 28, 1925, "Battle Fleet Convoy Screening Formation," *Records*, roll 3.

14. CINCUS memorandum to CNO, Mar. 14, 1926, "U.S. Fleet Problem No. 6—Report on," 2, *Records*, roll 6.

15. "Report on U.S. Fleet Problem No. VI, 15 February, 1926," *Records*, roll 7.

16. "Comment by Commander Aircraft Battle Squadrons, Battle fleet on Fleet Problem No. V, March 2 to March 11, 1925," *Records*, roll 3; "Critique of Fleet Problem Sixteen Held at San Diego, California 15 June, 1935," 33, *Records*, roll 18. Intercepted radio transmissions led to successful attacks on submarines during the 1935 fleet problem but in no others.

17. "Remarks of Commanding Officer—USS *Melvin*—re Critique in Connection with Fleet Problem No. 5, 14 March 1925," *Records*, roll 3.

18. CINCUS memorandum to CNO, Sept. 15, 1935, "Fleet Problem XVI—report on," 12, *Records*, roll 18.

19. O. Donn Grace, *Sonar and Anti-submarine Warfare*, 2. The acronym "ASDIC" was a security measure in itself. It stood for "Antisubmarine Defense Investigating Committee," which concealed the particulars of the technology being developed.

20. CINCUS memorandum to CNO, "Submarine Torpedo Attack on Fleet-Exercise No. 77 Week 4–8 April, Fleet Problem XIX, report of," 2–7, *Records*, roll 23.

21. Ibid, 8.

22. S. E. Moses (captain, USN), "Comment by Commander Aircraft Squadrons, Battle Fleet on Fleet Problem No. V March 2 to March 11, 1925," 1, *Records*, roll 3.

23. R. R. Paunack (unit observer, aircraft squadrons, battle fleet) report, Mar. 21, 1927, "Fleet Problem #7, Report on," 3, *Records*, roll 8.

24. "United States Fleet Problem Number Seven, Commander-in-Chief Blue Naval Forces, 3 January, 1927," part 4, "Operation Order No. 1, Task Organization," *Records*, roll 8; "Estimate of the Situation by Commander-in-Chief, Blue Naval Forces, Fleet Problem VIII, February 17, 1928," 26; "Fleet Problem XVI—report on," 8, *Records*, roll 11, 18.

25. Testimony of Mr. Starr Truscott to the General Board, Aug. 10, 1918, "Construction of Airships," 823–29, *Proceedings and Hearings of the General Board of the U.S. Navy*, roll 1; "Comments of Admiral Frank H. Schofield, U.S.N., Commander-in-Chief, Black Fleet on Problem XII Made at the Critique of Problem XII Held on March 2, 1931, Balboa, Canal Zone," 2, *Records*, roll 13; CINCUS memorandum to CNO, May 23, 1932, "United States Fleet Problem XIII, Report of the Commander-in-Chief, United States Fleet," 15, *Records*, roll 14. One reason for aviation's expanded antisubmarine warfare role was the demise of the rigid airship program. Three months prior to the end of World War I, Starr Truscott, chief engineer of the Army and Navy Airship Board, testified to the General Board that both the British and Germans looked favorably on airships as antisubmarine platforms. He cited reports from British submarine commanders of being attacked from zeppelins and from one report in particular, in which a submarine had been bombed while at a depth of seventy feet.

Truscott's confidence was not supported by operational success. The demise of the rigid airship program was examined in chapter 4. In February 1931, the airship *Los Angeles* was included in Fleet Problem Twelve as an antisubmarine scout for the Blue fleet. Her failure to locate any submarines led Black fleet commander and future-CINCUS Frank Schofield to generalize following the exercise that the cost of airships was "out of proportion to their usefulness," while their "appeal to the imagination was not sustained by their military performance."

26. Brodie, *Sea Power in the Machine Age*, 322–23.

27. "United States Fleet Problem XIII, Report of the Commander-in-Chief, United States Fleet, 23 May, 1932, " 6, 27; aircraft scouting plane squadron Two-B report, Mar. 18, 1932, "Operations of VS Squadron Two-B and VS Squadron 14-M during fleet Problem XIII," 19–20, *Records*, roll 14. Even U.S. Marine Corps aviators played a role in antisubmarine operations during the exercise. On March 13, a marine scouting unit spotted a submarine operating on the surface. Navy aircraft were alerted and located the submarine by homing in on the radio transmissions made by the marine aircraft.

28. "Operations of VS Squadron Two-B and VS Squadron 14-M during fleet Problem XIII," 41; "Comments on Operations by Fleet Umpire Blue, 13 March," *Records*, roll 14.

29. CINCUS memorandum to CNO, Sept. 15, 1935, "Fleet Problem XVI—report on," 1–12; "Remarks of Lieutenant Commander F.C. Denebrink [Flag Secretary, Staff of Commander-in-Chief, United States Fleet] at Critique of Fleet Problem Sixteen," 1–5, *Records*, roll 18.

30. "Fleet Problem XVI—report on," 12.

31. "Remarks of Lieutenant Commander F. B. Stump (Senior Squadron Commander, U.S.S. Saratoga) at Critique of Fleet Problem Sixteen," *Records*, roll 18.

32. Commander aircraft, battle force memorandum to CINCUS, June 4, 1937, "Comments and Recommendations—Fleet Problem XVIII," 1–5, *Records*, roll 22.

33. CINCUS memorandum to CNO, May 29, 1935, "Fleet Problem No. 5—Report on," 2, *Records*, roll 3. "Constructive" ships were simulated units assigned to a fleet.

34. "Fleet Problem XVI—report on," 17.

35. Robert Love Jr., "Ernest Joseph King, 26 Mar 1942–15 Dec 1945," *The Chiefs of Naval Operations*, ed. Robert Love Jr., 154; Brodie, *Sea Power in the Machine Age*, 320–21; Paul G. Halpern, *A Naval History of World War I*, 354–55. It was not just naval officers who expressed objections to the institution of convoys during World War I. British civilian merchant masters were equally skeptical of their utility. Some bridled at the notion of losing their independence. Others doubted whether civilian merchants could be expected to maintain the strict formation discipline demanded in a convoy.

36. CINCUS memorandum to CNO, Mar. 3, 1924, "UNITED STATES FLEET Problem No. 2," 2, *Records*, roll 1; CINCUS memorandum to CNO, Apr. 30, 1924, "United States Fleet Problem Number Four—Report on," 2, *Records*, roll 3; "CONVOY, ESCORT, AND SUPPORT FOR UTAH; CRUDIV 7; CARDIV 2; CRUDIV 5; LEXINGTON, FLEET PROBLEM XX, 15 March 1939," *Records*, roll 26; K. Jack Bauer, *A Maritime History of the United States*, 241–42, 298–99, 304–307. Another complicating factor was the dismal state of the U.S. merchant fleet. The decline began during the Civil War. Confederate commerce raiders, such as *Shenandoah* and *Alabama*, seized over 105,000 tons of U.S. shipping and drove another 800,000 tons of U.S. merchants to foreign flags. Postwar efforts to revitalize the U.S. merchant service were hampered by difficulties in recruiting American seamen, high wages, and protective tariffs.

Initiatives on the part of the U.S. government in the early twentieth century to reinvigorate the merchant service proved equally impotent. Less than one-sixth of the ships authorized by Woodrow Wilson's Shipping Act of 1916, for example, were actually built. Stagnation continued well into the interwar period. Substantive efforts at construction of new merchant ships did not begin until 1939.

Chapter 6. A Strategic Afterthought

1. John H. Russell (brigadier general, USMC), "A New Naval Policy," *Marine Corps Gazette* 18, no. 2 (Aug. 1933): 13–17.

2. The official history of the Marine Corps is Frank O. Hough (lieutenant colonel, USMCR), Verle E. Ludwig (major, USMC), and Henry I. Shaw, *History of U.S.*

Marine Corps Operations in World War II, vol. 1, *Pearl Harbor to Guadalcanal*. Other works include Clifford (lieutenant colonel, USMCR), *Progress and Purpose*, and Jeter A. Isely and Philip A. Crowl, *The U.S. Marines and Amphibious War*. Isely and Crowl bring the official and scholarly together. Their work was drawn from seminars whose members included Bernard Brodie, Lt. Gen. Victor H. Krulak, fleet Adm. Ernest King, Hanson Baldwin, Samuel Eliot Morison, fleet Adm. Chester Nimitz, and Adm. Raymond Spruance. Representative of works that offer a more scholarly examination of the USMC are Keith B. Bickel, *Mars Learning*, and Millett, *Semper Fidelis*.

3. Millett, *Semper Fidelis*, 316–18.

4. Spector, "Military Effectiveness of the U.S. Armed Forces," 70–74.

5. Robert Hugh Williams (brigadier general, USMC, ret.), *The Old Corps*; Merrill L. Bartlett, *Lejeune*, 8–10. Williams's book offers insights into the more colorful aspects of Marine Corps officer life during the interwar years.

6. *Landing-Force Manual, United States Navy, 1920*, 18–37, 144–227.

7. Bartlett, *Lejeune*, 37–63, 123–25.

8. John A. Lejeune (major general, USMC), "The United States Marine Corps," U.S. Naval Institute *Proceedings* 51, no. 10 (Oct. 1925): 1860–69; John A. Lejeune, "The Marine Corps, 1926," U.S. Naval Institute *Proceedings* 52, no. 10 (Oct. 1926): 1961–70.

9. Ballendorf and Bartlett, *Pete Ellis*, 21–27, 49–59, 97–123.

10. Earl Ellis (major, USMC), USMC 712H Operations Plan, "Advanced Base Operations in Micronesia, 1921" (Originally prepared by Intelligence Section, Division of Operations and Training, Headquarters USMC on July 23, 1921. Republished by Headquarters, USMC, as *Fleet Marine Force Publication* 12–46, 1992), 29–38.

11. Ibid., 1–7.

12. Ibid., 77–78.

13. Ibid., 39–50, 79.

14. Bartlett, *Lejeune*, 152–57.

15. Clifford, *Progress and Purpose*, 25–30, 36–40; Millett, *Semper Fidelis*, 323–28; Bickel, *Mars Learning*, 56.

16. Ballendorf and Bartlett, 9, 123–59. In early 1921 Ellis received tacit permission from Lejeune for a covert mission to the Mandates to investigate the extent of the island's defenses. Ellis spent almost two years traveling through the Marianas, Carolines, and Marshalls. His death while visiting the Palau Islands on May 12, 1923, was attributed initially to Japanese subterfuge. In fact, Ellis died from complications arising from his chronic alcoholism. No notes were recovered from his journey. There is no evidence that the Japanese were fortifying their possessions.

17. Headquarters of the chief umpire, USS *Seattle*, memorandum to Navy Department, Jan. 25, 1924, "Report on Joint Army and Navy Exercises, January 1924," *Records*, roll 2; commander, scouting fleet, "Black Estimate of the Situation, Operations Plan, Orders, 19 December 1923," *Records*, roll 2; commander-in-chief, battle fleet, memorandum, undated, "U.S. Fleet Problem Number Three (Joint Army and Navy Problem Number Two)," 1, *Records*, roll 2.

18. Ibid.

19. "U.S. Fleet Problem Number Three (Joint Army and Navy Problem Number Two)," 2.

20. Commander, control force report, undated, "Report of Operation of Control Force, Fleet Problem 3," *Records*, roll 2.

21. Ibid., 5.

22. Ibid., 5–6.

23. H. M. Smith (major, USMC), Jan. 23, 1923, "Report of Operations of Marine Brigade," *Records*, roll 2; "Report of Operation of Control Force, Fleet Problem Three," 7, *Records*, roll 2.

24. "Black Estimate of the Situation," 2; "U.S. Fleet Problem Number Three (Joint Army and Navy Problem Number Two)," 12–16; commander-in-chief, battle fleet, memorandum to CINCUS, Feb. 1, 1924, "U.S. Fleet Problem No. 3 (Joint Army and Navy Problem No. 2): Report on," 1–4, *Records*, roll 2.

25. "Remarks by Commander Aircraft Squadrons, Battle Fleet," Jan. 22, 1924, *Records*, roll 2.

26. "Conclusions of the Umpires Joint Army and Navy Problem Two," Jan. 24, 1924, 1–6, *Records*, roll 2.

27. Ibid., 11; E. K. Cole (brigadier general, USMC), "Operations Expeditionary force, Fort Randolph and Coco Solo, January 17–19, 1923," 1–5, *Records*, roll 2.

28. Miller, *War Plan Orange*, 149–52; CINCUS memorandum to CNO, Apr. 30, 1924, "United States Fleet Problem Number Four—Report On," *Records*, roll 3; "U.S. Fleet Problem Number Four, Blue Situation," 1–3, *Records*, roll 3.

29. "Navy Department Instructions Pertaining to U.S. Fleet Problem Number Four as Contained in CNO File Op-12S of 20 September 1923, Subject: Problems for the Maneuvers of the Winter 1923–24," *Records*, roll 3.

30. "United States Fleet Problem Number Four—Report On," 4.

31. "Estimate of the Situation Fleet Problem No. Four. 1924. Submitted by Rear Admiral M. M. Taylor, Commander Blue Control Force," 2, *Records*, roll 3.

32. "Estimate of the Situation Fleet Problem No. 4—1924, Submitted by Brigadier General Eli K. Cole, Commanding Marine Corps Expeditionary Force," 1–12, *Records*, roll 3; "Maneuvers of the Winter 1923–1924, U.S. Fleet Problem number 4, Black, Admiral Y's Estimate of the Situation," *Records*, roll 3; "Winter Maneuvers, 1923–1924, U.S. Fleet Problem No. 4, Estimate of the Situation by Colonel Williams, comdg, M.C.E.F., Culebra Force," *Records*, roll 3; "Marine Corps Expeditionary Force, U.S. Fleet, Operations, Training and Intelligence Report," 2, *Records*, roll 3.

33. "Estimate of the Situation Fleet Problem No. Four, 1924, Sequence of Operations"; "Marine Corps Expeditionary Force, U.S. Fleet, Operations, Training and Intelligence Report," *Records*, roll 3.

34. "Marine Corps Expeditionary Force, U.S. Fleet, Operations, Training and Intelligence Report," 6.

35. Headquarters, U.S. Marine Corps expeditionary force, Culebra, P.R., Feb. 5, 1924, "Report and Comments on Landing Operations, Blue Force, Culebra," 9–11, *Records*, roll 3.

36. "United States Fleet Problem Number Four—Report On," 4–5; "Critique of Fleet Problem No. Four. Submitted by Commander Control Force," 1–5, *Records*, roll 3.

37. Miller, *War Plan Orange*, 78–79, 116, 122–31.

38. Clifford, *Progress and Purpose*, 32–34; Joint Army-Navy Planning Committee memorandum to the Joint Board, Sept. 17, 1924, "Grand Joint Army and Navy

Exercise to be held in the Pacific during the Spring of 1925," *Records of the Joint Board, 1903–1947*, microfilm, roll 15; confidential memorandum from the chief umpire, Joint Army and Navy Exercise N0.3, to the adjutant general, U.S. Army, and chief of naval operations, May 6, 1925, "Grand joint Exercise Number 3—report on," *Records of the Joint Board*, roll 15; letter from Adm. E. W. Eberle to secretary of the navy, Jan. 14, 1926, "Joint Army and Navy Exercises, 1926–1927," *Records of the Joint Board*, roll 15; memorandum from chief umpire, grand joint exercise no. 4, to adjutant general, U.S. Army, and chief of naval operations, Feb. 18, 1932, "Report of the Chief Umpires—Grand joint Exercise No. 4," *Records of the Joint Board*, roll 16.

39. Isely and Crowl, *U.S. Marines and Amphibious War*, 28–29; John P. Campbell, "Marines, Aviators, and the Battleship Mentality, 1923–1933," in Bartlett, *Assault from the Sea*, 168–76; John A. Lejeune, *The Reminiscences of a Marine*, 475–77; Clifford, *Progress and Purpose*, 42–43; Millett, *Semper Fidelis*, 327–29.

40. George Barnett (major general, USMC, ret.), "Sea Training of Marine Officers," U.S. Naval Institute *Proceedings* 50, no. 6 (June 1924): 935–38; William Veazie Pratt (rear admiral, USN), "Discussion," U.S. Naval Institute *Proceedings* 50, no. 7 (July 1924): 1126–27.

41. *Landing-Force Manual, United States Navy, 1927*, 231–48.

42. Clifford, *Progress and Purpose*, 36–37.

43. E. W. Broadbent (lieutenant commander, USN), "The Selection of Advanced Bases," *Marine Corps Gazette* 14, no. 3 (Sept. 1929): 216–20.

44. Walter N. Hill (lieutenant colonel, USMC), "The Employment of Marine Corps Expeditionary Force in a Major Emergency," *Marine Corps Gazette* 15, no. 5 (May 1931): 16–20

45. E. B. Miller (colonel, USMC), "The Marine Corps: Its Mission, Organization, Power and Limitations," *Marine Corps Gazette* 17, no. 3 (Nov. 1932): 17–21.

46. Kenneth J. Clifford, *Amphibious Warfare Development in Britain and America from 1920–1940*, 100–101.

47. Hough, Ludwig, and Shaw, *History of U.S. Marine Corps Operations in World War II*, 13; Victor H. Krulak, *First to Fight*, 80.

48. Clifford, *Progress and Purpose*, 42–44; Bickel, *Mars Learning*, 206–12.

49. Clifford, *Progress and Purpose*, 42–48; T. A. Gibson, "Gallipoli, 1915," in Bartlett, *Assault from the Sea*, 142–45; Isely and Crowl, *U.S. Marines and Amphibious War*, 16–20; Arthur T. Mason (captain, USMC), "An Introduction to the Gallipoli Campaign," *Marine Corps Gazette* 20, no. 1 (Feb. 1936): 23–26; Arthur T. Mason (captain, USMC), "An Introduction to the Gallipoli Campaign, Part Two," *Marine Corps Gazette* 20, no. 2 (May 1936): 23–44; E. P. Jessup (captain, USN), "Failure at Gallipoli," U.S. Naval Institute *Proceedings* 61, no. 2 (Feb. 1935): 191–209; Walter S. Anderson (commander, USN), "The Strategy and Logistics of the Dardanelles Campaign," U.S. Naval Institute *Proceedings* 49, no. 7 (July 1923): 1127–41. The failed amphibious operation on the Gallipoli Peninsula in April 1915 informed much of the marines' doctrinal effort. Chief advocate for a campaign in the Dardanelles was Winston Churchill, who conceived the bold amphibious operation to drive the Turks out of the war. The operation began inauspiciously on March 18, 1915, when a force of British and French battleships failed to reduce the fortifications protecting the straits. Undaunted, the Allies continued to plan for an invasion of the peninsula. For over a month the cam-

paign experienced delays stemming principally from the convoluted logistics chain that stretched from England to the campaign headquarters in Alexandria, then seven hundred miles to the Dardanelles. When the Allies finally went ashore on April 23, the Germans and Turks had had plenty of time to shore up their defenses.

The operation was a failure for a variety of reasons. Delays and security breaches provided the Turks and Germans adequate time to prepare for the defense. Landings were made on four different beaches, none of which had been suitably reconnoitered. Coordination between the invading forces was nonexistent. The amphibious landings failed to move beyond the beachhead. Naval gunfire support proved ineffective. London lost confidence in the troops. The troops likewise questioned the commitment of the military and political leaders who had sent them to Gallipoli. The troops were withdrawn in August.

The articles from the *Proceedings* and *Marine Corps Gazette* provide an interesting insight into the differing perspectives on the operation. Articles written by naval officers for the *Proceedings* focused on the political aspects of the campaign. In their minds, the politician's indifference to the advice of military experts caused the disaster. In an ad hominem attack on Churchill, Captain Jessup argued that the campaign was forced upon the war council by "a civilian of such dominating character as to silence the technicians." Marines tended to emphasize the operational failures of the campaign. Captain Mason suggested that Churchill's idea was promising. It was faulty preparation and execution, he argued, that doomed the operation.

50. Isely and Crowl, *U.S. Marines and Amphibious War*, 32–44.

51. Hough, Ludwig, and Shaw, *History of U.S. Marine Corps Operations in World War II*, 8–14.

52. CINCUS report, May 23, 1932, "United States fleet Problem XIII, 1932," 1, *Records*, roll 14.

53. CINCUS report, June 1, 1935, "Report of Fleet Problem XV," 13, *Records*, roll 16.

54. Director of fleet training, memorandum to CNO, Nov. 16, 1933, "Fleet Problem XV as proposed by Commander-in-Chief, U.S. Fleet," 3, *Records*, roll 16.

55. "Report of Fleet Problem XV," 13–33.

56. Ibid., 33–34.

57. "Report of Fleet Problem XV," annex E, "Comments by Commander-in-Chief at Critique of Fleet Problem XV," 66, *Records*, roll 16.

58. CINCUS memorandum to CNO, Jan. 29, 1934, "Fleet Problem XV—1934," *Records*, roll 16; CINCUS memorandum to CNO, Sept. 15, 1935, "Fleet Problem XVI—report on," 3–4, *Records*, roll 18.

59. "Fleet Problem XVI—report on," 5, 14, 25; CINCUS memorandum to commanding general, Fleet Marine Force (Quantico, Virginia), Feb. 10, 1935, "Fleet Problem XVI—Participation of Fleet Marine Force," *Records*, roll 18.

60. "Fleet Problem XVI—report on," 36; "Remarks of Brig. General Lyman (Commanding General, Fleet Marine Force) at Critique of Fleet Problem Sixteen," *Records*, roll 18.

61. "Remarks of Brig. General Lyman," 2.

62. "Remarks of Chief of Staff, U.S. Fleet (Rear Admiral Bryant) at Critique of Fleet Problem Sixteen," *Records*, roll 18.

63. CNO memorandum to CINCUS, July 9, 1936, "Fleet Problem XVIII—Concept of," *Records*, roll 22; CINCUS memorandum to CNO, undated, "Fleet Problem XVIII, Proposed Problem—Forwarding of," 5, *Records*, roll 22; CNO memorandum to CINCUS, July 24, 1936, "Date of Fleet Problem XVIII," *Records*, roll 22; CINCUS memorandum to commander, battle force (commander, Black fleet, U.S. Fleet Problem XVIII), Mar. 1, 1937, "Black Admiralty—Instructions to Commander Black Fleet, U.S. Fleet Problem XVIII," 1, *Records*, roll 22.

64. Isely and Crowl, *U.S. Marines and Amphibious War*, 46–56.

65. *Landing-Force Manual, United States Navy, 1938*, 18–35.

66. Clifford, *Amphibious Warfare Development in Britain and America from 1920–1940*, 144–51; Hough, Ludwig, and Shaw, *History of U.S. Marine Corps Operations in World War II*, 15–22, 24–28, 32; Millett, *Semper Fidelis*, 331–33; Krulak, *First to Fight*, 90–100; O'Connor, "U.S. Marines in the 20th Century," 101–102.

Chapter 7. Re-examining Mahan

1. Mahan, *Influence of Sea Power upon the French Revolution and Empire*, 1:121–24.

2. Ibid., 126–37.

3. Ibid., 156–61.

4. John Major, "The Navy Plans for War, 1936–1941," in *In Peace and War*, ed. Kenneth Hagan, 242–43; memorandum from CNO to CINCUS, undated, "Fleet Problem XX—Concept of," *Records*, roll 25; annex "A" to U.S. Fleet Operation Order No. 38, "U.S. Fleet problem XX—Geographical, General situation, Special Restrictions and Assumptions, Assignment of Forces and Force Commanders," *Records*, roll 25. "Green" represented Brazil.

5. CINCUS memorandum to commander, Black fleet, undated, "Fleet Problem XX—Special Situation, BLACK," *Records*, roll 25.

6. Ibid. Paragraph three of the memo states; "The objectives of your prospective operations are; first, the interception of the WHITE UTAHS [a Utah-class battleship was used to represent the merchant convoy]; second, the gaining of command of the vital sea-areas off GREEN coast; and third, the establishment of an advanced fleet base in the Porto Rico–Culebra–Virgin Islands Area from which our forces can operate to protect our own lines of communications, while interrupting those of WHITE between Port SAIL and Para."

The final paragraph of the memo reads, "In the event of war, it is anticipated WHITE will contest the command of the sea in the area of projected operations, using his First Fleet immediately and relying on his Second Fleet to consolidate his position. [The Second Fleet was constructive in the exercise.] The importance of the early destruction of the WHITE First Fleet is paramount, as its successful operation in the Lesser Antilles, or westward, threatens our vital lines of communication to the Canal Zone and elsewhere." In the left margin of this particular paragraph appears a hand-scribed notation, "? See par 3." Additionally, the word "paramount" in the last sentence of the paragraph was underlined, presumably by the same person who made the marginal note.

7. "Fleet Problem XX Estimate of the Situation by Vice Admiral Andrews, Commander BLACK Fleet," Jan. 18, 1939, 1–26, *Records*, roll 25.

8. Commanding officer, Aircraft Battle Force memorandum to CINCUS, Mar. 31, 1939, "Fleet Problem XX, Comments and Recommendations," *Records*, roll 26.

9. Commander, Black fleet, memorandum to CINCUS, Mar. 28, 1939, "Fleet Problem XX—Comment and Recommendation," *Records*, roll 26.

10. William R. Braisted, "On the American Red and Red-Orange Plans," in *Naval Warfare in the Twentieth Century, 1900–1945*, ed. Gerald Jordan, 167–70, 178–82; Christopher M. Bell, "Thinking the Unthinkable: British and American Naval Strategies for an Anglo-American War, 1918–1931," *International History Review* (Canada) 19, no. 4 (1997): 794–802.

11. Bell, "Thinking the Unthinkable," 789–808; Sumida, *Inventing Grand Strategy and Teaching Command*, 82–92; Vlahos, *Blue Sword*, 99–102; Vlahos, "Wargaming," 17–19; George Questor, "Mahan and American Naval Thought since 1914," in *The Influence of History on Mahan*, ed. John Hattendorf, 192–93. Bell argues that War Plan Red was a serious initiative, "a sensible thing to do in a sensible way." U.S. military planners distrusted British intentions and were certain that imperial security would come at the expense of U.S. commercial interests. War planning against England, while never receiving official sanction, was nevertheless viewed as integral to preparedness.

On the other side of the debate are arguments that war with England was more an abstract concept than real probability. Jon Sumida observes that Mahan, one of the early architects of Red war planning, had changed his mind by the turn of the century. Given the propensity of liberal governments to abstain from massive naval construction, Mahan argued that U.S. security could just as easily be secured by transnational cooperation with England. Michael Vlahos argues that in the Naval War College's curriculum, war games against a Red enemy were means of reinforcing a "service ethos" and building confidence in the students. George Questor offers another perspective. He argues that War Plan Red was simply in the nature of the staff planner. Questor cites early RAF plans against France and even a very imaginative Canadian plan to invade the United States. Even Bell admits that while U.S. planners were preparing for an Anglo-American war, their potential adversary had no formal plans of its own. To the Royal Navy, it was becoming increasingly obvious that the security of the empire depended on cooperating with the United States.

12. Fleet Problems One (Feb. 1923), Three (Jan. 1924), Four (Jan. 1929), Ten (Mar. 1930), Eleven (Apr. 1930), Fifteen (Apr. 1934), and Twenty (Mar. 1939).

13. A contemporary example of geographic transposition occurred during Operation Desert Shield. U.S. and allied aircrews flew "mirror image" training missions, in which the geographic boundaries of Iraq were redrawn in Saudi Arabia.

14. James R. Leutze, *Bargaining for Supremacy*, 3–5; Baer, *One Hundred Years of Sea Power*, 33–42; Sumida, *Inventing Grand Strategy and Teaching Command*, 82–99. Examples marking the trend include British free trade policies in the mid-nineteenth century, British acquiescence to the U.S. Hay-Ponceforth Treaty of 1901 (which reversed America's long-standing agreement with Britain on maintaining the neutrality of the proposed isthmian canal.), and Prime Minister Arthur Balfour's formal acceptance of the Monroe Doctrine in February 1903. Sumida takes the trend even further. He argues that Mahan's argument for a "preponderant navy" in 1912 was based not on the strength of the Royal Navy but rather upon his fear of a possible defeat of the Royal Navy by the German fleet.

15. Leutze, *Bargaining for Supremacy*, 3–5.

16. Ibid.

17. Baer, *One Hundred Years of Sea Power*, 113–15; Roskill, *Naval Policy between the Wars*, 1:61–63; U.S. fleet confidential letter no. 12, July 14, 1930, "Fleet Problem Eleven," 1–5, *Records*, roll 13. U.S. Navy ships were hosted in Kingston, Jamaica, Port of Spain, Trinidad, St. George, Grenada, and Bridgeton, Barbados. The architect of Fleet Problem Ten was Adm. William Veazie Pratt, who shared President Hoover's belief in cooperation with the British. Pratt was instrumental in engineering an agreement with the British on continuing the battleship construction moratorium, as well as a compromise on cruiser strength, during the 1930 London Naval Conference.

18. Dudley W. Knox (captain, USN retired), "Our 'Stake' in Sea Power," U.S. Naval Institute *Proceedings* 53, no. 10 (Oct. 1927): 1089.

19. Leutze, *Bargaining for Supremacy*, 11–20.

20. Miller, *War Plan Orange*, 77–85; Edward Miller, "War Plan Orange, 1897–1941: The Blue Thrust through the Pacific," in *Readings in American Naval Heritage*, ed. Department of History, United States Naval Academy, 181–93.

21. Miller, *War Plan Orange*, 77–85; Miller, "War Plan Orange, 1897–1941," 181–93.

22. Miller, *War Plan Orange*, 114–21.

23. Ibid., 122–23.

24. Director of War Plans Division, memorandum to CNO, June 9, 1923, "Modification of Navy Orange Estimate," *Records of the Strategic Plans Division*, roll 17; U.S. Navy War Plans Division, "Estimate of the Situation Blue-Orange, September 1922," *Records of the Strategic Plans Division*, roll 17. While the June 9 memorandum from the War Plans Division was the only change recommended to the Blue-Orange estimate, in the upper right-hand corner of the document is a handwritten note: "Change #1, 10 July—1923," indicating that the changes had been approved. The Blue-Orange estimate cited is the original 1922 plan, with the changes from the June 9 memo incorporated on July 10.

25. "Estimate of the Situation, Blue-Orange," 15–15c.

26. Ibid., 24–25.

27. Ibid., 19–20.

28. CNO memorandum to Capt. William H. Standley, July 25, 1923, "Winter Maneuvers, 1923–24—Committee to prepare problems for," *Records*, roll 1; memorandum, July 31, 1923, "Minutes of Meeting of Special Board to Consider Problems for the Winter Maneuvers of the U.S. Fleet," *Records*, roll 1.

29. Albion, *Makers of Naval Policy*, 217–19; Davis, *Admirals' Lobby*, 19–23; Baer, *One Hundred Years of Sea Power*, 56–58; Miller, *War Plan Orange*, 81–85.

30. Baer, *One Hundred Years of Sea Power*, 116–17. CNO Adm. William Veazie Pratt (Sept. 1930–June 1933) best represents the split between shore and sea perspectives. His earlier support for the Washington Naval Treaty in 1922, and the London Naval Conference in 1930 (in which he was the lone navy representative), convinced big navy advocates within the service that Pratt was selected as CNO to further Hoover's pacifist policies. At the ceremony marking Pratt's promotion to CNO, Adm. Charles F. Hughes, whom Pratt was relieving, refused to shake his hand.

31. "U.S. Fleet Problem Number Two, Blue Situation," 1–5, *Records*, roll 1; commander-in-chief, U.S. fleet report, "United States Fleet Problem No. 2," *Records*, roll 1. Navy planners reoriented the geography of the eastern Pacific to fit the western Pacific scenario. In this "geographic transposition" Alaska represented the United States, San Diego became Oahu, and the Philippines were simulated by a stretch of the northern Chilean coastline.

32. Clark G. Reynolds, *Navies in History*, 1.

33. Vlahos, "Wargaming," 7–13; Vlahos, *Blue Sword*, 133–50; Michael Doyle, "The U.S. Navy and War Plan Orange, 1933–1940: Making Necessity a Virtue," *Naval War College Review* 33 (May–June 1980): 7–13. Vlahos points out that war games at Newport were highly scripted affairs that were dominated by a complex set of rules (160 pages) and managed by umpires Vlahos characterizes as "Olympian overseers." While the war games did play out aspects of War Plan Orange, Vlahos argues that their underlying purpose was to reinforce service ideology. Michael Doyle provides an interesting anecdote to further illustrate the problem with the Newport war games. In 1933, war college students were presented the problem of moving the fleet across the Pacific to relieve the Philippines. Capt. Ernest King, who was in charge of the Blue (U.S.) solution, recommended that the fleet take a northerly route to avoid submarines and aircraft operating from the Japanese Mandates. The NWC staff, believing that the southerly route would provide more beneficial training, rejected King's proposal. Doyle reports that King was furious with the alteration of his plan.

34. "Report on United States Fleet Problem Number One," 140, *Records*, roll 1; "Remarks of Admiral Laning at Critique of Fleet Problem Sixteen," 9, *Records*, roll 18; commander, Battle Force (commander, Black fleet, Fleet Problem XVIII), memorandum to commander-in-chief, U.S. fleet, June 23, 1937, "Comments and Recommendations on Fleet Problem XVIII," 2, *Records*, roll 22.

35. CINCUS memorandum to CNO, June 4, 1928, "Fleet Problem VIII—Report of Commander in Chief, United States Fleet," *Records*, roll 11; "Estimate of the Situation by Commander-in-chief, Blue Naval Forces," *Records*, roll 11.

36. CINCUS memorandum to CNO, Mar. 18, 1929, "United States Fleet Problem IX—Report of Commander-in-Chief, United States Fleet," 28–29, *Records*, roll 12.

37. Ibid., 103–107.

38. CINCUS memorandum to U.S. fleet, May 7, 1930, "Fleet Problem Ten," 5–8, *Records*, roll 13.

39. Ibid., 17–26, 43.

40. Mahan, *Influence of Sea Power upon History*, 4.

41. "Fleet Problem Ten," 55–89.

42. Ibid., 60.

43. CINCUS memorandum to U.S. fleet, July 14, 1930, "Fleet Problem Eleven," 1–64, *Records*, roll 13.

44. Ibid.

45. J. V. Chase (rear admiral, USN), "Fleets: Their Composition and Use," U.S. Naval Institute *Proceedings* 56, no. 10 (Oct. 1930): 895–901.

46. "Estimate of the Situation, Blue—Orange, September 1922," 9, *Records of the Strategic Plans Division*, roll 17.

47. Miller, *War Plan Orange*, 166–68; Spector, *Military Effectiveness*, 82. Miller argues

that Embick's criticism of Orange reflected the army's lack of enthusiasm for expending the resources to adequately defend the Philippines.

48. Plan O-1 Orange, July 1, 1934, "U.S. Joint Asiatic Operating Plan—Orange," 19–47, *Records of the Strategic Plans Division*, roll 17.

49. CINCUS memorandum to CNO, Sept. 15, 1935, "Fleet Problem XVI—report on," 4–17, *Records*, roll 18.

50. Ibid., 19; remarks of Adm. Harris Laning, in enclosure "F" to CINCUS Serial 5179, "Critique of Fleet Problem Sixteen Held at San Diego, California, 15 June 1935," *Records*, roll 18.

51. "Fleet Problem XVI—report on," 22–32.

52. Ibid.

53. Ibid., 32.

54. Black Fleet Operations Order No. 1, Mar. 17, 1937, "Task Organization," Records, roll 22; commander, Black fleet, memorandum to CINCUS, May 11, 1937, "FPXVIII—Narrative of Events and Track Charts," *Records*, roll 22.

55. Commander, Black fleet, memorandum to CINCUS, June 23, 1937, "Comments and Recommendations on Fleet Problem XVIII," *Records*, roll 23.

56. "U.S. Joint Asiatic Force Operating Plan—Orange," 9–11, 65.

57. Ibid., 64–69, 70–71.

58. CNO memorandum to CINCUS, Aug. 18, 1939, "Fleet Problem XXI—Concept of," *Records*, roll 31; extract from CNO letter to CINCUS, June 16, 1939, *Records*, roll 31.

59. CINCUS memorandum to CNO, Dec. 6,1939, "U.S. Fleet Problem XXI—Outline of," 1–8, *Records*, roll 31; annex "B" to U.S. Fleet Operation Order No. 2–40, Jan. 15, 1940, "General Plan for Fleet Problem XXI and Annual fleet Exercises, 1 April–17 May 1940," *Records*, roll 31.

60. Appendix "4" to annex "B" to U.S. Fleet Operation Order No. 2, Jan. 15, 1940, "Special Instructions to Commander Maroon Fleet, Fleet Problem XXI, Part VI," *Records*, roll 31.

61. "Fleet Problem XXI, Estimate of the Situation," Mar. 18, 1940, *Records*, roll 31; "Part VI—Fleet Problem XXI, Estimate of the Situation (Briefed) by Commander Purple Fleet," undated, *Records*, roll 31.

62. "Part VI—Fleet Problem XXI, Estimate of the Situation (Briefed)"; commander, Battle Force memorandum to CINCUS, May 8, 1940, "Remarks by Admiral C.P. Snyder, U.S. Navy, at Critiques of Parts II and VI, Fleet Problem XXI—forwarding of," *Records*, roll 36.

63. William D. Puleston (captain, USN), "A Re-examination of Mahan's Concept of Sea Power," U.S. Naval Institute *Proceedings* 66, no. 9 (Sept. 1940): 1229–36.

Chapter 8. Conclusion

1. CNO memorandum to CINCUS, undated, "Fleet Problem XX—Concept of," *Records*, roll 25.

2. Mark R. Peattie, "Japanese Naval Construction, 1919–1941," in *Technology and Naval Combat in the Twentieth Century and Beyond*, ed. Phillips Payson O'Brien, 93–109. Peattie argues that Japanese naval officers' own fixation on Mahan, as well

as their anticipation of numerical inferiority in a future war with the U.S. Navy, resulted in an interwar construction program that emphasized a qualitative capability to destroy U.S. surface forces. As a consequence Japanese destroyers were built primarily to conduct torpedo attacks against the U.S. fleet as it proceeded across the Pacific and not to protect merchant ships from submarine attack.

3. Thomas Buell, *Master of Sea Power*, 214–25.

BIBLIOGRAPHY

Albion, Robert G. *Makers of Naval Policy, 1798–1947.* Edited by Rowena Reed. Annapolis: U.S. Naval Institute Press, 1980.

Alden, John D. *The Fleet Submarine in the U.S. Navy: A Design and Construction History.* Annapolis: U.S. Naval Institute Press, 1979.

"Alfred Thayer Mahan, in Memoriam." U.S. Naval Institute *Proceedings* 41, no. 1 (January–February 1915): 1–9.

Allen, Joseph. *Battles of the British Navy.* Vol. 1. London: George Bell and Sons, 1900.

Allison, Graham T. *Essence of Decision: Explaining the Cuban Missile Crisis.* Boston: Little, Brown and Company, 1971.

Anderson, Walter S. (commander, USN). "The Strategy and Logistics of the Dardanelles Campaign." U.S. Naval Institute *Proceedings* 49, no. 7 (July 1923): 1127–41.

——— (captain, USN). "Submarines and Disarmament Conferences," U.S. Naval Institute *Proceedings* 53, no. 1 (January 1927): 50–70.

Andrade, Ernest J. "Submarine Policy in the United States Navy, 1919–1941." *Military Affairs* 35, no. 2 (1971): 50–56.

Annual Reports of Fleets and Task Forces of the U.S. Navy, 1920–1941. Washington, D.C.: National Archives and Records Service, 1974. Microfilm.

Annual Reports of the Navy Department. Washington, D.C.: GPO, 1902–1929.

Baer, George W. *One Hundred Years of Sea Power: The U.S. Navy, 1890–1990.* Stanford: Stanford University Press, 1994.

———. "U.S. Naval Strategy 1890–1945." *Naval War College Review* 44, no. 1 (winter 1991): 6–33.

Ballendorf, Dirk A., and Merrill L. Bartlett. *Pete Ellis: An Amphibious Warfare Prophet.* Annapolis: U.S. Naval Institute Press, 1997.

Barnett, George (major general, USMC, ret.). "Sea Training of Marine Officers." U.S. Naval Institute *Proceedings* 50, no. 6 (June 1924): 935–38.

Bartlett, Merrill L., ed. *Assault from the Sea: Essays on the History of Amphibious Warfare.* Annapolis: U.S. Naval Institute Press, 1983.

———. *Lejeune: A Marine's Life.* Columbia: University of South Carolina Press, 1991.

Bauer, K. Jack. *A Maritime History of the United States.* Columbia: University of South Carolina Press, 1988.

Beehler, W. H. (commodore, USN). "The Navy and Coast Defense." U.S. Naval Institute *Proceedings* 35, no. 2 (June 1909): 343–81.

Bekker, C. D. *Hitler's Naval War.* Garden City, Doubleday, 1974.

Bell, Christopher M. "Thinking the Unthinkable: British and American Naval Strategies for an Anglo-American War, 1918–1931." *International History Review* (Canada) 19, no. 4 (1997): 789–808.

Bickel, Keith B. *Mars Learning: The Marine Corps Development of Small Wars Doctrine, 1915–1940.* Boulder: Westview Press, 2001.

Biddle, Tami Davis. *Rhetoric and Reality in Air Warfare: The Evolution of British and American Ideas about Strategic Bombing, 1914–1945.* Princeton: Princeton University Press, 2002.

Bowing, R. A. "The Negative Influence of Mahan on Antisubmarine Warfare." *Journal of Royal United Services Institute for Defense Studies* 122, no. 4 (1977): 52–59.

Braisted, William R. "On the American Red and Red-Orange Plans." In *Naval Warfare in the Twentieth Century, 1900–1945: Essays in Honor of Arthur Marder,* edited by Gerald Jordan, 167–86. New York: Crane Russak, 1977.

Broadbent, E. W. (lieutenant commander, USN). "The Selection of Advanced Bases." *Marine Corps Gazette* 14, no. 3 (September 1929): 216–21.

Brodie, Bernard. *Sea Power in the Machine Age.* Princeton: Princeton University Press, 1941.

Bucholz, Arden. *Moltke, Schlieffen, and Prussian War Planning.* New York: Berg, 1991.

Buell, Thomas. *Master of Sea Power: A Biography of Fleet Admiral Ernest J. King.* Boston: Little, Brown and Company, 1980.

Burns, Richard Dean, "Regulating Submarine Warfare, 1921–1941: A Case Study in Arms Control and Limited War." *Military Affairs* 35, no. 2 (April 1971): 56–62.

Carr, Edward Hallett. *What Is History?* New York: Vintage Books, 1961.

Chase, J. V. (rear admiral, USN). "Fleets: Their Composition *and* Use." U.S. Naval Institute *Proceedings* 56, no. 10 (October 1930): 895–901.

Clausewitz, Carl Von. *On War.* Edited by Michael Howard and Peter Paret. Princeton: Princeton University Press, 1976.

Clifford, Kenneth J. *Amphibious Warfare Development in Britain and America from 1920–1940.* Laurens, N.Y.: Edgewood, 1983.

———. *Progress and Purpose: A Developmental History of the United States Marine Corps.* Washington, D.C.: USMC History and Museums Division, 1973.

Cohen, Warren I. *Empire without Tears: American Foreign Relations, 1921–1933.* Philadelphia: Temple University Press, 1987.

Cole, Eli K. (lieutenant colonel, USMC). "The Necessity to the Naval Service of an Adequate Marine Corps." U.S. Naval Institute *Proceedings* 40, no. 5 (September–October 1914): 1395–1401.

Coletta, Paolo E., and Bernarr B. Coletta. *Admiral William A. Moffett and U.S. Naval Aviation.* Lewiston, N.Y.: E. Mellen Press, 1997.

Compton-Hall, Richard. *Submarines and the War at Sea: 1914–1918.* London: MacMillan, 1991.

Conference on the Limitation of Armament: Washington, November 12, 1921–February 6, 1922. Washington, D.C.: GPO, 1922.

Coox, Alvin D. "Military Effectiveness of Armed Forces in the Interwar Period, 1919–1941." In *Military Effectiveness: The Interwar Period,* edited by Allan R. Millett and Williamson Murray. Boston: Allen and Unwin, 1988.

Corbett, Julian S., ed. *Fighting Instructions, 1530–1816.* London: Navy Records Society, 1905.

Cotton, Lyman A. (captain, USN). "Commerce Destroying in War." U.S. Naval Institute *Proceedings* 45, no. 9 (September 1919): 1495–1517.

———. "Unrestricted Commerce Destroying." U.S. Naval Institute *Proceedings* 45, no. 9 (September 1919): 1517–28.

Crowl, Philip A. "Alfred Thayer Mahan: The Naval Historian." In *Makers of Modern Strategy: From Machiavelli to the Nuclear Age,* edited by Peter Paret, 444–81. Princeton: Princeton University Press, 1986.

Davis, Burke. *The Billy Mitchell Affair.* New York: Random House, 1967.

Davis, Vincent. *The Admirals' Lobby.* Chapel Hill: University of North Carolina Press, 1967.

Dean, Francis H. *America's Navy and Marine Corps Airplanes, 1918–to the Present.* Atglen, Pa.: Schiffer Military History, 1999.

Douhet, Giulio. *The Command of the Air.* Translated by Dino Ferrari. New York: Coward-McCann, 1942.

Doyle, Michael. "The U.S. Navy and War Plan Orange, 1933–1940: Making Necessity a Virtue." *Naval War College Review* 33 (May–June 1980): 7–13.

Ellis, Earl (major, USMC). USMC 712H Operations Plan, 23 July 1921, "Advanced Base Operations in Micronesia, 1921." Republished by Headquarters, USMC, as *Fleet Marine Force Reference Publication 12–46,* 1992.

Farago, Ladislas. *The Tenth Fleet.* New York: Ivan Obelinsky, 1962.

Felker, C. C. "Airpower on the Offensive: The U.S. Army Air Corps versus the U-Boats in the Bay of Biscay." Master's thesis, University of Alabama, 1992.

Fiske, Bradley A. (commander, USN). "Air Power." U.S. Naval Institute *Proceedings* 43, no. 8 (August 1917): 1701–1705.

———. "American Naval Policy." U.S. Naval Institute *Proceedings* 31, no. 1 (March 1905): 2–34.

———. "Torpedo Plane and Bomber." U.S. Naval Institute *Proceedings* 48, no. 9 (September 1922): 1474–78.

———. "Why Togo Won." U.S. Naval Institute *Proceedings* 31, no. 4 (December 1905): 807–809.

Frost, Holloway H. (ensign, USN) "The Problem of Fighting a Fleet Under Way with Long Range Torpedoes." U.S. Naval Institute *Proceedings* 39, no. 2 (June 1913): 681–99.

——— (lieutenant commander, USN). "The Results and Effects of the Battle of Jutland." U.S. Naval Institute *Proceedings* 47, no. 9 (September 1921): 1335–54.

Fullam, William (lieutenant, USN). "The Organization, Training and Discipline of the Navy Personnel as Viewed From the Ship." U.S. Naval Institute *Proceedings* 22, no. 1 (1896): 83–116.

Grace, O. Donn. *Sonar and Anti-submarine Warfare.* Escondido, Calif.: Sage Publishing, 1999.

Halpern, Paul G. *A Naval History of World War I.* Annapolis: U.S. Naval Institute Press, 1994.

Hamer, David. *Bombers versus Battleships: The Struggle between Ships and Aircraft for the Control of the Surface of the Sea.* Annapolis: U.S. Naval Institute Press, 1998.

Hearings before the General Board of the U.S. Navy, 1917–1950. Wilmington: Scholarly Resources, Inc., 1982. Microfilm.

Higham, Robin. "Airpower in World War One, 1914–1918." In *The War in the Air, 1914–1994,* edited by Alan Stephens, 1–28. Maxwell AFB, Ala.: Air University Press, 2001.

Hill, Walter N. (lieutenant colonel, USMC). "The Employment of Marine Corps Expeditionary Force in a Major Emergency." *Marine Corps Gazette* 15, no. 5 (May 1931): 16–21.

Hoff, A. B. (lieutenant, USN). "The Submarine as an Enemy." U.S. Naval Institute *Proceedings* 31, no. 2 (June 1905): 383–400.

Holley, Irving B. *Ideas and Weapons: Exploitation of the Aerial Weapon by the United States during World War I: A Study in the Relationship of Technological Advance, Military Doctrine, and the Development of Weapons.* New Haven: Yale University Press, 1953.

Hone, Thomas. "Spending Patterns of the United States Navy, 1921–1941. *Armed Forces and Society* 8, no. 3 (spring 1982): 443–63.

Hough, Frank O., Verle E. Ludwig, and Henry I. Shaw. *History of U.S. Marine Corps Operations in World War II.* Vol. 1, *Pearl Harbor to Guadalcanal.* Washington, D.C.: GPO, 1958.

Hubbard, J. C. (lieutenant, USN). "Aviation and Control of the Sea." U.S. Naval Institute *Proceedings* 62, no. 1 (January 1936): 33–38.

Isely, Jeter A., and Philip A. Crowl. *The U.S. Marines and Amphibious War: Its Theory, and Its Practice in the Pacific.* Princeton: Princeton University Press, 1951.

Jessup, E. P. (captain, USN, ret.). "Failure at Gallipoli." U.S. Naval Institute *Proceedings* 61, no. 2 (February 1935): 191–209.

Johnson, David E. *Fast Tanks and Heavy Bombers: Innovation in the U.S. Army, 1917–1945.* Ithaca: Cornell University Press, 1998.

Karsten, Peter. *The Naval Aristocracy: The Golden Age of Annapolis and the Emergence of Modern American Navalism.* New York: Free Press, 1972.

Keegan, John. *The First World War.* New York: Alfred A. Knopf, 1999.

Kemp, Paul. *Convoy Protection: The Defence of Seaborne Trade.* London: Arms and Armour, 1993.

Kimball, W. W. (commander, USN). "Submarine Boats." U.S. Naval Institute *Proceedings* 27, no. 4 (December 1901): 739–46.

Knox, Dudley W. *The Eclipse of American Sea Power.* New York: Army and Navy Journal, 1922.

——— (commander, USN). "The General Problem of Naval Warfare." U.S. Naval Institute *Proceedings* 42, no. 1 (January–February 1916): 23–47.

———. "Our 'Stake' in Sea Power." U.S. Naval Institute *Proceedings* 53, no. 10 (October 1927): 1087–90.

Krulak, Victor H. *First to Fight: An Inside View of the U.S. Marine Corps.* Annapolis: U.S. Naval Institute Press, 1984.

Landing-Force Manual, United States Navy, 1920. Washington, D.C.: GPO, 1921.

Landing-Force Manual, United States Navy, 1927. Washington, D.C.: GPO, 1927.

Landing-Force Manual, United States Navy, 1938. Washington, D.C.: GPO, 1938.

Lejeune, John A. (major general, USMC). "The United States Marine Corps." U.S. Naval Institute *Proceedings* 51, no. 10 (October 1925): 1858–71.

———. "The Marine Corps, 1926." U.S. Naval Institute *Proceedings* 52, no. 10 (October 1926): 1961–70.

———. *Reminiscences of a Marine.* Philadelphia: Dorrance, 1930; reprint, New York: Arno Press, 1979.

Leutze, James R. *Bargaining for Supremacy: Anglo-American Naval Collaboration.* Chapel Hill: University of North Carolina Press, 1977.

Levitt, Barbara, and James G. Marsh. "Organizational Learning." *Annual Review of Sociology* 14 (1988): 319–40.

Love, Robert W., Jr., ed. *The Chiefs of Naval Operations.* Annapolis: U.S. Naval Institute Press, 1980.

Macintyre, Donald. *The Battle of the Atlantic.* New York: The MacMillan Company, 1961.

MacIsaac, David. "Voices from the Central Blue: The Air Power Theorists." In *Makers of Modern Strategy: From Machiavelli to the Nuclear Age,* edited by Peter Paret, 624–48. Princeton: Princeton University Press, 1986.

Mahan, Alfred Thayer. *The Influence of Sea Power upon History, 1660–1783.* New York: Dover, 1890. Reprint, New York: Dover, 1987.

———. *The Influence of Sea Power upon the French Revolution and Empire, 1793–1812.* 2 vols. London: Sampson, Low, Marston, 1892.

———. *Lessons of the War with Spain.* Boston: Little, Brown, and Company, 1899.

———. *The Life of Nelson, the Embodiment of the Sea Power of Great Britain.* 2 vols. Boston: Little, Brown, and Company, 1897.

———. "Reflections, Historic and Other, Suggested by the Battle of the Sea of Japan." U.S. Naval Institute *Proceedings* 32, no. 7 (June 1906): 447–63.

———. *Sea Power in Its Relations to the War of 1812.* London: Sampson, Low, Marston, 1905.

Major, John. "The Navy Plans for War, 1936–1941." In *In Peace and War: Interpretations of American Naval History, 1775–1984,* edited by Kenneth Hagan. Westport, Conn.: Greenwood Press, 1984.

Mallison, W. T. *Studies in the Law of Naval Warfare: Submarines in General and Limited War.* Washington, D.C.: GPO, 1968.

Marder, Arthur. *From the Dreadnought to Scapa Flow: The Royal Navy in the Fisher Era.* Vol. 2, *The War Years: To the Eve of Jutland.* London: Oxford University Press, 1965.

———. *From the Dreadnought to Scapa Flow: The Royal Navy in the Fisher Era.* Vol. 3, *Jutland and After.* London: Oxford University Press, 1966.

Mason, Arthur T. (captain, USMC). "An Introduction to the Gallipoli Campaign." *Marine Corps Gazette* 20, no. 1 (February 1936): 23–26.

———. "An Introduction to the Gallipoli Campaign, Part Two." *Marine Corps Gazette* 20, no. 2 (May 1936): 23–44.

McAdoo, William. "The Navy and the Nation." U.S. Naval Institute *Proceedings* 20, no. 2 (1894): 401–22.

McBride, William M. "Challenging a Strategic Paradigm: Aviation and the U.S. Navy Special Policy Board of 1924." In *Readings in American Naval Heritage,* edited by Department of History, United States Naval Academy, 121–39. Needham Heights, Mass.: Simon and Schuster, 1998.

———. *Technological Change and the United States Navy, 1865–1945.* Baltimore: Johns Hopkins Press, 2000.

McDowell, C. S. (captain, USN). "Anti-submarine Work during the World War." Washington, D.C.: National Archives, 1977. Electrostatic copy of unpublished typescript, located in National Archives and known as Record Group 45. Originally received in December 1919.

McFarland, Stephen L., and Wesley Phillips Newton. *To Command the Sky: The Battle for Air Superiority Over Germany, 1942–1944.* Washington, D.C.: Smithsonian Institution Press, 1991.

Meigs, Montgomery. *Slide Rules and Submarines.* Washington, D.C.: National Defense University Press, 1990.

Melhorn, Charles M. *Two-Block Fox: The Rise of the Aircraft Carrier, 1911–1929.* Annapolis: U.S. Naval Institute Press, 1974.

Merli, Frank. *The* Alabama, *British Neutrality, and the American Civil War.* Edited by David M. Fahey. Bloomington: Indiana University Press, 2004.

Miller, E. B. (colonel, USMC). "The Marine Corps: Its Mission, Organization, Power and Limitations." *Marine Corps Gazette* 17, no. 3 (November 1932): 10–21.

Miller, Edward S. "War Plan Orange, 1897–1941: The Blue Thrust through the Pacific." In *Readings in American Naval Heritage,* edited by Department of History, United States Naval Academy, 181–93. Needham Heights, Mass.: Simon and Schuster, 1998.

———. *War Plan Orange: The U.S. Strategy to Defeat Japan, 1897–1945.* Annapolis: U.S. Naval Institute Press, 1991.

Millett, Alan R. *Semper Fidelis: The History of the United States Marine Corps.* New York: Free Press, 1991.

Mitchell, William. "Has the Airplane Made the Battleship Obsolete?" *The World's Work,* April 1921, 550–56.

———. *Winged Defense: The Development and Possibilities of Modern Air Power—Economic and Military.* New York: G. P. Putnam's Sons, 1925. Reprint, Dover Publications, 1988.

Moore, Samuel Taylor. *U.S. Airpower: Story of American Fighting Planes and Missiles from Hydrogen Bags to Hydrogen War-heads.* New York: Greenberg, 1958.

Morison, Elting. *Men, Machines and Modern Times.* Cambridge, Mass.: MIT Press, 1966.

Morison, Samuel Eliot. *History of United States Naval Operations in World War II.* Boston: Little, Brown and Company, 1948.

Morrow, John Howard. *The Great War in the Air: Military Aviation from 1909 to 1921.* Washington, D.C.: Smithsonian Institution Press, 1993.

Nimitz, Chester W. *Triumph in the Atlantic: The Naval Struggle against the Axis.* Englewood Cliffs, N.J.: Prentice-Hall, 1960.

O'Brien, Phillips Payson, ed. *Technology and Naval Combat in the Twentieth Century and Beyond.* London: Frank Cass, 2001.

O'Connell, Robert L. *Sacred Vessels: The Cult of the Battleship and the Rise of the U.S. Navy.* Boulder: Westview Press, 1991.

O'Connor, Raymond G. "The U.S. Marines in the 20th Century: Amphibious Warfare and Doctrinal Debates." *Military Affairs* 38, no. 3 (October 1974): 97–103.

Padfield, Peter. *War beneath the Sea: Submarine Conflict, 1939–1945.* London: John Murray, Ltd., 1991.

Peattie, Mark R. "Japanese Naval Construction, 1919–1941." In *Technology and Naval Combat in the Twentieth Century and Beyond,* edited by Payson O'Brien, 93–109. London: Frank Cass, 2001.

Pelz, Stephen E. *Race to Pearl Harbor: The Failure of the Second London Naval Conference and the Onset of World War II.* Cambridge, Mass.: Harvard University Press, 1974.

Posen, Barry R. *The Sources of Military Doctrine: France, Britain and Germany between the World Wars.* Ithaca, N.Y.: Cornell University Press, 1984.

Potter, E. B., ed. *Sea Power: A Naval History.* 2d edition. Annapolis: U.S. Naval Institute Press, 1981.

Pratt, William Veazie (rear admiral, USN). "Discussion." U.S. Naval Institute *Proceedings* 50, no. 7 (July 1924): 1126–27.

Proceedings and Hearings of the General Board of the U.S. Navy, 1900–1950. Washington, D.C.: National Archives and Records Service, 1987. Microfilm.

Puleston, William D. (captain, USN). "A Re-examination of Mahan's Concept of Sea Power." U.S. Naval Institute *Proceedings* 66, no. 9 (September 1940): 1229–36.

Questor, George. "Mahan and American Naval Thought since 1914." In *The Influence of History on Mahan: The Proceedings of a Conference Marking the Centenary of Alfred Thayer Mahan's The Influence of Sea Power upon History, 1660–1783,* edited by John Hattendorf, 177–93. Newport, R.I.: Naval War College Press, 1992.

Records of the Joint Board, 1903–1947. Washington, D.C.: National Archives and Records Service, 1986. Microfilm.

Records of the Strategic Plans Division, Office of the Chief of Naval Operations and Predecessor Organizations. Wilmington, Del.: Scholarly Resources, Inc., 1991. Microfilm.

Records Relating to United States Navy Fleet Problems I to XXII, 1923–1941. Washington, D.C.: National Archives and Records Service, 1974. Microfilm.

Register of Commissioned and Warrant Officers of the United States Navy and Marine Corps. Washington, D.C.: GPO, 1923–1941.

Reynolds, Clark. *Admiral John H. Towers: The Struggle for Naval Air Supremacy.* Annapolis: U.S. Naval Institute Press, 1991.

———. *The Fast Carriers: The Forging of an Air Navy.* New York: McGraw-Hill, 1968.

———. *Navies in History.* Annapolis: U.S. Naval Institute Press, 1998.

Rickover, H. G. (lieutenant, USN). "International Law and the Submarine," U.S. Naval Institute *Proceedings* 61, no. 9 (September 1935): 1213–27.

Roland, Alex. *Underwater Warfare in the Age of Sail.* Bloomington: University of Indiana Press, 1978.

Ropp, Theodore. *The Development of a Modern Navy: French Naval Policy, 1871–1914.* Edited by Stephen S. Roberts. Annapolis: U.S. Naval Institute Press, 1987.

Rosen, Stephen Peter. "Military Effectiveness: Why Society Matters." *International Security* 19, no. 4 (spring 1995): 5–31.

Roskill, Stephen. *Naval Policy between the Wars.* Vol. 1, *The Period of Anglo-American Antagonism, 1919–1929.* London: Collins, 1968.

———. *Naval Policy between the Wars.* Vol. 2, *The Period of Reluctant Rearmament, 1930–1939.* London: Collins, 1976.

Russell, John H. (brigadier general, USMC). "A New Naval Policy." *Marine Corps Gazette* 18, no. 2 (August 1933): 13–17.

Seager, Robert, II. "Ten Years before Mahan: The Unofficial Case for the New Navy, 1889–1890." *The Mississippi Valley Historical Review* 40, no. 3 (December 1953): 491–512.

Showalter, Dennis E. *Railroads and Rifles: Soldiers, Technology, and the Unification of Germany.* Hamdon, Conn.: Archon Books, 1975.

Spear, Lawrence. "Submarine Torpedo Boats: Past, Present and Future." U.S. Naval Institute *Proceedings* 29, no. 4 (December 1902): 1000–13.

Spector, Ronald H. *At War at Sea: Sailors and Naval Combat in the Twentieth Century.* New York: Viking Press, 2001.

———. *Eagle against the Sun: The American War with Japan.* New York: Free Press, 1985.

———. "The Military Effectiveness of the U.S. Armed Forces, 1919–1939." In *Military Effectiveness: The Interwar Period,* edited by Allan R. Millett and Murray Williamson, 70–98. Boston: Allen and Unwin, 1988.

———. *Professors of War: The Naval War College and the Development of the Naval Profession.* Newport, R.I.: Naval War College Press, 1977.

Stephens, Alan. "The True Believers: Airpower between the Wars." In *The War in the Air,* edited by Alan Stephens, 29–68. Maxwell AFB, Ala.: Air University Press, 2001.

Stimson, Henry L. *On Active Service in Peace and War.* New York: Harper, 1948.

Stirling, Yates (rear admiral, USN). "Naval Preparedness in the Pacific Area." U.S. Naval Institute *Proceedings* 60, no. 5 (May 1934): 601–609.

——— (captain, USN). "The Place of Aviation in the Organization for War." U.S. Naval Institute *Proceedings* 52, no. 6 (June 1926): 1100–10.

——— (rear admiral, USN). "Sea Power." U.S. Naval Institute *Proceedings* 61, no. 6 (June 1935): 767–80.

——— (commander, USN). "The Submarine." U.S. Naval Institute *Proceedings* 43, no. 7 (July 1917): 1371–1390.

Sumida, Jon. *Inventing Grand Strategy and Teaching Command: The Classic Works of Alfred Thayer Mahan Reconsidered.* Washington, D.C.: Woodrow Wilson Center Press, 1997.

Trimble, William F. *Admiral William A. Moffett: Architect of Naval Aviation.* Washington, D.C.: Smithsonian Institution Press, 1994.

Turnbull, Archibald Douglas. *History of United States Naval Aviation.* New Haven, Conn.: Yale University Press, 1949.

U.S. Department of State. *London Naval Treaty of 1930.* Washington, D.C.: GPO, 1930.

U.S. Naval History Division. *Dictionary of American Naval Fighting Ships.* Vol. 6. Washington, D.C.: GPO, 1976.

Van der Vat, Dan. *The Atlantic Campaign: World War II's Great Struggle at Sea.* New York: Harper and Row, 1988.

Vlahos, Michael. *The Blue Sword: The Naval War College and the American Mission.* Newport, R.I.: Naval War College Press, 1980.

———. "Wargaming; An Enforcer of Strategic Realism: 1919–1942." *Naval War College Review* 39 (March–April 1986): 7–22.

Wainwright, Richard (captain, USN). "The Battle of the Sea of Japan." U.S. Naval Institute *Proceedings* 31, no. 4 (December 1905): 779–805.

———. "Our Naval Power." U.S. Naval Institute *Proceedings* 24, no. 1 (March 1898): 39–87.

Warren, Lee P. (lieutenant commander, USN). "The Battleship Still Supreme." *The World's Work* (April 1921): 556–60.

Wead, Frank W. (lieutenant, USN). "Naval Aviation Today." U.S. Naval Institute *Proceedings* 50, no. 4 (April 1924): 561–74.

Weir, Gary E. "The Search for an American Submarine Strategy and Design, 1916–1936." *Naval War College Review* 44, no. 1 (1991): 34–48.

Westcott, Allen F., ed. *Mahan on Naval Warfare: Selections from the Writings of Alfred Thayer Mahan*. Boston: Little, Brown and Company, 1942

Wildenberg, Thomas. *Destined for Glory: Dive bombing, Midway, and the Evolution of Carrier Airpower.* Annapolis: U.S. Naval Institute Press, 1998.

———. "In Support of the Battle Line: Gunnery's Influence on the Development of Carrier Aviation in the U.S. Navy." *Journal of Military History* 63, no. 3 (July 2001): 697–713.

Williams, Robert Hugh. *The Old Corps: A Portrait of the U.S. Marine Corps between the Wars.* Annapolis: U.S. Naval Institute Press, 1982.

INDEX

Page numbers in *italics* indicate photographs.

Printed in the USA
CPSIA information can be obtained
at www.ICGtesting.com
LVHW040932300923
759403LV00058B/59